Learning from others in groups

Learning from others in groups

Experiential learning approaches

Cary L. Cooper
University of Manchester
Institute of Science and Technology

GREENWOOD PRESS
WESTPORT, CONNECTICUT

English language edition, except the United States and Canada,
published by Associated Business Press, London

Published in the United States and Canada by
Greenwood Press, Inc., Westport, Connecticut

First published 1979

Library of Congress Cataloging in Publication Data

Cooper, Cary L
  Learning from others in groups.

  Includes bibliographical references and index.
  1. Group work in education. 2. Education—Experimental
methods. I. Title.
LB1032.C59 1979   371.3   78-26987
ISBN 0-313-20922-7

Library of Congress Catalog Card Number: 78-26987

ISBN: 0-313-20922-7

Printed in Great Britain

Contents

Acknowledgements

The author would like to thank the following journals and publishers for allowing him to reproduce articles published by him:

Human Relations and Plenum Publishing Corporation.
Interpersonal Development and S. Karger AG.
Psychological Reports.
British Journal of Social Work.
Group and Organization Studies and *Annual Handbook for Group Facilitators: 1976* and University Associates.
Advances in Experiential Social Processes and John Wiley & Sons.
Psychology Teaching and the Association of Teachers of Psychology.

In addition, the author would like to thank the colleagues who worked with him on some of these papers; Iain Mangham, John Hayes, Ned Levine, Koichiro Kobayashi and Ken Harrison.

Introduction

Experiential learning groups of all kinds—T-groups, encounter groups, *Gestalt* groups, etc. — have had colossal growth over the last two decades. Many people believed in the late Fifties and early Sixties that these forms of human relations or social skill training were a temporary, fad-like phenomenon, which would only attract the 'borderline neurotic' or the 'intra-psychical adventurer'. While some people who take advantage of these experiences are pursuing this training for 'personal growth' purposes, the vast majority of participants who attend such programmes do so to enhance certain of their interactive skills necessary for the performance of their work: managers—to develop their skills in working with colleagues and subordinates, particularly in groups; social workers — to explore their interrelationships with clients, their motives in making particular client decisions, and to improve their working relationship with colleagues; health administrators — in trying to create and facilitate more effective inter-group relationships in hospital and other health-related settings. The list of occupational groups responding to this type of training is unending, as more and more training and personnel officers in industrial, public service, and social service organisations begin to realise the importance of experiential group training activities in improving the social skills of people whose job necessitates dealing with and helping other people. Indeed, Carl Rogers, the father of modern psychology, said, 'these groups are the most rapidly spreading social phenomenon in the country' (Rogers, 1970). The purpose of this book, therefore, is to explore some of the main issues and research generated by one of the most influential human relations training techniques of this century, the T-group or experiential learning group.

The book is divided into five main sections. In the first section of the book we will be exploring a number of general issues related to experiential learning methods. In the first instance, we will look at the objectives of these approaches and their main learning constituents. That is, we will be attempting to highlight how these experiential techniques differ from conventional learning methods. Next, we will explore the values inherent in experiential learning, the value conflicts that emerge in such groups and the manner in which an understanding of the underlying assumptions and values can help in planning effective group experiences. And finally, we will be discussing some of the important learning characteristics in experiential groups which we must consider in their design and execution.

In the second section we will be looking at how effective are experiential learning groups. We will focus in on the characteristics of these groups which lead both to adverse and growthful changes in individual behaviour. Since the most important characteristic of the learning experience of these groups lies in the behaviour of the trainer, we will explore the links between his interventions and participant change. Although in the late 1950s and early 1960s T-groups and other experiential methods were used primarily in the West they are spreading further and further East. We conclude this section by examining the impact of these techniques on three different cultures, England, Turkey and Japan.

The third section of the book will look at the use of groups in four different contexts: in developing more effective and coherent relations between executives on the board of a company; in cementing better relationships between teachers and students; in changing the work and outside behaviour of social workers; and in developing the social skills of personnel working in the restaurant industry.

The fourth section will look at some research done on different aspects of the learning environment of experiential groups: examining the personality profiles of group participants and leaders; exploring the effect of physical contact on self-disclosure of participants; and isolating the impact of structured exercise-based groups and more unstructured experiential approaches and their impact on the psychological conditions of learning.

In the fifth section, in this extended essay, the author is attempting to provide a prognostication of the future of experiential learning techniques by a detailed examination of four socio-economic trends: Anglo-American orientation of the movement, production and growth trends of advanced capitalist economies, shifting age structure and the changes in the expression of middle-class needs.

All these chapters are based on conceptual and empirical work published by the author in a variety of scholarly journals. It reflects ten years of systematic research into the effects and characteristics of experiential learning methods.

Section A
Issues in experiential methods

In this section of the book we will be exploring a number of general issues related to experiential learning methods. In the first instance, we will look at the objectives of these approaches and their main learning constituents. That is, we will be attempting to highlight how these experiential techniques differ from conventional learning methods. Next, we will explore the values inherent in experiential learning, the value conflicts that emerge in such groups and the manner in which an understanding of the underlying assumptions and values can help in planning effective group experiences. And finally, we will be discussing some of the important learning characteristics in experiential groups which we must consider in their design and execution.

1 Understanding individual and group behaviour: experiential learning groups

'At the fifth meeting the group's feelings about its own progress became the initial focus of discussion. The talkers participated as usual, conversation shifting rapidly from one point to another. Dissatisfaction was mounting, expressed through loud, snide remarks by some and through apathy by others.

'George Franklin appeared particularly disturbed. Finally pounding the table, he exclaimed, "I don't know what is going on here! I should be paid for listening to this drivel? I'm getting just a bit sick of wasting my time here. If the teachers don't put out — I quit!" George was pleased; he was angry, and he had said so. As he sat back in his chair, he felt he had the group behind him. He felt he had the guts to say what most of the others were thinking! Some members of the group applauded loudly, but others showed obvious disapproval. They wondered why George was excited over so insignificant an issue, why he hadn't done something constructive rather than just sounding off as usual. Why, they wondered, did he say their comments were "drivel"?

'George Franklin became the focus of discussion. "What do you mean, George, by saying this nonsense?" "What do you expect, a neat set of rules to meet all your problems?" George was getting uncomfortable. These were questions difficult for him to answer. Gradually he began to realize that a large part of the group disagreed with him; then he began to wonder why. He was learning something about people he hadn't known before. ". . . How does it feel, George, to have people disagree with you when you thought you had them behind you? . . ."

'Bob White was first annoyed with George and now with the discussion. He was getting tense, a bit shaky perhaps. Bob didn't like anybody to get a raw deal, and he felt that George was getting it. At first Bob tried to minimize George's outburst, and then he suggested that the group get on to the real issues; but the group continued to focus on George. Finally Bob said, "Why don't you leave George alone and stop picking on him. We're not getting anywhere this way."

'With the help of the leaders, the group focused on Bob. "What do you mean 'picking' on him?" "Why, Bob, have you tried to change the discussion?" "Why are you so protective of George?" Bob began to realize that the group wanted to focus on George; he also saw that George didn't think he was being picked on, but felt he was learning something about himself and how others reacted to him. "Why do I always get upset", Bob began to wonder, "when people start to look at each other? Why do I feel sort of sick when people get angry at each other?" . . . Now Bob was learning something about how people saw him, while gaining some insight into his own behaviour.' (from *Leadership and Organization: A*

Behavioral Science Approach by Tannenbaum, Weschler, & Massarik, McGraw Hill, New York, 1961.)

This short extract taken from a course in group behaviour for undergraduate students illustrates some of the features of an educational technique referred to as the Sensitivity Training or T-group. It is an approach to understanding group behaviour which, broadly speaking, provides individuals with an opportunity to learn more about themselves and their impact on other people, and about group dynamics. In Britain as well as in the US there is increasing use of these groups by universities and professional bodies in teaching, by the social administration departments and welfare agencies in training social workers, and by industry in attempting to improve managerial effectiveness.

The T-group is a method which relies primarily on the 'individual achieving insights into the nature of social behaviour by discovery rather than by formal instruction'. This normally means bringing together a group of people (for whom learning about themselves, their impact on others, and small group behaviour are relevant) for the purpose of studying the behaviour of their own group, with the aid of a staff member (who is usually a clinical or social psychologist).

In general, there are certain features that distinguish this type of learning experience from a conventional discussion seminar on group behaviour. Tannenbaum, Weschler, and Massarik (1961) have outlined these distinctions. First, the training is primarily 'process-orientated' rather than 'content-orientated'. That is, the primary stress is on the feeling level of communications between people rather than on the informational or conceptual level. Individuals are encouraged to deal with their feelings about themselves and about others and to explore the impact they have upon each other. They examine feelings, expressions, gestures, and subtle behaviours which in everyday life often are taken for granted. Second, the training is not structured in a conventional manner. The staff member does not provide the group with a topic of conversation. The individual members must decide themselves what they want to talk about, what kinds of problems they wish to deal with, and what means they want to use in reaching their goals. As they concern themselves with these problems, they begin to act in characteristic ways: some people remain silent, some are aggressive, some tend consistently to initiate discussion, and some attempt to structure the proceedings. With the aid of the staff member, these approaches or developments become the focal points for discussion and analysis. The staff member draws attention to events and behaviour in the group by occasional interventions in the form of tentative interpretations which he considers will provide useful information for study. He encourages members to focus attention on behaviour in the group *here-and-now.* Who is behaving in what way and what feelings are being generated as a result? Third, the heart of a T-group experience is found in small groups, allowing a high level of participation, involvement and free communication. These groups therefore consist of between eight to twelve members.

As Smith (1967) has suggested, any T-group, as any natural group, has a number of problems toward which its attention is focused. Some of these are:

The problem of distribution of power and influence. Shall the group be tightly structured? Shall it be informal and unplanned. Who shall determine this? How shall the group deal with the staff member's power and influence?

The problem of intimacy. How much of my private thoughts and feelings is it right to tell the group? How close shall the group members become to one another?

The problem of identity. What sort of person am I? How do I compare with these other group members? What is the 'real' me — me as I see me, or me as they can see me?

As the group works on these problems, it develops a normative structure or set of rules governing the range of permissible behaviours, a more open and trusting environment, and a less defensive one. When this occurs it is possible for group members to give and receive feedback with regard to one another's behaviour. The feedback process is one whereby a member of the group is told by the others what effect his behaviour has had on them. Individuals in the group learn that the sort of feedback that is usable by the receiver does not comprise general value judgments (I think that you are an aggressive s.o.b., etc.) but specific statements as to what feelings and behaviour followed an act of the receiver's ('When you proposed that you should be chairman, I was very angry, but I said nothing because I feared the consequences'). In this way each member of the group builds up a picture of how the others respond to his customary behaviour. 'Accurate communication necessitates this kind of checking of messages which is rarely possible in ordinary everyday life' (Smith, 1969).

In the future, some form of self-awareness as it relates to our participation in groups may come to be seen as a prerequisite for anyone who spends his working life among *groups* of people. For the present, the full potentialities of the T-group method have certainly not been worked out, although much research evidence (Cooper & Mangham, 1971) is now available to support its use as a highly important method of enhancing self-awareness and the awareness of the dynamics of group behaviour. Little is known, however, about all aspects of the T-group that lead to its effectiveness, but more research in this area is now being undertaken. The importance of the T-group method is that it recognises that the findings of social psychology are more likely to be understood and internalised if they are rediscovered anew by each individual.

References

Cooper, C.L. and Mangham, I.L., *T-groups: A survey of research,* London: John Wiley, 1971.
Smith, P.B., The use of T-groups in effecting individual and

organisational change, *Psychological Scene,* 1, 1967.
Smith, P.B., *Improving skills in working with people,*
London: Department of Employment and Productivity,
1969.
Tannenbaum, R., Weschler, I.R. and Massarik, F.,
Leadership and organisation: A behavioral science approach,
New York: McGraw-Hill, 1961.

2 Implicit values in experiential learning groups: their functional and dysfunctional consequences

Experiential learning groups have been available as a method of social skill training for nearly thirty years (Bradford, Gibb and Benne, 1964; Cooper 1972), (we will from time to time refer to the experiential activities as T-groups, as a shorthand phrase). In that time, they have blossomed into a wide range of different applications with different populations (Siroka, Siroka, and Schloss, 1971; Blumberg and Golembiewski, 1976). They have also been subsumed under a host of different labels — T-groups, sensitivity groups, encounter groups, *Gestalt* therapy groups, Esalen groups, personal growth groups, sometimes indicating a different orientation, but more often not (Mills, 1976). Nonetheless, there has been a common core of values which has cut through these groups and made them a distinct type of group experience (Levine and Cooper, 1976). They have been one of the major educational innovations of the last thirty years and they have affected substantially the development of other educational techniques over that period. Our purpose in this chapter is to discuss explicitly the values inherent in experiential learning groups, the value conflicts that emerge frequently in such groups and the manner in which an understanding of the underlying assumptions and values under which practitioners are operating can help in the planning of a more internally consistent and effective group experience.

Values in groups

In the last few years, there have been a number of criticisms levelled against these group-learning techniques, many of which raise serious questions about goals and values involved (Back, 1967; Lakin, 1969; Back, 1972). While some of these criticisms have been wide off the mark, others have struck at the core of assumptions and values upon which this movement has legitimated itself. Group practitioners have been accused of being anti-scientific, unconcerned with the problems of society, of not showing an awareness for ethical issues, and of not making careful selection of prospective participants. The strength of the criticisms, it appears, paralleled the growth of the group movement. As it expanded into different areas, allowing more and more persons to participate in various group experiences, the criticisms levelled against it increased. This was exacerbated by experiential group proponents, who often made the criticisms more scathing by retreating occasionally into Messianic positions ('We are creating a new way'), more often into self-fulfilling justifications ('You have to go through this experience to understand it'), and quite commonly into conceptually sloppy and mystifying rationales for their purpose.

Very rarely did the 'group people' systematically try to study the group phenomenon that they had created and to subject it to the type of evaluation that most other educational approaches are eventually forced to accept. The research, naturally, did show that participants in group situations could change under certain circumstances (Cooper and Mangham, 1971). People could learn to be more open with others (Rubin, 1967), more sensitive to social situations (Bass, 1962), more understanding of how other people see them (Burke and Bennis, 1961), have more insight into human behaviour (Argyris, 1965), more aware of their own feelings (French, Sherwood, and Bradford, 1966), and more adaptable and flexible in social situations (Cooper, 1972). In short, experiential learning groups could be meaningful experiences for people *under certain circumstances*. The key here, however, is 'under certain circumstances', for there is sufficient research to show that the trainer, the group context, the personalities of the members are all critical dimensions in determining whether a group experience is valuable or not (Cooper, Levine, and Kobayashi, 1976; Cooper, 1977). There is a great deal of research evidence showing that group experiences can be neutral in their effect (Cooper and Mangham, 1971) and some even show that such experiences could be harmful under certain circumstances (Cooper, 1975; Smith, 1975).

Groups as technology

Experiential learning groups, just like any other educational or programmatic techniques, have to be evaluated continuously in order to improve their effectiveness as a technique. Consciousness of the process grows slowly as mistakes are made, as criticisms are levelled, and as a growing level of sophistication about selectivity of participants and methods is obtained. The effect of all of this is to provide practitioners with a great insight into the whys and wherefores of the technique. If we want to put this more abstractly, we can say that any educational technique has a set of assumptions and a set of values inherent in it. The assumptions take the form of operating rules, whereby the practitioners need guidelines to respond to their participants, and the values emerge in the form of desired ends or goals for which the technique is aimed (Levine, 1971; 1972). It may take a while before practitioners can verbalise explicitly the values and assumptions upon which they operate, but eventually with experience this emerges. There are, of course, alternative values and assumptions possible, and they have their own techniques associated with them. But this is in the nature of all technologies. Technologies always have particular values, goals and assumptions, and the manner in which choice between technologies is made is at this theoretical level, rather than as a technical decision.

This might seem relatively straightforward, and somewhat pedantic at that, if we did not realise that practitioners of experiential learning group techniques have been extremely guilty of not facing up to the assumptions and values inherent in the types of group they operate; and at times these practitioners have even gone to the other extreme and insisted that they operate according to 'no values and assumptions'! (Clark, 1962). The experiential learning group was, after all, conceived of in the context of allowing a free interchange of communication, of focusing on 'emergent' problems in a group (the 'here and now') rather than on external 'structural' problems, on being open to all kinds of different feelings, on acknowledging the impact of people as they occur, and on learning to be flexible and adaptive in relating to others. Their whole focus has been on spontaneity and creativity, rather than on structured cognition. People go to groups to 'discover things', to be surprised, to be active, to try out different behaviours, to experience intense emotions (to be angry, to fall in love, to be free, to be childlike and happy again); they do not go to groups to be lectured to, to learn formal material(s), to have to 'work hard', to have to accomplish things, to have to behave in structured ways. Experiential learning groups are 'fun' and are not supposed to be 'hard work'. They are innovative and creative, not formalised. They have their own 'experiential logic', not a mathematical, nor a social conventional, nor even an 'ideal behaviour' logic.

Such feelings often underlie participation in group experiences by practitioners and members alike. It is, however, one thing to say that experiential learning groups do not have structured activities, and another to pretend that they do not have 'structure' to them — a set of assumptions, values and goals. For it is our contention here that such groups are highly structured, that the practitioners and members both act in accordance with this structure, and, more importantly, that their awareness of the inherent structure can allow a greater degree of planning of the part of practitioners. Making more explicit assumptions, goals and values is the first step towards planning how this process is to be effectively handled. The more explicit one is about the process, the clearer one can be about how to plan it, the more open one can be about mistakes in the design, the quicker a rectification will occur, and the more effective the technique will become in the long run. In short, what we are saying is that experiential learning groups form a technology just like any other technology, and thus the same rules and logic can be applied towards improving this technology as any other.

Experiential learning groups as value systems

In an earlier article (Levine and Cooper, 1976), we attempted to define some of the expressed common goals that are often stated in experiential learning groups and some of the underlying social conditions that have created this movement. Basically, we argued that a T-group is a type of group in which there is a commitment towards involvement, towards relating the group to its outside environment. These four or five values, as a composite, form roughly a type of group that can be distinguished from other types of group. This does not mean that all experiential learning groups are the same (they certainly are not) nor that there are not differences in style, goals, purposes between groups. Rather, virtually all of the experiential group movement has accepted these values in their general form, as well as adding new ones depending on the context.

The T-groups and the common values expressed by them, however, must be seen as a product of four societal conditions which created the demands for this type of group. The T-group movement emerged as a function of an Anglo-American dominance in social science after the Second World War, as a product of an advanced capitalist economy in which there was a concern for improving administrative and organisational skills, as a function of a young age structure due to the high birth rates after the war, and as an expression of middle-class needs. The experiential learning group or T-group was the child of post Second World War Anglo-American society (Levine and Cooper, 1976). Experiential learning groups emerged as a sought-after technology. The state of society at the time they emerged was one dominated by large organisations (both private and public), which had complicated problems of planning, organising, producing, and distributing their product (Galbraith, 1967). A whole range of new managerial and administrative problems emerged in this context, and the interests of group-training people, who were beginning to discover a number of principles of small group behaviour, were aimed in this direction. The demand for these applications came primarily from these large organisations, for without them the group movement would never have grown and developed as it did.

Also, people were concerned about their sense of 'being' in this new advanced, corporate society. The increasing bureaucratic organisation of America and Europe after the war created new roles for people (Reisman, 1950). There were strong pressures towards improving one's living standard, and the means for doing this were suddenly more available for a higher proportion of the society than was the case previously. There were less strong, but developing, pressures towards social equality, which started to show themselves in the late 1950s (Civil Rights movement, equal opportunity, etc.). There was a negative side to this, of course. New roles created confusion over expected behaviour, and people started to question how they were supposed to act (Erikson, 1950). In the 1950s and especially during the 1960s, there was suddenly a widespread concern in American-European society over finding a sensible style of relating to other people. This concern was shown by the increase in books and films on behaviour, psychology, therapy, and liberation, on seeking out new ways of 'relating to one's body', on 'discovering ourselves', and so forth. Participants, and trainers, were attending the groups partly to obtain skills in relating to large organisations, but also towards discovering hidden aspects of themselves and new ways of behaving towards others. The problem was perceived at an individual level — discovering oneself, developing one's personal resources, eliminating neurotic behavioural patterns — but the stimulus for such a problem was rooted in the society, and the values implicit in this behaviour were social (Erikson, 1956).

This brings us up against one of the most important implicit assumptions of the whole experiential learning group movement, namely that change is to be sought through 'individuals' rather than through 'collectivities' (Bradford, Gibb, and Benne, 1964). The new large organisations that have emerged slowly throughout this century, and which blossomed after the Second World War, were assumed to be permanent, 'fixed' entities. Change, if it had to occur, had to be through 'individuals'. Thus, people are brought to groups to learn about behaviour, to learn about their behaviour in social situations, to learn how to be more flexible, etc. When we make such a commitment towards 'individual education', we are implicitly accepting the *status quo* of the society. Society is all right; individuals must change. There is nothing wrong, of course, with working with individuals; the whole education system is set up on similar premises, after all; but there is an aspect of this that we must accept if we are properly to understand the values and assumptions inherent in an experiential group process. This is namely that education always has a strong socialising component — a normative dimension; education teaches knowledge and skills, but it also teaches attitudes, values, and roles which are part of a social formation. And, that, therefore, we are learning to fit into a social system in learning these. Even the knowledge and skill components are social to a large extent. Knowledge is not created abstractly, but by specific individuals working within specific institutions, existing in specific places, etc. Similarly with skills; skills must be acted out in certain places and on certain materials and in certain relationships with specific people. We live in a real world, not an abstract one, so that education is always social in form.

This emphasis on the individual, however, brings up an important complication, which is that individual change must be consistent with the given organisations within which a person works or lives. Many people involved in group work, especially those concerned with organisational development, soon discovered the limits of the group approach when the attempted to push participants to express behaviours that were inconsistent with the norms in which these individuals worked (Harrison, 1972). A potential conflict between the values pursued in a T-group and the values existing in a social organisation emerges because the limits for change of the organisation are so narrow. Most large organisations are economic-based; they either produce something, distribute that produce, or else give services and collect their income from other producing organisations (e.g., the Government). Economic relationships tend to be relatively stable, for people have too much to lose by changing these frequently. Thus, economic organisations are essentially conservative. The T-group, on the other hand, argues for flexibility on the part of participants, on openness to new experiences, on confronting people who are not communicating, and generally on individual change. What happens, then, when an individual working within an organisation tries to change his behaviour? If that change is inconsistent with the existing norms, the chances are that he will have to accept the norms or else become a deviant in that situation.

All of this is a way of saying that experiential learning groups are specific groups which occur in a specific social context. To talk about such groups as if they are removed from that context, as if the goals and values that they express are 'universal' ones (free of social sanctions), as if people can act any way they want without impunity, is to create a myth about groups, and a very antisocial one at that — which is incapable of being enacted on in any real society. Unstructured groups, which allow total freedom to individuals to act and express anything they want, cannot produce any permanent change in individuals; the groups can only exist by themselves, and as soon as the group disbands the reality of the behaviour disbands.

Sources of values

Values become important to experiential learning groups because they affect the way people behave and they affect what people learn in the groups. Therefore, we will have to explore these values in more depth — what values are important, how these are expressed in the group, and how a trainer or facilitator can incorporate value-analysis in setting up and planning the design of experiential learning group experiences.

Values which affect T-groups can have five different sources:

1. They can come from the society at large, and be general values.
2. They can come from the organisational context of the group.
3. They can come from the trainer.
4. They can come from the members themselves.
5. They can emerge in the process of the interaction.

Let us take each of these in turn.

Societal values

Societal values come from the society at large. Sometimes these values are made explicit; other times they are not. But they are always *potential* — they emerge if someone violates them. For example, there are social conventions that are normally followed in groups, such as the wearing of clothes. This convention is so accepted and commonly understood that it deserves little comment in a group, except when it is explicitly violated as in the case of nude marathon groups (Appley and Winter, 1973).

Aside from these normal conventions, there are a number of social values which are important in affecting the behaviour of members in an experiential group. The most obvious are the perceived status characteristics of the members. All societies acknowledge age and sex differences, and they usually also acknowledge class, ethnic, racial, educational, and sometimes religious differences. Most groups have to work through these differences, and yet they have not been properly discussed by 'group people'. Older persons command more respect by virtue of their age. Sometimes this is made explicit by members, especially if it proves to be a problem, but often it is not. Similarly, sex differences are usually acknowledged, sometimes worked on, but often played down. Sex differences usually create a double-edged problem for groups. On the one hand, there are the usual assumptions about sex-role differences. In some (e.g., managerial groups), women are not expected to play an equal role with men, especially as it relates to power and decision-making, but are encouraged to play social-emotional or integrative roles. But more often than not, this *role typing* is questioned, usually by women, and the group is pushed to handle the issue. The social value of sex roles emerges here because that value is itself undergoing a change in the society, and new roles for men and women are being created. Thus, what one often observes inside a group is the acting out of this role transition in mirror form. The submissive/social-emotional female is transformed into the assertive/aggressive female trying to overcome this passive role, while the aggressive/dominant male is transformed into a more passive/accepting male trying to overcome guilt feelings about being dominant. The T-group does no more than highlight the social conflict outside by creating a microcosm inside.

The other side of the sex difference problem, however, is the question of sexuality. Men and women are naturally attracted to each other, and the relative freedom of the T-group and the strong pressure on expression of feelings quickly brings such feelings out. How this is expressed, however, varies according to the type of sex-role model accepted by the group. In 'Male Chauvinistic' groups, women are usually in the minority anyway, so the traditional role of men competing to 'capture' the women is played out in a symbolic way. By the nature of the situation, however, this game must end in negating sexual advances, so that sex-role equality emerges as a means of controlling sexuality (see Freud, 1918, for an analogous model). In other cases, however, when the participants generally accept more egalitarian and less stereotyped sex roles, and in situations where women are in the majority, the groups may shy away from expressing such feelings. Usually group pressures are such as to discourage the overt expression of sexuality in the public area.

Groups often handle these two types of issue, at least superficially. But other status-issues usually do not emerge, if only because T-groups are run with such a homogeneous population. Class differences rarely occur because of the over-dominant middle-class orientation of the groups, nor do ethnic or racial differences, which often interrelate with class differences (see Rubin, 1967; Olmosk and Graverson, 1972; Smith and Wilson, 1975 for examples of groups run along these lines). Religious differences often do not occur because these are becoming less important, especially in the more developed countries.

To the extent that these differences do not appear, however, they tend to reinforce particular class values and fail to confront these with broader, more egalitarian social values. If participants are never exposed to class or racial differences because working-class and various racial minority group persons rarely come to T-groups, then members of groups — white, middle-class people — are never exposed to other perceptions of the society and have difficulty in grasping or understanding the position of more exploited people.

In addition, the intimate, involved atmosphere of the T-group creates strong pressures towards minimising social conflict when it appears. Groups quickly agree that 'women are equal to men', 'blacks' have been discriminated against and ought to be 'integrated', 'workers are human just like everyone else and ought to receive their fair share of the social wealth', and then go on to deny such differences. In doing this, however, groups are playing down the existence of these social conflicts, which actually do exist in the society (and are taking sides in doing so). They are saying 'we are all white middle-class at roots', a myth which is so blatantly wrong as to be obvious. In this sense participants are not learning anything useful, and in fact, are actually helping to perpetuate the problem.

Another type of social value which emerges in T-groups, often in a very disguised form, is the notion of the 'well-adjusted Man'. Groups make assumptions about psychological 'normality' and then expect participants to conform to these assumptions (Szasz, 1961; Laing, 1965). Participants are assumed to be healthy, emotionally well-adjusted individuals (normative people), as distinct from 'sick', pathological individuals seeking help (for example, as in therapy groups). People who do not act in these 'normal' ways are considered 'deviant', 'undersocialised', 'disturbed', or a whole host of other labels which can be applied. Now, quite clearly, 'normality' is a set of normative behaviours which varies by society, by social class, by subculture, and there may be differences in the interpretation of members over what is acceptable behaviour and what is not. Young people tolerate sexuality, aggression, drugs, the expression of positive feelings far more easily than do older, pre-Second World War persons. On the other hand, materialistic motives, competition, power-seeking are far more acceptable norms to express for the older than for the younger generation. Nonetheless, in spite of these subcultural differences, there is still a great deal of overlap and communality on what is considered 'normal' behaviour. In particular, participants will become very disturbed when confronted by bizarre behaviour on the part of one member. If they cannot attribute the behaviour to events which occurred inside the group, or to role-playing, then the members become very uncomfortable and feel an inadequacy to deal with the situation. Participants are expected to act within normal limits, and if someone goes outside these limits no one knows how to handle the situation. Sometimes, of course, the individual is actually play-acting, and other times the individual may be threatening the group (e.g. as if he or she was saying 'I'm going to get you people. I'm going to throw a schizophrenic episode at you and see how you handle it. I'm going to freak out'), but this type of behaviour is always disturbing to the members. It is hard to give rules-of-thumb on what to do in such a situation if one is a group leader, but we have often found that confronting the situation in just these terms has often alleviated the tension. We point out to the group that the members are making assumptions about normality, and that person X is challenging those assumptions. Often this has allowed the group to redefine the situation and perhaps reintegrate person X back into the group. For example, this person may have been acting this way because he or she felt excluded from the group. Or the behaviour may have occurred because the person could not handle the trust being shown, or, more likely, the person may be acting this way just because there is a lack of trust in the group and this is the manner in which this individual can express that. Pointing out the implicit norms of normality can be a fruitful way of opening up members towards greater flexibility and innovative behaviour by a group, especially those used to rigid hierarchies.

Organisational or contextual values

A second source of values for experiential learning groups, and possibly the least recognised by trainers, is the organisational context. Groups always develop and operate in a specific environment. Starting with the recruitment into the group, through assembling the group at a time and place, to the actual interaction of the members there is always a specific context which surrounds the group. In some cases, this context may be explicit (e.g., managers from a single company, members of a course structure), but more often than not it is implicit. Yet even where the context does not seem to be the overriding issue in a group, there are many contextual assumptions and values. The most basic one is the idea of 'relevance'. The behaviour in the group, and the learning to be achieved, must be 'relevant'. Relevance, of course, has a specific meaning, one defined by the contextual environment. For an OD group, relevance is behaviour and learning that will help individuals adapt to their specific work environment. For a more individualistic group, relevance is behaviour-orientated towards self-knowledge, and attitudes and beliefs related to a specific social group. Seeking intimacy is relevant for groups in which intimacy is valued. Showing aggression may be relevant for social groups which value aggression. Showing aggression may be bad, for other social groups which play down competition and aggression. Psychological states are very circumscribed by societal and situational norms. Even the most universalistic of human expressions, such as love, intimacy, trust, acknowledgement, positive regard are meaningful at certain times and places. For a manager attending an OD group, exploring his deeper feelings of intimacy and love for his wife will be irrelevant for the organisational purpose which he joined the group in the first place.

But relevance has other meanings than just the situational appropriateness of various behaviours. It also has the idea of loyalty attached to it. In order for behaviour to be relevant for a setting, one must belong to a group in which that behaviour is expressed. This point has not been properly grasped by many group facilitators who have insisted on pushing certain behaviours as if they were universal and relevant for every group and every situation. 'Be more open' is like the Eleventh Commandment in many group leaders' eyes. But why? Is it always appropriate to be open? What about when a person meets an enemy? Should he be open then? What happens to a poor black person when he is confronted with a hostile white policeman wanting to know what he is doing? Should he be open? In fact, *can* he be open? Openness requires that the other person is willing to tolerate openness, and in some situations it is better to be a little bit paranoid if one is going to be adaptive to a situation.

Do not get us wrong. We are not advocating that people do not have to be open, that they should be defensive and manipulative, that they should mistrust their fellow men. We know the full value of openness and honesty, of expressing one's feelings (or knowing how to express one's feelings); these are all valuable states and the group movement has done much to encourage these social values. All we are saying is that the appropriateness of a behaviour pattern must be relevant to the context in which it occurs, and a trainer should pay attention to this (see Cooper, Levine, and Kobayashi, 1976). The establishment of trust and openness are two-way communications, after all, and pushing these values on only one side may not be enough. For example, managers often complain that they cannot communicate with their bosses, that either their bosses do not understand them or feel afraid that they will be superseded by their subordinate. Clearly the organisational setting in which such a perception occurs is a competitive one in which loyalty to the firm and self-promotion are delicately balanced in a semi-stable equilibrium. How can one expect one's boss to be open and accepting if he or she fears that his job may be lost if he does? In this case, 'openness', as a behavioural value, has to be modified so that it becomes relevant for the situation. Perhaps the manager would do well to test limits slowly and see if it is possible to open up the dialogue over a long period rather than prematurely exposing himself.

One of the most pressing problems of relevance in any group situation concerns the question of divided loyalties. If, in particular, the members happen to come from a single institution, there may be a split between a feeling of loyalty to the whole institution and a loyalty to one of its parts. This is more obvious with participants from a formal organisation, especially a large one. Commitment to the particular subdivision that one belongs to (such as a production unit, or a sales unit inside a large company, or a particular academic department inside a university) often takes priority over a commitment towards the organisation as a whole. This can be seen in terms of the necessities inherent in a job — that certain demands are required in order to satisfy the role requirements of the job — or it can be as a reaction to the particularism of another subdivision. For example, academic departments often feel maligned by university administrations for looking after themselves only. The behavioural consequences of such particularism should be fairly evident — the functioning of the whole may be disrupted by the particularism of the parts. In the above example, the academic department tries to hang on to as much money as possible in the annual budget allocated to it, even if it will not spend all its funds sensibly. There may be a long-standing history which has created mistrust between units, and it may be necessary to recreate trust before units will accept the goals of the whole organisation first. Such a problem creates substantial material for any T-group wanting to look at such issues.

Even with groups that are not obviously from a single institution, the issue of particular versus holistic loyalty emerges. There is a conflict over more individual values being followed compared to more social ones. Within the group interaction itself, group members must negotiate a balance between allowing individuals to satisfy their own needs as opposed to creating a group structure that allows more interdependency. 'Giving to others', after all, means 'denying to oneself', in the short run at least. Groups may confront certain individuals with the idea that they are attempting to satisfy their own needs at the expense of others. Members may be accused of 'dominating the group', 'not listening to others', 'cutting out certain members', and so forth. As group trainers, we usually advocate a group-orientated approach on the grounds that once an effective, trustful, communicative group structure has been built, then individuals can more easily satisfy their own individual needs. But still this does not solve the issue; different groups achieve more group-orientated structures than others. In fact, the different approaches to experiential groups often break down on this issue. Personal expression-type groups are far more individualistic than the traditional T-group, and both are much less so than OD groups (Mills, 1976).

The issue of particularism appears, however, on an even more social level. To what extent do the members of the group see themselves as belonging to a broader collectivity? T-groups with students often show this dilemma (Levine, 1973). Especially in America and Great Britain, students tend to treat their experiences as students in isolation from the university context in which they participate. It is as if they were saying 'I am an individual trying to get along in the world. I can't be bothered with other people's needs. All I want to do is satisfy my own needs.' Sampson (1975) has called this 'self-contained individualism' and he sees this as emanating from a capitalistic economy that pits people against each other in a competitive manner. It is very hard for a person to see himself as part of a broader collectivity, especially when that collectivity is so loosely defined. Yet we do live in a society, and how we act does affect others in that society. Perhaps we have been too guilty of encouraging individualism at all costs, and not paying enough attention to one's role in the social world in which we live.

Trainer's values

There are a number of ways in which experiential group leaders can communicate values that can influence individual learning. First and foremost, values are highlighted and communicated by the intervention behaviour of the group facilitator, that is, his behaviour serves as a 'value model'. For example, a passive, interpretative authority-orientated trainer (in the Tavistock mode) is modelling and could be seen to be advocating 'emotional distance', 'patriarchial relationships', and 'low involvement and participation' (Cooper, 1976). In addition, an aggressive, dominant and highly active group leader could be positing control, confrontation, low social support, etc. On the other hand, an interactive or congruent one could be advocating a democratic process, collective decision-making and collective responsibility. It is terribly important for trainers to be aware that their behaviour reflects, communicates, and in many cases, models certain values which can influence immediate learning and subsequent behaviour of participants. Second, trainer values are also expressed in the design of the training experience; how structured or unstructured the sessions are, how the trainer's role is defined in the sessions, the nature of the role that the trainer adopts *vis-à-vis* the participants outside the group, the degree of involvement of the constituents in the design of the programme, etc. This is to a large extent related to the motives of the group leaders, in the first place, in engaging in experiential group activity. Each trainer behaves in ways that create the conditions for both psychological success and failure, which are related to his own needs and psychological make-up (Argyris, 1965). The group facilitator can exploit his role in the pursuance of these needs, particularly in his desire to be liked or to exercise power. As Schein and Bennis (1965) have emphasised: 'The possibilities for unconscious gratification in the change-agent's role are enormous and because of their consequences (for the health of the client as well as the change-agent) they must be examined.' It is essential that training programmes be developed that focus on the trainer's motives and values and how these may enable or prevent participants from learning in their own way.

Members' values

A fourth source of values comes from the participants of experiential learning groups. Group member values take the form of 'needs' and 'desired goals'. Needs refer of various personal and interpersonal predispositions and 'desired goals' as to what is expected to be obtained from participating in a group (e.g., specific help to solve an organisational problem, learning to assert oneself better, learning to communicate better, learning to be more open to one's feelings, etc.). The 'desired goals' may be implicit and not recognised at the start of an experiential group by the member — he/she may discover them as the group unfolds. The needs, desired goals, and implicit goals will play a very important part in the development of group climate, the effectiveness of the group experience, etc. More importantly, where we have trouble with member values is when they come into conflict with trainer values. Trainers have a way of imposing their own values on the participants; in fact, this frequently stems from the lack of awareness of trainee needs or from an overwhelming need to express their own values. Group members may go along with this imposition, but will resent it later if they do not satisfy their own needs through the intervention (for example, the trainer wants to push an encounter exercise, while members want to integrate or conceptualise the experiences thus far acquired). We must distinguish here between situations when the trainer can perceive some needs that the group will discover and, thus, he/she structures the group in order to demonstrate them versus situations where the trainer is trying to use the group to satisfy his own needs, irrespective of what the members want.

Nevertheless, the understanding of member values are critical to the success of the group experience — unfortunately these are not always conscientiously considered.

Emergent values

A fifth source of values involves values which are discovered during the process of the interaction, which were neither planned by the trainer nor defined by the members; they are, so to speak, 'spontaneously' discovered. One of the best illustrations of these values is conclusions the group may reach as a consequence of actions that have developed during the interaction. For example, at large group sessions, there is often a fragmentation that takes place partly because of the large size and partly because of a lack of integration. A subgroup of this larger group may decide to 'act out' on their

own, and the consequence of this will be further
fragmentation. Such behaviour may come back to haunt the
subgroup as a chain of events it triggered off that soon affects
the initial fragmentation (i.e., subgroup A breaks off,
subgroup B then follows, the subgroup C fragments, and
soon there is no large group any more). The members may
come to the conclusion that action on the part of a subgroup
fundamentally threatens the overall cohesiveness of the large
group, unless it has been discussed and agreed on by the
larger collectivity. Thus, a value emerges — the need for
macro-planning as a consequence of the interaction.

Other examples can be given of emergent values, for they
constitute one of the major learning experiences in T-groups.
People discover principles because they can view the
consequences of certain actions. A person who controls his
feelings and does not communicate with others may learn
that by doing so other people will not trust him. If he can see
the consequences of his actions, then he may take an
important value from the group. A dominant member may
learn that he/she is not trusted or followed, again because
other members will not accept his/her leadership when
he/she is mistrusted. We learn very much through the
consequences of our actions, if we are lucky enough to see
them, and one of the important purposes of a T-group is to
provide this type of learning.

Value conflicts

So far we have discussed values as if they emerge naturally in
the group and are quite compatible with each other. Quite
clearly this is wrong and it is more likely that there are values
which are in direct conflict with one another, as well as a
normal competition between alternative values for priorities
in the group. If we think of the group as a sort of market-
place to values, then we can better understand some of the
interaction that is occurring. The trainer and the members are
competing to push their own values, and it may take time

before the group achieves a consensus over which values take higher priorities.

Conflicting values occur periodically in groups, and in the normal course of social life. Conflict over external values — political, economic, religious — may enter into the interaction, as they do outside the group. But there may also be a conflict over values which relate directly to the behaviour of the members. Some members or trainers place greater value on the satisfaction of individual needs within the group, while others emphasise more social needs. This is not just a question of competing values, but one of fundamental emphasis. Is it better to express one's feelings towards someone or is it better to be sensitive to the needs of others? There are times when these are conflicting values which are not reducible to a common theme. As trainers, we like to believe that the open expression of feelings will necessarily lead to better interaction between members, but it does not always follow. Sometimes the expression of feelings will push the group in a certain, individualistic direction, and it becomes difficult, if not impossible, to get the group moving in a more social direction. There are certain critical periods in a group's life when there is a fluidity of direction. At these points, a trainer has a lot of influence and can push the group in a number of different directions; this has been even simulated in experiments of group-training style (Cooper, 1969). If the trainer is more individually orientated, the group will go in that particular direction, whereas if the trainer is more socially orientated, the group will move accordingly. The choice of values is between conflicting ones, not congruent values. Usually trainers decide on some kind of trade-off between these two values, but in all cases this involves a conscious choice.

Some other conflicts which occur frequently in OD groups are an emphasis on adapting towards the institutional framework of the organisation versus emphasising fundamental change in the organisation. Do we encourage people to be flexible and adaptable when they return to their organisation or do we want them to be more radical in their approach? At times, social class conflicts also have a great bearing on the way OD groups are run. Whom do we encourage the members to identify with? The management? The total organisation? The workers? To the extent that such conflicts do not emerge within the organisation, this will not be an issue, but most organisations periodically do go through 'class conflicts', especially at wage negotiation time, and a T-group caught in the middle of this will be divided by this issue. Which side will the trainer opt for in encouraging the group to move in a certain direction? Or let us take another example. Frequently, large private industrial corporations pursue economic goals which may at times conflict with larger societal goals. For example, an industrial company may wish to expand its production which increases pollution in the environment and thus may bring harm to the society. How does the trainer handle this issue, especially when the trainer is usually an organisational outsider, while being a member of the society? Does the trainer pretend that the issue does not exist, and tries to avoid it inside the group? If so, the trainer is taking sides — with the company against the society! Or does the trainer confront the group with his own values? It takes a lot of courage to confront a group such as that, considering that one may not be invited back to run any more groups. Yet a trainer is forced to choose one of two conflicting social values at this point by his behaviour.

These are extreme examples, but they do illustrate the value limits within which we work as trainers. We are not valueless people, but thinking, feeling, acting people who have a place in a social world. At times we will be periodically called upon to express our values, and to implement them into action, and a T-group is a very likely place where this might happen, given the open, fluid, permissive milieu.

More often than not, however, trainers and members will be forced to choose between competing values in defining priorities. Very often this occurs in the recruitment process. A group which is advertised as 'Encounter Group', *'Gestalt* Therapy Group', 'Self-Actualising', or 'Personal Growth Group' will convey a very different set of priorities that one which is advertised as 'Group Dynamics Group', 'Sensitivity Group', 'T-Group', or 'OD Group'. Regardless of what the trainer had in mind (and research has shown that labels are not particularly good guides to trainers' values [Mills, 1976]), the first type of group will conjure up in the mind of the potential participant an image of very individualistic goals, whereas the second type of group will convey a promise of more 'groupy' activities. Participants will select themselves partly on the basis of these images, and some of the goals for the group will be defined already.

But even within the group interaction, there will be a need to choose between competing values: between emphasising the expression of feelings in contrast to emphasising perceptions of each other; between emphasising our senses (such as touch, hearing, seeing) compared to emphasising our intellect (that is, better understanding of the dynamics); between emphasising more activity in contrast to emphasising more awareness and sensitivity; between emphasising role behaviour and role awareness in contrast to emphasising the breaking-out of roles; between emphasising orderly and rational planning compared to emphasising spontaneity and adaptive/decision-making. We are continually faced with choices where we have to order our priorities. We have to say that some behaviours or ideas are more important than others, and we have to structure our behaviour accordingly. And not only are trainers doing this, but members are doing it as well in their interaction. The main difference, however, is that the trainer is the most important person in the group, at least in the sense that the trainer structures the group, takes responsibility for its planning and execution, continually intervenes in order to point the group in certain directions, and has to acknowledge any outcomes of the group. If the members are satisfied, then the trainer receives praise. If the members are not, then blame is attributed accordingly.

Values and planning

The point we have been trying to make throughout this chapter is that an experiential learning group can be designed with more explicit and conscious decision-making processes. Values are being selected and chosen and brought into the group, or rejected, resulting in the group seeking an outcome for its efforts. Any group has an elaborate structure to it, comprising the assumptions, goals and values of the society reflected in the trainer and the members. The trainer, furthermore, is given the responsibility and power to plan and guide the group in a certain direction, and therefore he or she must choose between alternative values. The more explicit the group leader can be about the values involved, the more effective the group experience will be by virtue of the 'means having been adapted to fit the goal'.

Many trainers would reject this philosophy as being 'too intellectual' or 'too structured' and would prefer instead a philosophy that is 'more open' or 'more accepting of what happens'. 'Whatever happens, happens!' might be a convenient label for such a philosophy. There is a reluctance to acknowledge that group situations are structured with many values. But in adopting such a position, a trainer is accepting an extremely fatalistic philosophy, one that is denying that we have the ability to structure our own future. After all, one of the major values of T-groups is to show people that they can structure their prospects and behaviour to some extent, that they can influence other people, and that they can change their behaviour when necessary. Surely it is a little bit inconsistent, therefore, for a trainer to advocate active, purposeful behaviour on the part of the members of the group, but to adopt passive and aimless fatalism on the part of himself or herself?

In this section, therefore, we would like to discuss some possible planning techniques and the manner in which values might be incorporated into the group process. Planning, of course, takes different forms. It usually involves the trainer(s) sitting down with the organisers and conceptualising why, how, where, and when the groups will take place. Then it usually involves the trainer sitting down before the group begins and planning an overall structure and schedule for the group, be it a residential, marathon, or weekly group. But planning also takes on an evaluative role as the trainers will take stock of the group situation periodically to check on the effectiveness of the design, to analyse barriers that have emerged in the groups, to incorporate new goals that may have emerged, and to organise interventions that might facilitate the process. Planning in this sense is really a flexible procedure whereby the initial goals are continually re-evaluated and adjusted in order to incorporate the unique characteristics of each group. Finally, planning has a *post hoc* nature whereby the trainers sit down after the group has finished and take stock of the outcome of the group experience. This type of activity is planning for future groups, to incorporate the lessons of the past. In this sense, research on group experiences is, or should be, part of planning as it can provide feedback on the process and outcome of groups.

Decision-tree approach of planning

How one plans, of course, varies from situation to situation, depending upon what kind of group is being run, how many trainers and groups there are, where the group is being run, what outcomes are anticipated and so forth. Nonetheless, there are certain guidelines that one can lay down, and we have put these into a decision-tree (see Figure 2.1).

The key to planning is to start with the outcome — the participants. We start with certain questions about the population (step 1). Who are they? Where do they come from? This then raises the next issue: what is the organisational context in which the group operates? We have to, at this stage, ask questions about the purpose of the group (step 2). Why is the group being held? Who has sponsored the group? Why have the participants volunteered to come?

Answering these questions helps us define the third step, which is what are the expectations of the members? What do they want to learn from the group? This defines the members' goals in the group.

At this point, the trainers' skills become important because a technical assessment must be made of the feasibility of developing these goals (step 4). We have to ask, 'Is it realistic to push these expectations?' For the sake of simplicity we divide the answer to this question into two parts, 'yes' and 'no'. If the answer is 'yes', then our next stage is to think about how this can be done (step 6a); our focus at this point is a 'technical' one. But if the answer is 'no', then we have to assess why it is not realistic to push these goals (step 5b). Again, we can simplify the answer to this question into two branches: (1) that it is impossible to handle these goals in this context (step 6c), and (2) that other values might also be important to push for (step 6b). In the first instance, the trainer might assess whether the time and resources allotted is sufficient to carry out the task. Knowing the limits to a group experience is perhaps one of the most important skills a trainer can ever learn, because it means being realistic about what is possible. For example, many participants come to groups expecting to gain therapy from the group. A wise trainer must be sensitive to this issue because, first, there may be insufficient time really to handle this kind of issue, and, second, the trainer may not be qualified to go into such depth. It would be very harmful indeed to try to raise emotional issues in a group situation if there was not enough time or sufficient skills available to do this. We must be realistic about what we are capable of doing in a group, and it is better to reject such goals at the beginning than to create false expectations among the participants that we cannot fulfil.

The second branching to this question (step 6b) involves bringing in our judgement about which other values are important. We may agree to accept some of the expected goals of the participants, but add some more, or we may decide to override some of these expectations. In both cases,

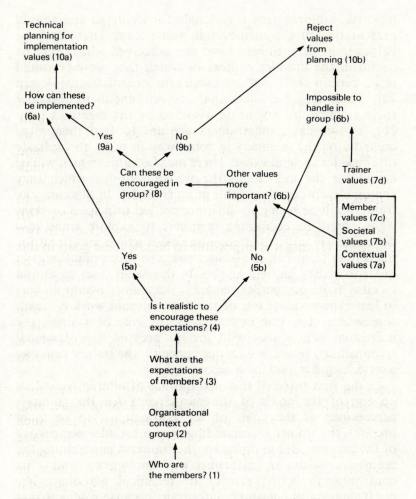

Figure 2.1 Decision-tree of planning decisions on value premises

however, trainers need a rationale for doing so and should present this to the members in some way. There may be values that the members have not perceived which may be useful in the broader context in which they were recruited (e.g., certain skills that are useful for organisations — step 7a). There may be values that are relevant in the broader society which are not being assumed by the members (step 7b); in this case, the trainers are apt to find themselves confronting the members in some way in order to explicate this broader societal value. There may be values which will be useful for the individuals themselves, but for which they cannot clearly perceive at this point (step 7c). In this case, the trainers will be trying to illustrate certain principles or skills while trying to encourage members to explore some new directions. Finally, there may be values which are useful for the trainer (step 7d); the trainer needs to do certain things in order to satisfy his/her psyche. In this latter case, as should be clear from our earlier remarks, the trainer would do well to leave these values out of the situation and work on them somewhere else. For in accepting the role of trainer, the individual who works with groups accepts a professional responsibility to act in a service capacity; the trainer provides a service (and is paid for it accordingly).

In the first three of this juxtaposing of alternative values on top of the goals of the participants (or the trainer's perceptions of the goals of the participants, to be more precise), the trainer is responding with a broader perspective of the process. But in doing so, the trainer is confronting the members with an alternative framework, and this confrontation is the essence of technical planning. The confrontation dimension is important because it means that we somehow have to show participants a different way, a new approach. We do this all the time in other activities (for example, a teacher tries to orient a student towards some new dimensions), but there is always some resistance brought by this confrontation. We feel that trainers should be conscious of this confrontation and should try to make it public in some way, to explain to the participants why it is that you are

confronting them. This is one way in which making one's
values explicit about a group situation can make it easier to
integrate these values into the process.

Logically, the next step (step 8) involves testing these new
values for feasibility, as we did in step 4, and then, depending
on the answers (steps 9a, 9b), either rejecting the value as
being impossible to build into the experience or else accepting
it and concentrating on technically developing it (step 10a).
What we have done, therefore, is logically to prune our
values so that we have some idea of what we are doing as we
approach a group. Obviously, the better we know the
situation of the participants, the better we know ourselves as
trainers, and the more experience we have had as trainers, the
clearer our planning will be and the more effective will be the
outcome.

Some methods for exploring value themes

We would like to end this discussion by briefly introducing a
few methods that would be appropriate for exploring value
themes. We will not go into detail, but will outline the general
form.

Creating conflicting values

Conflicting values are common in the real world outside
experiential learning groups, but have not been explored very
adequately by group trainers. The most basic method in
developing conflict is to create a division in a membership.
The criteria upon which the division is made then become
critical in focusing the members' awareness on this issue. This
division can be built into the formal design or it can be
introduced at a latter stage. But the more formal the division,
the more attention will be focused on the criteria of division.

Let us start with a division that already exists after a group
has developed to a certain point. For example, the group may
be dominated by a small subgroup while a larger subgroup is

very uninvolved. One technique is to make this division explicit and have the 'quiet' subgroup form a discussion group with the 'noisy' subgroup watching them. A less obvious way is to force the group to divide itself. The trainer poses the problem of a division (e.g., 'Let's split into quartets for one hour in order to explore our perceptions of each other') and let the group divide itself. Such a division may bring out the underlying division, or it may backfire and create two 'feudal armies' — the 'noisy' members capturing a couple of 'quiet' ones each and forming groups around them. The technique used will depend upon what is more appropriate to the situation; the trainer can usually get a sense of what might work, but the basic logic is the same.

Other subgrouping techniques that have been used by trainers are to break into pairs, trios, quartets, or even quintets. But the smaller subgroupings will usually focus attention on individual issues and less on conflict issues. Two divisions serve best for focusing attention on conflict, and three on coalition formation, a point noted long ago by Simmel (1908).

Conflict can usually be explored more fruitfully by deliberately building it into a design at the beginning. The earlier example gives one possibility. Another basis for division would be to choose some theme around which a division could be made; this, of course, would depend on there being enough individuals to fulfil the conditions of the theme. So, for example, one could create two or three groups on the basis of class, religion, nationality, sex, course structure, age, income, or any other social indicator. Splitting the group along these lines forces the group to face up to this issue; often the members may initially resent the division, for it brings conflict into the open. But in the end such a division will pose a problem for the members which they must try to solve. Self-divisions, as illustrated above, are often good for focusing attention on implicit divisions in a community of members. Similarly, one might want to focus the attention of the conflict on the intragroup process, rather than on the intergroup process.

A technique which is useful for exploring social conflict in a more sociological context is the use of simulation. In this case, a whole role structure has to be elaborated on in order to focus awareness on this, and participants become actors playing a role, rather than people playing themselves. Simulations were first developed as a form of war-gaming, but they have developed over the years to include political, economic, social and even psychological conflict situations (Guetzkow, 1959; Levine, 1973; Kolb *et al.,* 1974). The simulations can be full-blown (e.g., a decision-making exercise in a fictitious company; a student-administration conflict in an imaginary university) or they may be introduced as a part of a broader design (e.g., a production exercise within an OD laboratory). More details on simulations can be found in Kanderdine and Keys (1974), and Kibbee, Craft, and Nanus (1962).

Creating integrating values

The obverse of conflict is stability and integration, and there are a host of techniques available for creating these. In fact, much of the development of techniques in the group movement has concentrated on supporting these values (such as trust exercises, building better communication exercises, creating openness, etc.). But there are some common themes which run through these methods which distinguish them clearly from methods aimed at exploring conflict. First, divisions are discouraged, either by having only one group or by leaving the groups relatively autonomous if there is more than one group in an experiential design. Second, the method must encourage members that they will gain something by co-operating together, or lose something by not co-operating. Third, the method must encourage members to step out of social roles in their interaction, since social roles often have built-in conflicts, and if members continue to act out these social roles conflict will emerge. These methods are useful for developing skills for changing situations, or for developing behaviours not circumscribed by social roles. In this sense, they are appropriate for behaviour that constitutes most of our informal life; family, social life, informal communication, even some of our organised life.

The most important skills are methods designed to improve trust between people. Trust is a basic dimension of human life, and has many aspects: openness, honesty, dependability, predictability, love, protection, and acknowledgement. It is a dimension fundamental to all social interaction, even to role-defined behaviour (Erikson, 1950; Levine, 1971). But within formal roles, trust has an institutional component which is usually lacking in informal behaviour (i.e., one gains trust by effectively carrying out a role). The basic technique for creating trust in a group is to build a link between people. This can take many forms: establishing a talking relationship, establishing a physical relationship (for example, 'blindwalk', holding hands, other intimacies), creating a work-role relationship, creating an experiential relationship (i.e., experiencing something at the same time and place). The relationship thus established must be a predictable one; individuals must act according to expectations. The relationship does not have to be a very intimate one (though, of course, that may help), for many trust relationships are not intimate.

Putting trust somewhat mechanistically like this forces us to see it in a different light than the way we normally view it. For if a division and role behaviour constitute ingredients of conflict, while lack of division and role (and a predictable relationship) create trust, then it is clear that conflict and trust could alternate within the same person and could even affect the same relationship. In the basic 'division technique' outlined earlier, conflict is created between the divided groups while trust is created within the groups. As long as the members agree to play the roles involved, this polarity will exist. Conversely, if some members decide to break up the intergroup division by redefining the situation (for example, 'they are not really different from us'), this may bring the conflict back into a group because these members have violated the basic assumption holding the group together. Conflict and trust stand on a knife's edge equilibrium with one another and are very easily disrupted, as all couples know. Even with the same relationship, trust and conflict can alternate quickly. Take a couple as an example. The couple's intimacy holds the relationship together — they trust each other. If one or both of them suddenly starts reverting to formal roles usually external to the household (such as concentrating too much on work, 'staying out with the boys too late, getting too involved in the women's organisation'), then the potential for conflict is enormously increased, since the basic assumptions holding the pair together are violated; if there are children involved so that multiple linking assumptions exist, then the tension created by the role behaviour may be magnified more intensely.

'External' and 'internal' roles compete with one another for priority, making us both sociological and psychological creatures at the same time, though in a tenuous balance between the two. Changes in external roles may disrupt the internal equilibrium in a relationship, and the consequences may be so great that the result may be a splitting up of the group. This is why we observe that marriage and divorce patterns change with the ups-and-downs of the economy; economic growth creates higher aspirations and opportunities, thereby disrupting relationships; whereas stagnation creates dependency and stability (Levine, 1975).

There are other skills which are important for integrating groups. Communication is one such basic skill, so basic that we usually take it for granted. Communication involves keeping channels open so that information can be interchanged. Usually this involves talking and listening, but there are other methods. The great interest shown by the group movement in non-verbal communication attests to the desire to strengthen some 'not-very-used' channels. Written communication is another form which has not really been developed by the group movement. Writing is useful for communicating complicated, technical information, for communicating deeper feelings and thoughts, for communicating structured thinking, for making difficult requests in which face-saving is an important aspect of a relationship, for giving instructions, and so forth. These are important dimensions of social life, too, and perhaps the 'experiential movement' should pay more attention to this mode.

Symbolic communication is another form which is very undeveloped in the group movement. We are all aware that groups often create their own symbol system, a codified language which refers to specific events, people, and roles in the group. But we rarely think of using symbols in a more sociological sense as a mode for group communication. The United States, in fact, is a very bad place for developing symbolic communication, as there is a somewhat nihilistic rejection of symbolic forms. Probably this developed because the 'Americans' were from so many countries that they were required to drop many of their ethnic symbols in order to be accepted in that society. But the point is, such a mode of communication is very useful to develop, at least for societies other than the United States. Symbols have certain common elements: an agreed-upon meaning, belonging to a group or community of some sort, a sense of commitment of this group, a commitment to action on the part of the group in order to defend it, a commitment from members of the group for help in order to defend oneself, and certain level of trust which can be expected from members of the group. Communication of these symbols is often subtle; they can be stated verbally or non-verbally, but more than not, they involve a complex pattern relating the two, so that 'outsiders' cannot intervene as imposters. The communication is 'flashed' on suddenly by one person who then waits for an appropriate 'signal' back from the other. This interchange continues until it is accepted by both that they both belong to the group. The bases for symbolic communication are many, but they usually have a strong sociological dimension to them: ethnic communication, religious communication, political communication, social class communication, and so forth. But there are also some psychological dimensions to symbolic communication, too, usually involving an expression of certain linguistic forms. One can, with proper use of language, convey to others different types of self-definitions and motive structure (for example, 'I am a sensitive, turned-on person who is open to new experiences. Do you want to have a new experience together?'; 'I am a hippy-yippy, freaked-out social deviant looking for drugs. Do you happen to have any?'; 'I am a member of the ——, a semi-secret organisation which promises help to all its members. Can you help me?'). Thus, symbolic communication is an important mode of expression for group loyalties and serves to communicate motives and needs as well. In this sense, there is a lot of material here for social learning in groups, of which the group movement has barely touched.

These examples illustrate the wide range of possible methods for defining integrating values, and how they are contrasted with conflict values. They all have the characteristic of defining a group boundary, of encouraging mutual satisfaction, and of discouraging the introduction of external roles.

Creating individual values

We will look briefly at one final form of values — individual values — and explore, somewhat generally, the form of method used to create these in a group situation. The previous two types of value were group-based values in that they assumed a relationship to a group, either antagonistic or supportive. Individual values, on the other hand, isolate the individual from a group by focusing on his or her unique characteristics. The methods developed for exploring individual values, therefore, will aim to isolate the individual from the group. Either the individual is selected to perform some task or to receive feedback from the group, or else the individual's behaviour is isolated from that of the other members and explored. This can be done in an informal or formal way.

Most groups spend some of their time looking at

individuals in the group during the normal give-and-take of group interaction. At times there may be special exercises which can do this: role plays, *Gestalt* exercise, personal feedback exercises, acting out exercises, etc. But it is at this point that the value argument becomes important, because in focusing on individuals, many values are being expressed. These can be values that are considered necessary for mental health (such as increasing trust, openness, self-awareness), values that are necessary for interaction with others (such as interdependency, mutual reciprocity, increasing awareness of others) or values that are useful for oneself (such as increasing one's potency with others, improving one's ability to express oneself, increasing one's ability to accept feelings, increasing one's spontaneity). Some of these values may be consistent with social values that are being expressed, but others definitely may contradict social values. Some groups seem to take a very anti-social perspective, emphasising individualism at all costs. It is as if they are saying, 'Save yourself. No one is going to help you at all in this world. And don't waste your time helping others.' The group process becomes, 'How am I, an individual, different from everyone else here?', a theme which already creates a division between people. This kind of group very often has a directive trainer who very actively guides the group process, a style made necessary, possibly, in order to prevent the potential conflict from coming out in such a group.

If we emphasise strong social values, then we create conflicts with other groups. If we emphasise strong individual values, then we create divisions within a group. If we try to make a trade-off between these two by emphasising the group and the individual in interaction, then we may mollify conflict to some extent but also may create an unreal situation in which transfer of learning to the outside world is minimal. 'Happy' group situations are, after all, not necessarily realistic ones, and since one of our major purposes in running groups is to teach participants about social skills, emphasising smoothness of social interaction may not necessarily be a good thing. Our feeling is that values are inherent in social life, whether they be social or individual values. They achieve their meaning in a social framework and are fought for within that framework. Without values, in fact, it would be impossible to give feedback to members in a group. We would not be able to say, 'Hey, look what you're doing!', because without accepting values, there would be no means of evaluating behaviour. Values are essential to our existence and we would do well to make these as explicit as possible.

Conclusion

We have tried in this chapter to focus attention on the nature of values in experiential learning groups, because we feel that group trainers have not properly acknowledged the importance of these in their group work. Trainers have tried to act as if they worked outside the real world, or were creating an alternative society to the one that already existed. And while this goal of isolating human behaviour from its natural social context may be a noble one, and filled with idealistic and humanitarian overtones, it is unrealistic. For we as trainers live in that society and are part of the same contradictions that confront everyone else. Values, after all, become important when there are alternatives available. They derive their meaning from conflict, not consensus, for if we all were to agree, there would be no reason to be concerned. Thus, it is the essential nature of social conflict which focuses attention on values as the conflict shifts to an ideological level.

T-groups were created as a consequence of a corporate society in an advanced state of conflict. At the time, they fulfilled the felt need to provide some new skills for administrators who would run these large corporations. The issues posed to big corporations spilled over into the broader society in the form of questions concerning appropriate behaviour and norms. This has been the case in the last thirty years. But history is a progressive force in which social forms create their own antagonisms and alternative models become available. The growth of large corporations in the United States and Europe created a shift from an entrepreneurial society to a bureaucratic one (Baron and Sweezy, 1966). Industry became capital-intensive, thereby producing a shift towards a more service-orientated labour force, and in addition reduced the chances for upward mobility of some groups (e.g., the blacks, and American Indians in the United States, and to a lesser extent the West Indians in Britain). These changes also polarised international relations with the poorer countries of the world. A polarisation of values emerges from such an economic polarity, as the high standards of affluence being demanded within the developed countries were seen to be achieved at the expense of the lesser developed countries. 'I want to achieve a greater understanding of myself', as seen by one person, becomes 'you are achieving your greater understanding at my expense' by another. For it is an old cliché that freedom is a relative concept. Freedom cannot be 'absolute freedom' if it is given to some people and denied to others. And yet this is where many of our social values in the developed world have taken us. Extreme individualism shows a contempt for humanity when it becomes anti-social, when it encourages individuals to pay attention only to themselves. If that freedom is socially guaranteed so that all humanity benefits from it, then the satisfaction of individual needs will not be at the expense of others. Freedom, in order not to be sectarian, must be a social concept first, and not just an individual one.

Experiential groups are, of course, no place to handle the conflicts of the world. We cannot tell participants, 'Do not concern yourself with yourselves, but only with the poor unfortunates of this world!' Such a mandate would be absurd and silly, and would do more than make people feel mildly guilty for acknowledging their own needs. But in T-groups we can encourage a sensitivity to other people, if only to the other members of the group. For that sensitivity underlies a greater sense of social responsibility. Thus, in being sensitive, we learn to adjust our behaviour to acknowledge the needs of other people, with the end-product being a kind of compromise to a broader commitment to social freedom, for it gives to the other person the right to exist and be happy. And if we all could act in such a way, would this not be a good thing for humanity, too?

References

Appley, D.G. and Winter A.R. *T-groups and therapy groups in a changing society,* San Francisco: Jossey-Bass, 1973.

Argyris, C., Explorations in interpersonal competence, *Journal of Applied Behavioral Science,* 1973, **1,** 58—84.

Bach, G.R., Marathon group dynamics: I. Some functions of the professional group facilitator, *Psychological Reports,* 1967, **20,** 995—99.

Back, K.W., *Beyond words,* New York: Russell Sage Foundation, 1972.

Baron, P.A. and Sweezy, P.M., *Monopoly capital,* New York: Monthly Review Press, 1966.

Bass, B., Reactions to twelve angry men as a measure of sensitivity training, *Journal of Applied Psychology,* 1962, **46,** 120—24.

Blumberg, A. and Golembiewski, R.T., *Learning and change in groups,* Harmondsworth Middx: Penguin, 1976.

Bradford, L.P., Gibb, J.R. and Benne, K.D., Two educational innovations. In L.P. Bradford, J.R. Gibb, and K.D. Benne (eds.), *T-group theory and laboratory method,* New York: Wiley, 1964.

Burke, R.L. and Bennis, W.B., Changes in perception of self and others during human relations training, *Human Relations,* 1961, **14,** 165—82.

Clark, J.V., Some troublesome dichotomies in human relations training, *Human Relations Training News,* 1962, **6,** 3—6.

Cooper, C.L., Influence of the trainer in T-groups, *Human Relations,* 1962, **22,** 515—30.

Cooper, C.L., *Group training for individual and*

organizational development, Basel: S. Karger, 1972.

Cooper, C.L., *Theories of group processes,* New York: Wiley, 1975.

Cooper, C.L., *Developing social skills in managers,* London: Macmillan, 1976.

Cooper, C.L., Adverse and growthful effects of experiential learning groups, *Human Relations,* 1977, **30,** 1103-1129.

Cooper, C.L. and Mangham, I.L., *T-groups: A survey of research,* London: Wiley, 1971.

Cooper, C.L., Levine, N. and Kobayashi, K., Developing one's potential: from west to east, *Group and organizational studies,* 1976, **1,** 43—55.

Erikson, E.H., *Childhood and society,* New York: Norton, 1950.

Erikson, E.H., The problem of ego identity, *Journal of the American Psychoanalytic Association,* 1956, **4,** 56—121.

French, J.R.P., Sherwood, J.J. and Bradford, D., Changes in self-identity in a management training conference, *Journal of Applied Behavioral Science,* 1966, **2,** 210—18.

Freud, S., *Totem and taboo,* London: Routledge and Kegan Paul, 1918.

Galbraith, J.K., *The new industrial state.* Boston: Houghton-Mifflin, 1967.

Guetzkow, H., A use of simulation in the study of international relations, *Behavioral science,* 1959, **4,** 183—91.

Harrison, K., Chapter in Cooper, C.L., *Group training for individual and organizational development,* Basel: S. Karger, 1972.

Kanderdine, J. and Keys, G., A rationale for the evaluation of learning in simulation and games, Paper presented to the National Gaming Council, 1974.

Kibbee, J., Craft, C. and Nanus, B., *Management games,* New York: Rineholt, 1962.

Kolb, D., Rubin, I.M. and McIntyre, J.M., *Organizational psychology,* Englewood Cliffs, N.J.: Prentice-Hall, 1974.

Laing, R.D., *The divided self,* Harmondsworth, Middx.: Penguin, 1965.

Lakin, M., Some ethical issues in sensitivity training,

American Psychologist, 1969, **24,** 923—29.

Levine, N., Emotional factors in group development, *Human Relations,* 1971, **24,** 65—89.

Levine, N., Group training with students in higher education, In C.L. Cooper (ed.), *Group training for individual and organizational development,* p. 40—67. Basel: S. Karger, 1973.

Levine, N., Divorce in Turkey, Paper presented at the Second Turkish Demography Conference, Izmir, Turkey, 1975.

Levine, N. and Cooper, C.L., T-groups — twenty years on: a prophecy, *Human Relations,* 1976, **29,** 1—23.

Mills, C. Chapter in C.L. Cooper, *Developing social skills in managers,* London: Macmillan, 1976.

Olmosk, K. and Graverson, G., Group training for community relations. The community workshop, In C.L. Cooper (ed.), *Group training for individual and organizational development.* Basel: S. Karger, 1972.

Rubin, I., The reduction of prejudice through laboratory training, *Journal of Applied Behavioral Science,* 1967, **3,** 29—50.

Sampson, E.E., *Ego at the threshold,* New York: Delta Books, 1975.

Schein, E.H. and Bennis, W.G., *Personal and organizational change through group methods,* New York: Wiley, 1965.

Simmel, G., *Conflict,* New York: Free Press of Glencoe, 1908.

Siroka, R.W., Siroka, E.K. and Schloss, G., *Sensitivity training and group encounter: An introduction,* New York: Grosset and Dunlap, 1971.

Smith, P.B., Are there adverse effects of sensitivity training, *Journal of Human Psychology,* 1975, **15,** 29—47.

Smith, P.B. and Wilson, M., The use of group training methods in multiracial settings, *New Community,* 1975, **4,** (2), 218—31.

Szasz, T., *The myth of mental illness,* New York: Harper, 1961.

3 Designing and facilitating experiential group activities: variables and issues*

In designing and implementing experiential group activities, certain types of variable need to be considered. These variables can be seen in three major groups: initial, emergent, and evaluative (see Figure 3.1). Discussed here are the various subdivisions within each type, with specific points of consideration suggested for the facilitator designing an experiential group activity.

INITIAL VARIABLES

Factors to be considered prior to the group activity consist of aims (learning objectives) and the learning environment, including participants, group structure, and the training staff.

*Reproduced by special permission of John E. Jones and J. William Pfeiffer, University Associates and the *Annual Handbook of Group Facilitators,* 1976, pp 157-69.

Learning objectives

In designing a group experience, it is important to consider first the general aims or outcome desired and then the specific ways in which people should change, develop, or behave. The following points should be determined:

Standards

- Who should set learning standards.
- Who should judge the results (participants, facilitators, both of these, outside individuals or groups).

Affective/conceptual aims

- The extent to which aims are emotional (usually personal) or conceptual (cognitive).

Short-term/long-term aims

- How long the group learning is intended to have an effect (days, months, years).

Question of authority

- Who should set learning objectives (facilitator, participants, or both).

Remedial/developmental aims

Remedial work tends to focus on a participant's weaknesses, problems, or lacks; developmental work aims on building a participant's strengths. The extent to which the activity is focused in either direction should be considered, as well as the implications of this focus.

Initial variables

Learning objectives (general and specific aims)

> Standards
> Affective/conceptual aims
> Short-term/long-term aims
> Question of authority
> Remedial/developmental aims
> Predetermined/emergent aims
> Experimental/experiential aims

Learning environment

Participants

> Homogeneity/heterogeneity
> Family/strangers
> Background dissonance/consonance
> Initial state of participants

Group structure

> Essential/instrumental/incidental
> Group size
> Timing and life span
> Physical arrangements

Training staff

> Personality and style variables
> Mechanistic/organic approaches
> Modelling/scanning
> Skills repertoire
> Group or personal growth
> Multiple staff

Figure 3.1 Design and operational variables for group training

Emergent variables

Management of differences
Depth of intervention — training vs. therapy
Ambiguity
Degree of confrontation
Subject/method dissonance
Distributive/integrative situations
Surface validity
Valid/invalid data
Projection/introjection
Extent of closure
Group splitting
Flow/blocking

Evaluative variables

Presentation of self
Feedback
Supportive climate
Experimentation
Practice and application
Interdependence and authority
Goal clarity
Group growth
Group maintenance
Communication
Structure and procedure
Cognitive map

Predetermined/emergent aims

- The extent to which learning aims can be determined prior to the experience.
- The possibility of additional aims emerging during the experience.
- The extent to which the facilitator imposes, consciously or otherwise, some aims by his own values and by setting norms.

Experimental/experiential aims

The choice between these aims has implications for the training design (e.g., use of observers, data collection, process reviews) and for the facilitator's learning theory or models (e.g., one can experience something and 'learn' without discussing that experience afterward). Points to consider:

- The extent to which the activity will be a joint learning experiment, in which the facilitator has a special responsibility (e.g., for helping the group examine data in reviewing its work).
- The extent to which the facilitator allows participants to experience the activity without reviewing their experience.

Learning environment

The principal components of the learning environment — participants, group structure, and training staff — must often be considered in relation to learning objectives.

Participants

The nature of participants and, especially, the similarities and differences among participants need to be considered. The following items are particularly significant:

Homogeneity/heterogeneity. Heterogeneity can lead to greater confrontation but can also provide the group with a wider range of resources. Homogeneity, on the other hand, may lead to greater intimacy/affection, but promote less variety. This effect can restrict the number of learning possibilities available to the group.

Family/strangers. Groups with established relationships (e.g., work groups and family groups) might achieve a greater transfer of learning but might also be reluctant to be entirely open. Instead, participants who are strangers (and unlikely to continue their relationship after the training) may gain greater intimacy and openness at the possible expense of a less effective transfer of learning.

Background dissonance/consonance. It is important to consider whether group training is dissonant with the norms and culture of the institutional background within which the activity is to take place. The participants may learn and change their attitudes in ways that are contrary to the ideology of their back-home situations, and the implications of this should be considered. Also, the organisational climate of the aegis under which training is organised may be supportive, hostile, curious, frivolous, sceptical, anxious, or impatient toward group training.

Initial state of participants. If the initial state of the participants is inaccurately judged, learning may not be optimised. It may be necessary for the facilitator to find ways to check out his initial-state assumptions. Items to be determined:

• The amount of information the facilitators have.
• The assumptions facilitators make about the initial goals, needs, and readiness of the participants.

Group structure

In assessing design issues, decisions must be made about whether the group is essential, instrumental, or incidental to the learning process; the group size; the timing and life span of the group; and the physical arrangements.

Essential/instrumental/incidental. In some training experiences (e.g., interpretive groups) the group itself is a central and essential part of the learning model. In others (e.g., T-groups, encounter groups, etc.) the group is instrumental in the learning process by providing both interaction opportunities and support. In yet other experiences (e.g., *Gestalt* and counselling), the group is largely incidental, since valuable work can be done as well in pairs, trios, etc. The group may, however, represent an economy or provide further opportunities for participants to learn by observing other individuals and identifying with them.

Group size. The size of the total group-training population is important in designing various learning experiences. One should seriously consider the number of participants desired and the ways in which this population can be divided to achieve various objectives.

Timing and life span. Spaced sessions (e.g., two-hour weekly sessions) may produce a less intimate and less person-centred experience, whereas more condensed or intensive sessions (e.g., a one-week residential session) may offer more personal growth. Spaced sessions may allow greater analysis of group dynamics and encourage members to 'work through' between sessions (e.g., a couples' group). Defined time limits may encourage participants to express useful information by the end of the allotted time period, but can also establish the facilitator's role as the locus of control or authority of the group. Norms will develop as a result of the following timing parameters:

- The total time allocated to the group experience.
- The time distribution (sessions at regular intervals, one intensive week, etc.).
- Session time limits and adherence to limits.

Physical arrangements. The physical arrangements are a significant consideration in facilitating the learning objectives. For example, a small-group session held in a lecture theatre would have an entirely different atmosphere from one held in more intimate surroundings. Physical arrangements include:

- Where the groups will work.
- What kind of atmosphere the physical surroundings create (e.g., easy chairs, cushions, etc.).
- How the physical environment can be arranged to support learning objectives.

Training staff

Issues about staff include personality, style, potential role conflicts, learning models, philosophies, and assumptions. The resolution of these issues is critical to the successful fulfillment of the learning objectives.

Personality and style variables. Some facilitators work more readily with their own aggression, some with their affection, and others remain somewhat detached and unemotional. These differences may be justified or rationalised as differences in role perception and style, but they may really be due to personality differences among the staff. Since the models of role conflict and resolution of interpersonal differences in the staff team could influence participants' learning, it is important to review style preferences when selecting a training staff.

Mechanistic/organic approaches. If one staff member insists on structuring a group experience, and another wants to respond to group needs spontaneously, the entire experience may suffer. It would be possible, however, to synthesise these two approaches into a more productive compromise.

Modelling/scanning. Trainers who adopt a learning theory based on modelling might find that they are encouraging noticeable but short-term change. If, instead, they encourage group members to use one another as learning sources, through an approach based on scanning the interaction of group members, participants may *show* less change, although this approach may also prompt major internalised change.

Skills repertoire. The trainer/facilitator's ability to handle certain types of group experience and his range of competence should be a training consideration.

Group or personal growth. Staff disagreement about the level of intervention may create normative problems in that participants receive conflicting messages about the learning objectives of the group. On the other hand, the conflict may provide participants with a wider range and greater breadth of learning. Issues of concern:

• The orientation of the trainer/facilitator toward understanding the dynamics of the group or toward developing the growth potential of the individual.
• Whether both orientations can co-exist.

Multiple staff. The composition of the staff will influence somewhat the norms and learning objectives of the participants. The inclusion of women may provide opportunities for focusing on issues that otherwise might not surface. Items for this variable:

• The number of staff involved.
• The compatibility of the staff.
• Inclusion of both men and women.
• Inclusion of staff with specific occupational identifications.

EMERGENT VARIABLES

A number of dynamic variables emerge during the learning process in group work. Emergent variables include management of differences, depth and level of interventions, vagueness of direction, confrontation, dissonance in subject and method, distributive/integrative situations, credibility, validity (or nonvalidity) of data, projection and introjection, closure, subdivision of groups, and flow and blocking in learning and communication.

If the facilitator is aware of these variables, he may be more effective in dealing with them as they arise. However, he may also be more likely to provoke or precipitate such issues.

Management of differences

There are likely to be differences in the starting states, needs, personalities, learning rates, and moods of the participants. Differences and conflict can be a source of creativity. In particular, some participants may want to learn about their own aggression or style of conflict resolution. Occasionally, however, it may be better temporarily to avoid conflict by providing other sources of learning that may ultimately help to resolve the differences, e.g., by splitting the group into compatible subgroups to develop feedback skills before coping with the total group conflict. The facilitator should consider how he and the group cope with differences and conflict — by ignoring them, debating, arguing, fighting, compromising.

Depth of intervention — training versus therapy

The group may intend to work on issues (e.g., the level of competence in group work) and not become involved in personal or therapeutic issues, but suddenly or gradually the group members may become more introspective, and the hazy boundary between training and therapy is reached.

'Interpretive' interventions would facilitate useful therapy work, whereas 'behavioural-data-based' interventions leave options open. Focusing on there-and-then contributions from one member of the group and his personal problems will encourage a therapy-type group; interventions about the here-and-now skills and interpersonal relations between members encourage a training focus.

Therapy is concerned with a person's sense of who he is, how he is, how he got to be that way, and what he could do to change. *Training* is concerned with what a person can do with what he is, how he behaves toward others, and his skill or competence.

Ambiguity

In discovery learning one must cope with ambiguity and uncertainty. Yet some common, recurring themes can be distinguished in T-groups. For example, when the trainer deliberately refuses to be a leader in the group, participants feel the leadership and structure vacuum and usually work to fill it. Participants often expect that the trainer/facilitator should give the group direction and help because he has had previous similar group experience; yet some training models include anxiety as a necessary force in the learning process.

Degree of confrontation

As an integral part of many learning processes, people are confronted with feedback, evidence, and feelings from other group members and the facilitator. Judging the level of the confrontation is like gauging the difficulty of a jump across a gap — it must not be so small that it is unnoticeable, nor so large that one balks or fails. A confrontation level that is too low may lead to *assimilation* ('That's common sense, I already do/know that'). Too high a level of confrontation may lead to *rejection* ('That's nonsense, I don't agree'). The appropriate level of confrontation leads to *accommodation* ('How can I make sense of that? I am going to work on that'). The facilitator needs to determine:

• Elements in the process that provide confrontations.
• How the degree of confrontation can be optimised.

Subject/method dissonance

It is reasonable and comfortable — consonant — to learn about group dynamics in a group or about interpersonal relations while relating to others. However, it is uncomfortable — dissonant — to tell people to participate or to ask people to discuss their dependence. In the experiential situation, the contract, structure, and method should not be dissonant with the learning aims. Considerations for the facilitator:

• The balance (or lack of it) between what the group is doing and the issues it is working on.
• Problems that might arise with a high level of consonance.

Distributive/integrative situations

Distributive situations tend to be either analytical (e.g., subdividing issues and distributing the parts among people) or competitive and evaluative (e.g., allocating blame and attributing results to individuals). Integrative situations are usually co-operative or concerned with the *Gestalt*. Particularly in the use of structured experiences, participants' socialisation toward competition can bias group work toward distributive activities. Integration is, however, central to the philosophy of group work. The facilitator needs to consider whether group work and particularly any structured experiences he may use as interventions are likely to work toward distribution or integration.

Surface validity

Issues of validity and credibility appear very early in group life but become less important later. Unless people feel able to commit themselves initially to the work and life of the group (at least to the extent of making a start), it is difficult to gain their acceptance/commitment. Considerations;

* Whether tasks, issues, exercises, and the setting of the group work appear realistic or valid to participants.
* Whether members seem credible to each other.
* Face credibility of the facilitator — influenced by such factors as age, sex, experience, manner, dress.

Valid/invalid data

It is useful for the facilitator to be clear about the ground rules for the validity of data and for him to share and compare his criteria with group members. The most valid data are descriptions of actual behaviour ('You sat next to me in every session') or expressions of personal feelings ('I feel warm and strong'). Less valid but complementary data are interpretations ('You sit by me because you feel isolated') and guesses about motives ('You sit by me because you are trying to get to know me'). Interpretations and conjectures about motives cannot be verified — they can only be accepted or denied in comparison with the evidence offered. Their acceptance or denial, however, becomes another valid behaviour. Still less valid data are 'we' statements where 'I' statements would be more accurate ('We all feel anxious, don't we?'); old feedback, which is less valid the farther away from the event it is ('yesterday I felt angry with you when you talked so much'); and non-specific generalisations ('Some members of the group just don't listen'). Some tests of data:

- The kind of data valid for the work in progress.
- Whether the current data flow in the group is valid or invalid.

Projection/introjection

In projection, people disclose their own ideas, attitudes, feelings, assumptions, values, skills, and styles to the group and to one another. In introjection, people absorb ideas, feedback, data, etc., from other group members. Projection and introjection can be conscious or unconscious. Often the work in a group proceeds in phases of projection followed by introjection. If this occurs, it may be useful periodically to review the group's progress in these terms.

Extent of closure

The degree of closure for any issue or incident in the learning process may vary from total open-endedness to a high degree of closure. Both approaches have their difficulties. Low closure can be frustrating and can raise more issues and questions than answers. High closure can lead to encapsulation and elimination — allowing fewer possibilities for individuals to internalise learning. Learning is ultimately personal, and the results of the group's work are vested in individual members as they leave the group. Whatever level of closure the facilitator decides to aim for is likely to be a compromise, based on a judgment of the extent to which closure affects learning and resolution.

Group splitting

As the group process continues, the initial group-structure variable of size shifts to become an emergent variable. One manifestation is lateness or absenteeism, an issue related to the functioning of the group as well as to the particular individuals. A more obvious form of this issue occurs when members or facilitators suggest that the group split into subgroups or when the group splits spontaneously. In some models (e.g., Bion), it can be considered either as an avoidance mechanism or, if handled as a dichotomy, as a creative polarity. In other models (e.g., encounter), no such negative interpretation is associated with splitting. Dividing into pairs and subgroups is used as a facilitative structural intervention. This issue is related to the initial essential/instrumental/incidental variable, because splitting is less acceptable if the group itself is essential.

Flow/blocking

At times, the group or some individuals become blocked. They cannot progress and learn only how it feels to be frustrated, impotent, or lacking in skills. These can be useful learning issues, particularly if various styles of responding to a block are explored. At other times the work must flow, feelings must be expressed, and there must be movement.

Flow can be facilitated by such devices as exercises, acting-out, physical and non-verbal expression, and games. Although these may appear 'phony' to participants, such contrived measures can often activate genuine results.

The facilitator must be able to cope with learning while he is blocked and must also know how to facilitate flow. He can then determine the implications of his interventions, basing them on the needs of the group and the members, rather than on his own skill bias.

EVALUATIVE VARIABLES

Although the facilitator/trainer has to make certain judgments and decisions before and during group work, the extent to which these judgments should be conscious is debatable. However, the assumption is that more skilled trainers will welcome raising rather than lowering their level of consciousness about their judgment. Such an evaluation is not meant, however, to suggest that intuitive skill and spontaneity are unimportant. This discussion does not recommend any particular model for group work. Rather, it suggests that whatever conscious or unconscious models a facilitator has should be utilised as effectively as possible.

The following are not issues about which the facilitator must make a decision; instead, they offer *criteria* useful in making appropriate judgments about initial and emergent variables. Presenting such a list aims at increasing the clarity with which a facilitator confronts a particular issue and at raising possible alternatives.

Presentation of self

Until the individual has and uses opportunities to reveal how he perceives, feels, and does things, he has little basis for learning about himself. Often silent members claim they learn by observing and listening to others. In a way this is true, but they are presenting only the 'non-included' part of themselves. With various results, groups put pressure on silent or non-participant members to join in. An effective group climate allows and facilitates self-presentation and does not force conformity to group norms in the method of that presentation.

Feedback

If people learned from experience, older people would clearly be more skilled at relationships and behaviour than younger people. How people use their experience is more important than the experience itself. Individuals learn through developing behaviour patterns guided by clear and accurate feedback about the effectiveness and appropriateness of their actions. Feedback may come from other participants, the trainer, observers, data-collection instruments, audio- and videotape playback, or task-success elements in a structured experience.

Feedback must be valid data (see emergent variables) and be related to events and actions. Feedback is also more useful if it is relevant to behaviour and situations that can be changed or modified. It is easier to change what one *does* than to change what one *is*. For example, 'You are a hostile person and should change' is less useful than 'If you were less hostile to me, I could work better with you'. Negative motives, such as to punish the receiver or to establish the giver's superiority, can often reduce the validity of feedback.

Supportive climate

An atmosphere of trust and non-defensiveness is necessary for people to risk their ideas and feelings, behave openly, and accept feedback. Each person must be able to risk being himself, right or wrong, effective or ineffective, without feeling he is risking his membership in the group and the acceptance of others. This does not necessarily mean that conflict, anger, or differences should be avoided. Such emotions, indeed, are more acceptable in a supportive climate.

Experimentation

An important possibility in many group-training situations is the testing of alternative patterns of behaviour and personal relations. Within a supportive climate and with valid feedback, experimentation can be a key element in changing behaviour. Participants may, however, use experimentation defensively: 'I did not really feel like that; I only behaved that way to see what you would do'. The difference between useful and useless experimentation is that *useful* experimentation concerns one's personal behaviour; experimentation with others' behaviour is 'playing games'.

Practice and application

To gain confidence in his newly acquired behaviour, an individual needs to practise it. New behaviour needs to be transferred to and retained in situations external to the training situation. This is sometimes referred to as the 're-entry' problem. It is possible and profitable to test actual application if group work is set at intervals (e.g., weekly meetings), since the individual may receive valid feedback on his behaviour. Simulated application can be used to deal with an issue concerning the facilitator, including fantasies about applying a new approach to the issue.

Interdependence and authority

It is important for the group to confront and understand its relationship with the group's authority figure — usually the facilitator/trainer. When this happens, it is a good indicator of progress in the group. If it never occurs, the quality of interdependence is questionable. Overdependency on the facilitator allows members to avoid taking responsibility for their actions and learning. Changes in behaviour are then likely to fade when the authority person is not present or if he loses credibility. Interdependence between group members and facilitator is more healthy.

Goal clarity

It is helpful when participants, groups, and facilitators have some clear goals and purposes. A lack of clear learning goals produces two problems: differences in individual learning needs cannot be handled, and it becomes difficult to determine the extent of progress. Goals are more helpful if related to specific behaviours and actions and checked against feedback. Although clear goals cannot be expected immediately, goal clarification and review should be a continuing process for individuals and for the group.

Group growth

A group has development needs beyond the collective needs of its members; it needs time and assistance to become mature, effective, and cohesive. A group will often require more man-hours than the same number of individuals working separately or in small subgroups — achieving different, but valued, results. 'One-shot' groups are of limited or specialised significance.

Group maintenance

The need for group maintenance is closely related to group growth. In many group learning models, members can use group maintenance to develop their skills in group diagnosis and group facilitation. Energy invested in group building and maintenance as a preventive rather than repair measure is a positive indicator of group growth.

Communication

Usually only a small proportion of what is said in a group is heard or understood by many of the members. Participants may be thinking about what they want to say next, what they would like to say but will not, what they think the speaker is really saying, or what they are feeling at the moment. Any of these distractions reduce the probability of listening. A positive correction is for group members to slow down the verbal communication rate or make shorter statements that others can check to insure understanding. Checking and non-verbal communication activities are useful in this process.

Structure and procedure

'Unstructured' groups do not exist. All groups have norms and procedures, and even anarchy is a structure. For example, a T-group is based on certain norms about its form and function.

It is not always sufficiently clear how formal the structure should be and whether it is imposed externally or derived internally. Structures are related to assumptions and values, as well as to participants' abilities to cope with ambiguity. When a group can establish and maintain the degree of structure it needs for effective work and can change the structure as its needs and issues change, group growth is evident.

Cognitive map

In some group training, theories and conceptual schemes may help participants understand the experience. The behaviour of an individual can be seen as based on his interior 'map' or schemata, which are not necessarily conscious. However, great benefit and little danger lie in developing a more conscious understanding of one's behaviour.

Conceptual material can be introduced by readings, films, lecturettes, and short theory interventions. One of the benefits of using theory material is that it may replace 'folklore' notions about a group, e.g., 'In any group there will always be one person who will emerge as a leader'. One danger in encouraging cognitive development is that some members may use conceptual material inappropriately to defend against or to avoid the experience. Nevertheless, it is usually beneficial for people to comprehend their experience and articulate their insights.

CONCLUSION

The issues and variables we have discussed here are valuable in a number of practical ways. First, they should provide an explicit and systematic guide to help facilitators focus on the issues (initial and evaluative, mainly) that should be considered in *designing* any experiential group activity. Second, they help the training staff of a particular group become more conscious of issues that might *emerge* during the life of the group and identify more clearly the situation in which they currently find themselves. This can also provide a laboratory staff team with a source of comparison to facilitate cohesion in the total learning community. Third, many of these variables and issues can help to highlight issues that should be considered in the designing of a trainer/facilitator *development* programme. Also, a careful consideration of these issues can be useful to the individual facilitator in his own development by serving as a possible framework for *self-appraisal*. Finally, many of these variables and issues raise interesting *research* questions about the processes of group functioning. For example, the differentiated effects of space versus massed training sessions or one structure versus another structure of design might be considered.

The authors' intention here is not to suggest a more mechanistic approach to the design and operation of group training. Experience, intuition, and spontaneity are considered valuable elements in a facilitator's approach. Rather, specific issues have been discussed and clarified to help facilitators consciously analyse some of the significant variables in group training in order to improve their own effectiveness and skill.

Section B
Research into experiential group effects

In this section we will be looking at how effective are experiential learning groups. We will focus in on the characteristics of these groups which lead both to adverse and growthful changes in individual behaviour. Since the most important characteristic of the learning experience of these groups lies in the behaviour of the trainer, we will explore the links between his interventions and participant change. Although in the late 1950s and early 1960s T-groups and other experiential methods were used primarily in the West, they are spreading further and further East. We conclude this section by examining the impact of these techniques on three different cultures: England, Turkey and Japan.

4 Adverse and growthful effects of experiential learning groups: the role of the trainer, participant, and group characteristics

*The purpose of this study was to examine the characteristics of experiential learning groups associated with adverse and growthful effects. Data were collected on trainer behaviour/ personality, participant personality/conditions of participation, and group process characteristics, and these were linked to two generic outcome measures (i.e., other trainee perceptions and work colleague reports). It was found that both positive and negative effects of such groups are (a) strongly related to the trainer's behaviour and personality, (b) unrelated to group process and structured variables (e.g., degree of confrontation, level of intimacy in the group, etc.), and (c) associated with trainees' personality predispositions in the short run but not in the long term. The implications of these findings are fully discussed. ***

* This research was supported by the UK Training Services Agency; the author would like to thank all the staff of the agency, the staff of the training programmes concerned, and the participants for their help in this project.

Introduction

As Back (1974) has suggested, there has been an enormous growth in experiential small-group training programmes (e.g., T-groups, structured exercise-based groups, etc.) over the last decade. As these methods of human relations or social-skill training grow in popularity and use, they tend to attract more and more suspicion and criticism. A number of people involved in (and outside of) the field of group training have suggested that these techniques 'disrupt on-going personality functions', 'encourage inappropriate levels of intimacy which may destroy rewarding psychological relationships with other people', and, therefore, may be potentially destructive and dangerous (Gottschalk, 1966; Crawshaw, 1969; Mann, 1970). Although a great deal of the early available evidence was based on anecdotal reports or very simplistic studies (Jaffe & Scherl, 1969), more recently there has been an increasing number of more controlled empirical investigations (for a comprehensive review see Cooper, 1975a). Many of the latter studies have primarily attempted to identify the casualty rate of these group methods. Of the five major studies assessing the *incidence* of damage, two have found *high* casualty rates among participants in experiential groups. Gottschalk and Pattison (1969) reported that in a sample of three groups of thirty-one participants, there were eleven 'obviously acute pathological emotional reactions' (six of these occurred in a single group). The symptoms they noted among the eleven casualties were psychotic reactions (two), acute anxiety and temporary departure from group (two), isolation and withdrawal reactions (four), depressive reactions (two), and sadistic-exhibitionist behaviour (one). The authors acknowledge that their groups may have been atypical and, in addition, that the effects may have been only transient since they were reporting on behaviour 'during' training. Although their figure of 30 per cent adverse effects is very high, there are several aspects of this research we should take into account. First, the assessments of trainees were done on the completion of training, so we do not know what the long-term effect was, particularly in the participants' family and work environments. Second, the judgments of pathological emotional reactions were made by the authors themselves, who were psychiatric clinicians. There may be a tendency for psychiatrists, however, to attribute greater clinical significance to behaviour than is warranted. For example, Weiss (1963) found differences between a group of fifty physicists and fifty-one clinical psychologists on their ability to predict future behaviour of several people on whom they were given data. The physicists' predictions were consistently more accurate when checked against actual subsequent behaviour of the person judged. The clinical psychologists significantly more often overestimated the difficulties the person would encounter and underestimated their ability to cope with them. And finally, behaviour such as 'isolation and withdrawal reactions' in a group context could have quite different significance than in a two-person psychotherapeutic interview (a situation these clinicians were more used to) (Smith, 1975). The second study, which found a relatively high proportion of casualties, is the most widely publicised one by Lieberman, Yalom, and Miles (1973), in which they claim 'no less than 9 per cent of participants in the eighteen groups studied became casualties'. Immediately after the group experiences they reported something like 8 per cent casualties and 8 per cent negative changers (defined as such if they showed negative changes on three or more psychometric and other rating criteria), a total of 16 per cent. Six months after training they found a 10 per cent casualty rate and an 8 per cent negative changers rate for a total of 18 per cent. There were several reasons why we should be cautious of these results as well (Cooper, 1975a). First, the random assignment of students to groups may have increased the risk of psychological disturbance. Second, the decision to categorise the 'suspect' students into 'casualties' was based on subjective criteria, that is, self-report by the students and the authors' judgments of 'psychological decompensation' and not on measurable observed behaviour. No evidence is

given to validate the authors' judgements as in the Gottschalk and Pattison (1969) study. Third, it is arguable that informing experiential group participants about the possibilities of 'considerable emotional upsets' before the start of the experience minimises the psychological risks to participants. It may, in fact, have the reverse effect by creating an expectation of intensive psychotherapy, which may not have been established without this intervention. Fourth, they had data which indicated that 23 per cent of their control group were negative changers immediately after training and 15 per cent six months later. This is as high if not higher than the experiential groups. Although we have to be cautious when drawing firm conclusions from this study, as we must from any large-scale study in this field, it still provides well-controlled evidence of adverse effect as a result of experiential training.

There are three studies which indicate results opposite of the above, that is, show smaller casualty rates. Ross, Kligfeld, and Whitman (1971), for example, carried out a survey in the city of Cincinnati, Ohio, a community with extensive experiential group activity. They sent questionnaires to 162 psychiatrists asking them to report any cases in which a patient's 'psychotic reactions or personality disorganisations, whether transient or long-lasting, seemed to be consequent to participation in non-structured groups (e.g., T-groups, etc.) in the preceding five years'. Of the 91 per cent of the psychiatrists who responded only nineteen separate patients were reported as becoming psychotic or acutely disorganised after training. The authors were given figures for numbers of persons participating in such groups over the preceding five years, which totalled 2900. Thus, the nineteen represented .66 per cent of the population thought to be 'at risk'. Of the participants thought to have been through T-groups, 1150 in all, fourteen were identified as casualties, an adverse effects rate of 1.2 per cent. In another study Batchelder and Hardy (1968) carried out an evaluation of group training among 1200 YMCA participants. Interviews with known critics of experiential small-group training in the YMCA turned up four cases of allegedly severe adverse effect. After further in-depth work with these participants, trainers, work colleagues, etc., the authors came to the conclusion that in at least three of the cases the ultimate, long-term outcome was beneficial rather than harmful. National Training Laboratory (1969) also reports some thirty-three participants out of 14200 (less than 1 per cent) who may have been 'at risk' from their training. These later two studies are very weak ones indeed, but the one by Ross *et al.* (1971) provides some very important large-scale support for low casualty rates from experiential learning groups.

Although these and other studies of adverse effect are focusing on an important area for research and are indirectly providing some useful information about the processes of experiential learning techniques, there are at least two fundamental reasons why this type of research orientation may not be very fruitful or helpful in the longer term. First, concentrating on identifying casualty rates is not really very meaningful in the absence of an adequate base rate of comparison. None of the above-mentioned studies set up adequate control groups and/or examined relevant comparative data, with the exception of Lieberman *et al.* (1973), but even they did not examine the casualty rates among their control subjects (only the proportion of negative changers). In any case, what is the appropriate comparison group: (1) untrained matched control subjects; (b) participants in some nonexperiential training programme (e.g., lecture, case studies, etc.) attempting to achieve similar objectives; (c) incidence rates of mental illness in the general population at large? We should probably be examining all of these alternative controls, but not much comparative data of this sort (particularly of types b and c) are available to draw on. Second, even if these data were accessible, concentrating our main focus on the rate of casualty will inevitably lead people to want to draw firm conclusions about the desirability or not of this form of training. That is, to reach definitive decisions that experiential group methods are dangerous and should be abolished or are safe/growthful and should be encouraged. Research effort into experiential small-group methods, or for that matter any educational technique, is likely to be more productive if it avoids the temptation to support the desirability or undesirability of a particular approach to learning. Rather, researchers should concentrate on identifying the learning processes and dynamics which create both the conditions for potential damage and success of a particular method/approach and what could be done to either minimise the risks or enhance its beneficial consequences. It was the purpose of this study to avoid the 'high visibility' of casualty rates and to concentrate on learning processes associated with adverse and growthful effects. The basic question we were attempting to answer in this research, therefore, was: 'What are the antecedent learning conditions that lead to positive and negative effects of small-group training programmes based on experiential methods?' The implications of the results for the future design and implementation of group training are also discussed.

Methods

Subjects

The subjects of the study were 227 male participants and thirty-two trainers in twelve management-development training programmes using small-group methods. Each of the programmes was broken down into a number of small groups, so that participants were working generally in groups of eight to twelve fellow trainees. The participants were middle- to senior-level managers from a variety of industrial organisations. They were drawn from five different generic group-training programmes, organised by management consultancy organisations or other institutions very well known for their work in experiential small-group training in the United Kingdom. All the individual programmes of these five training organisations and institutions over an eighteen-month period were evaluated. They were organised on approximately a one-week residential basis and had a number of important characteristics in common which Cooper (1973) suggests are essential to all experiential learning groups. First, they were designed so that learning took place primarily in small groups, allowing a high level of participation, involvement, and free communications. Second, they were all to some extent or another 'process' as distinct from 'content' orientated, that is, the primary stress was on the feeling level of communications rather than solely on the informational or conceptual level. Third, they were all orientated towards improving the human relations or social skills of managers as distinct from their task or technical skills. All programmes in one form or another were attempting to provide the manager with a better understanding of the dynamics of social interaction, communications between people, social sensitivity, etc. The means they used to achieve some of these objectives were, however, very different, notably in some of the following dimensions: degree of structure of the experience, directiveness of trainer, balance of 'content' and 'process', level of interpersonal intimacy, degree of participant choice of leaning tools, person-centred versus group-centred orientations, etc. Indeed, these five programmes were selected because they represented a good cross section of the small-group training experiences for managers in the UK in these very dimensions. Some of the programmes were known to have a high degree of structure through preplanned, time-linked exercises while others were known to be relatively unstructured (e.g., T-group). Other programmes were known to be 'group-process-orientated' as opposed to 'person-centred' and so on.

Adverse and positive outcome measures

Two central criteria of psychological disturbance or growth were used in this study to assess the effects of small-group training: *self and peer/trainee nominations* of who was 'hurt' and 'helped' by the training, and *work colleague reports* on the impact of training on work performance and work relationships at six weeks and seven months after training.

Self/peer nominations of 'hurt' and 'helped'. Lieberman *et al.* (1973) found in their study that the most accurate mode of identifying casualties in experiential groups (from among a large number utilised) was peer or trainee ratings of those who were 'hurt' as a direct result of their group experience. For example they found that of the sixteen psychiatrically diagnosed casualties in their study, twelve had high peer nomination ratings, whereas a significant drop in self-esteem ratings predicted only three casualties. It was on the basis of these findings that it was decided to use their measure here. All participants in the small-group training programme studied were asked the following question after the last session of training:

> 'Can you think of people in your group who were hurt (made worse, became overly upset) by the experience? Please describe *what happened* and to *whom* it happened. Include yourself, if this question is appropriate to you.'

We were also interested in the opposite side of the 'evaluation coin', that is, whether people were helped or not, so each participant was also asked to identify those participants who were *helped* by the experience (the word 'helped' replaced the words 'hurt, made worse, became overly upset'). For each trainee, therefore, data were available on the number of times he was named as being hurt and helped by the other trainees (and himself). Data were available for all trainees in all programmes.

Work colleague report on participants. The data collected on the effects of small-group training on the work performance and work relationships of the participants were obtained by using an adaptation of Bunker's open-ended behaviour change questionnaire (1965). This questionnaire was sent to the participant and two or three of his work colleagues six weeks and seven months after training. Each of the work associates was asked to respond to the following questions:

'Do you believe that the course (referred to in the letter attached), which your colleague attended, has affected his
(a) Work performance
(b) Relationships with work colleagues
in any positive or negative way? If so, please provide details in the space below. All information will be treated as strictly confidential.'

Two independent raters examined each of the two open-ended responses on the questionnaire for each participant and (1) determined whether it was a positive or negative change and (2) assessed the degree of directional change on a five-point continuum. Interrater reliability coefficients were calculated for the participants in each training programme separately, and they ranged from an $r = .77$ to $r = .90$. The response rates for the work colleagues were 81 per cent at six weeks and 80 per cent at seven months. This corresponds well with Bunker (1965), Moscow (1971), and other similar studies. Even though this is very good as far as postal surveys are concerned, it remains possible, as Smith (1975) suggests, that those 'adversely affected' may be among the small proportion who failed to respond. Moscow (1971), using the Bunker work colleague questionnaire (1965), did a study in which he attempted to see if the non-respondents in his evaluation project (into the effects of T-groups on managers back at work) were more 'adversely affected' by the group experience than the responders. He sent a postcard to those who had not responded to his 'work colleague questionnaire' asking them to check which of various reasons for non-response held true for them. The most frequent reasons were change in job, lack of job associates, and mistrust of the researcher's promise to maintain confidentiality. There was no suggestion that non-response was correlated with adverse programme effects.

Group characteristic or process variables measures

In this section we will be presenting some of the measures utilised to assess the respective independent or process variables which may be contributing to the reported positive or negative change in the training programmes examined. Five main process or group characteristic variables were used: participant personality predisposition, as measured by the 16PF Inventory; trainer personality, as measured by 16PF Inventory; trainer style, as measured by participants' perception of trainer behaviour during the training; characteristics of type of group training programme (e.g., level of intimacy, confrontation, structure, etc.) as judged by independent observers; and participants' conditions of participation (i.e., reasons for attending the training).

Participant personality predispositions. Lakin (1969) has suggested that one of the main reasons experiential learning groups may be dangerous is that they attract people who are seeking and in need of therapy, that is, individuals who are personally vulnerable and capable of being damaged. Although most of the research in this area, which concentrates on trainee vulnerability specifically, is equivocal (Cooper, 1975b), it was felt that this factor in conjunction with others may create the conditions for either psychological damage or growth. It was decided to use the Sixteen Personality Factor (16PF) Questionnaire (Cattell, Eber, & Tatsuoka, 1970), which was administered to all trainees just before the start of the first session of the training week. The 16PF was chosen because it was felt to be one of the most comprehensive and widely validated of the personality inventories, because it contains several subscales (C, H, L, O, Q3, and Q4) which seem to be reliably related to various aspects of anxiety (second stratum factor of adjustment versus anxiety), and because it could be easily and quickly administered. Form C was used, which is self-administering and consists of 105 three-alternative-choice items, comprising sixteen scales (four scales were omitted because of their low reliability). The following twelve source trait personality factors were used (the first of the bipolar traits mentioned for each factor represents the low-score end of the continuum):

Factor A: the sizothymia versus affectothymia source trait, which corresponds most closely to reserved, detached, critical, aloof versus warmhearted, outgoing, easy-going, participating, respectively; Factor C: the higher ego strength versus emotional instability trait, which is one of dynamic integration and maturity as opposed to uncontrolled, disorganised, general emotionality; Factor E: the submissiveness versus dominance trait, which can be dichotomised as obedience, docile, accommodating, as opposed to assertive, aggressive, and competitive; Factor F: the trait of desurgency versus surgency, or the differentiation between the sober and serious personality and the enthusiastic, happy-go-lucky one; Factor H: the threctia versus parmia source trait, the shy, timid, threat-sensitive, as opposed to the adventurous, socially bold personality; Factor I: the harria versus pramsia trait, which is comparable to Eysenck's tough-minded versus tender-minded typology; Factor L: the alaxia or 'trusting and free of jealousy' versus protension, or 'suspicious and hard to fool' trait; Factor O: the untroubled adequacy versus guilt-proneness trait, ranging from self-assured and confident to apprehensive and troubled; Factor Q1: reflects the continuum of conservatism to radicalism, or from rigidity and upholding established ideas to experimenting and free-thinking; Factor Q2: assesses the dichotomous trait of being group adherent at one end of the continuum to self-sufficient at the other; Factor Q3: low self-concept integration (undisciplined self-concept) to high self-concept control (following self-image); Factor Q4: low ergic tension, or relaxed and unfrustrated, to high tension, or frustrated and overwrought. Test, retest reliability, and validity data can be found in Cattell *et al.* (1970).

Trainer personality. Lieberman *et al.* (1973) found that the most predictive 'process variable' was the trainer's behaviour and style. It has been suggested elsewhere (Cooper & Mangham, 1970) that the trainer's personality predispositions and needs may also contribute to success or failure of experiential or social-skill training. Schein and Bennis (1965) emphasised this: 'Possibilities for unconscious gratification in the change agent's role (e.g., T-group trainer) are enormous and because of their consequences (for the health of the client/participant as well as the change agent) they must be examined.' Although Lieberman *et al.* (1973) explored trainer style during training they did not fully explore the psychometric predispositions of experiential group trainers. It was felt useful to examine this phenomenon here, particularly since it may have implications for both the selection of trainers and for their training and development. It may also provide additionally more negative information on perhaps 'who should not' be involved in a training role in experiential learning groups. The 16PF Inventory was filled out by all trainers prior to all training programmes.

Participants' perception of trainer style. The behaviour of the trainer during training in any social skill or experiential learning group is very important to its success or failure (Culbert, 1968; Cooper, 1969; Bolman, 1971). Indeed, Lieberman *et al.* (1973) found that this was the single most critical variable in assessing group casualties. In their study, trainer behaviour was determined by a relatively simple and short participant questionnaire (designed to get at the symbolic value of the group leader to participant), and by observer ratings of trainer behaviour, style, and primary focus. They came up with seven basic styles, which cut across group ideology: aggressive stimulators, love leaders, social engineers, *laissez-faire* leaders, cool aggressive stimulators, high structure leaders, and encountertape (self-learning Bell and Howell encountertapes) leaders. They found that the aggressive stimulator style of leadership produced 44 per cent of their experiential group casualties. Although this kind of global characterisation of trainer behaviour and style was a useful conceptual aid, it failed to provide a more detailed breakdown of trainer behaviour as seen by the participant.

Lieberman *et al.* (1973), however, had used the Personal

Description Questionnaire (PDQ) to get at participants' perception of themselves and other trainees and we felt that an adaptation of this instrument would be ideal as a measure of participant perception of trainer behaviour. Our version of the trainer style questionnaire therefore was an adaptation of the PDQ thirty-five-item bipolar adjectival scale, with the addition of five-point Likert-type ratings. It included some of the following semantic differential items: comfortable with others versus uncomfortable, genuine versus artificial, lenient versus strict, shows feelings versus hides feelings, rejects suggestions versus accepts suggestions, irresponsible versus responsible, high ability versus low ability, unenthusiastic versus enthusiastic, influential versus uninfluential, relaxed versus tense, sincere versus insincere, well-adjusted versus maladjusted, incompetent verses competent, etc. Each participant was asked to fill in a trainer style form for each trainer in the programme (at the end of training) and to indicate the proportion of the time spent with that particular trainer. In programmes where the participant had contact with more than one trainer, for over 30 per cent of the contact time, the perception of trainer style scores were averaged to provide the participant with a single score for each item. In order to minimise acquiescence response set half the trainer style items were reversed, so that a positive response reflected a negative trainer behaviour.

Groups of the thirty-five variables contained in the Trainer Style Questionnaire are likely to be intercorrelated and form overall trainer behaviour/style syndromes; it was decided therefore to carry out a factor analysis of all the data. Varimax rotation and a maximum of ninety-nine iterations were specified for this analysis. The six factors which emerged could be (in order of percentage of variance) described as reflecting the following characteristics: trainer openness and congruency (the responsibility/dependability items here reflect a consistency in behaviour which is an indigenous aspect of 'congruence'); trainer supportiveness; trainer authority profile; trainer extraversion/intraversion orientation; trainer tranquility; and trainer task competence.

These six factors will be used in the analysis that follows.

Conditions of participation: reasons for attending training. It has been suggested in the literature (Cooper, 1975c) that one of the possible contributory causes of disturbance from experiential learning groups may stem not only from the inappropriate motivations of participants but from the 'compliance to attend' imposed on them by their employing organisation. Many organisations send their managers on social-skill training programmes not only to help them improve their 'people skills', which may have long-term payoffs for the company itself, but also because certain managers may be deficient in their human-relations skills to the extent of creating departmental or organisational difficulties. In the latter case, managers may be sent on these training programmes without any real explanations as to why they are being sent or what senior management hope it will do for them. This may create frustration in the manager, which he may convert to hostility to the training programme. Ultimately he either 'refuses to learn' or, alternatively, since he has not 'selected the experience for himself', he may find it too threatening and suffer psychologically destructive consequences. Indeed, it has been suggested (Smith, 1975) that individuals who feel they cannot tolerate the dynamics of group training frequently, when they have the opportunity, *self-select* themselves out of such experiences. Neither 'refusing to learn' nor being 'adversely affected' bodes well for the success of the training. We felt here that it would be useful therefore to attempt to assess participants' condition of participation, that is, their reasons for attending. All participants were asked at the end of the training programme which of four alternatives with respect to their attendance applied to them. The alternatives moved from the condition of the organisation finding out about the programme and obliging the participant to attend (against his wishes) to the participant finding out about the training himself and being under no obligation to attend. A roughly equal number of participants fell into each of the four categories, with the

Table 4.1 Factor analysis of trainer style questionnaire (percentage of variance)

Factor 1:	Congruent/open/self-actualised 58.8 per cent	Factor 2:	Personal/social support 13.9 per cent
	Genuine		Accepts suggestions
	Responsible		Sympathetic
	Sincere		Frank and open
	Accepts help		Accommodating
	Reliable		
	Thorough		
	Dependable	Factor 4:	Outgoing
	Interested		6.3 per cent
	Optimistic		
	Happy		Shows feelings
			Outspoken
Factor 3:	Low-authority profile/'laissez-faire' 8.6 per cent		Demonstrative
	Lenient	Factor 6:	Task competence
	Undemanding		4.4 per cent
	Low prestige		
	Low status		High ability
			Enthusiastic
			Influential
Factor 5:	Relaxed/tranquil		Well-adjusted
	5.1 per cent		Competent
	Relaxed		Involved
	Unworried		Informed

category of 'participant self-selection' slightly less than the others. An open-ended question was included if none of the four alternatives were appropriate. In the few cases that this category was used, the responses were easily identifiable as one of the original four categories (on the basis of two independent observer judgments) and they were reclassified. A low score meant high compulsion to attend.

Observations of group process. Another very important aspect of experiential learning groups in terms of potential adverse or growthful effects are the group processes or dynamics of particular types of programme. It has been suggested by researchers and practitioners alike that groups which are unstructured, confronting, unsupportive, intimate, and highly person-centred may be potentially damaging under certain circumstances. It was felt necessary therefore to attempt to collect some data on the learning dynamics of these programmes. It was obviously inappropriate to rely on brochure material provided by the training organisations to assess their training approach or to discover what went on during training; on the other hand, it was financially impossible systematically to observe all training programmes — which would have been the optimal solution. It was therefore decided to assess a sample of each of the main training programmes. Two trained group observers (social psychologists with group training and research experience) were used in the study to assess the group approaches of the training programmes. They attended one of each of the main training programmes in their entirety. They were introduced along with the researcher at the beginning of the first session and the conditions of their attendance were 'contracted' with the trainees (which is consistent with norms in experiential groups). These conditions made it clear that participants could ask an observer to leave a particular session if they wished and could ask to see copies of the observer ratings referring to a particular session (in the event, no-one asked the observers to leave or to examine their ratings).

A group Rating Schedule was devised by the author for the observations. It comprised twenty-one different aspects of the group processes thought to contribute to either stress- or growth-related effects of experiential learning. The observer was asked to rate each session on the basis of the twenty-one point Likert-type scales ranging from 'to a very great extent' to 'not at all'. Some of the following dimensions were assessed: degree of focus on social interaction, nature of relationship between trainer and participant, degree of trust between participants and between trainer and participants, degree of focus on here-and-now behaviour, degree of confrontation in the group, degree of structure of the experience, degree of intimacy, level of personal support, etc.

Overall means were calculated from the observer ratings on each of the sessions to provide a group rating in each of the twenty-one dimensions and these were assigned to each participant in that particular group. Interrater reliability coefficients were calculated on a randomly selected number of sessions and they ranged from between $r = .75$ to $r = .81$. These twenty-one items were factor-analysed and five internally consistent factors emerged: process orientation, social atmosphere, trainer involvement, relationship between trainer and participant, and participant emotional cohesiveness. These factors were used in all subsequent analyses.

Results

In order to analyse the relationship between our criteria or outcome variables (e.g., self/peer nominations of 'hurt' and 'helped'; work colleague reports on participants) and our independent or process variables (e.g., participant personality, trainer personality, trainer style, group characteristics, and participants' conditions of participation), we used a stepwise multiple regression analysis. This type of analysis provides us with the best linear prediction equation between each of our outcome variables and sets of our process variables. The SPSS multiple regression subprogramme with a stepwise procedure was utilised, which provides considerable control over the inclusion of independent variables in the regression equation (Nie, Hull, Jenkins, Steinbrenner, & Bent, 1975). In trying to isolate process variables which will yield the optimal prediction equation, our cut-off point was determined by two statistical criteria (Kerlinger & Pedhazer, 1973). First, that the overall F for the equation was significant. And second, that the partial regression coefficient for the individual process variable being added was at a statistically significant or approaching significance level. Below this point not only is the coefficient

Table 4.2 Factor analysis of group observation scores (percentage of variance)

Factor 1:   *Process orientation*
               41.8 per cent

               Reactions to one another
               Focus on social interaction
               Focus on here-and-now feelings and behaviour
               Degree of confrontation

Factor 2:   *Social atmosphere*
               20.9 per cent

               Relations between trainers and participants
               Relaxed social atmosphere
               Pleasant social atmosphere

Factor 3:   *Trainer involvement*
               12.8 per cent

               Frankness and openness between trainers and
                   participants
               Trainer involvement

Factor 4:   *Nature of relationship between trainer and*
                   participant
               11.2 per cent

               Degree of support by trainers
               Degree of rejection by trainers
               Degree of intimacy between trainers and
                   participants

Factor 5:   *Participant emotional cohesiveness*
               8.3 per cent

               Trust between participants
               Degree of emotions shown
               Support by participants
               Intimacy between participants

Table 4.3 Stepwise multiple regression analysis of peer nominations of 'hurt' trainees with group characteristics and process variables[a]

Step	Process variable	Multiple R	R-square	R-square change
1	Trainee personality: Factor E 'independent'	.308	.095	.095
2	Trainee personality: Factor O 'self-assured'	.389	.151	.056
3	Trainer style: Factor 4 'withdrawn'	.443	.196	.044
4	Trainee personality: Factor Q4 'tense'	.484	.235	.038
5	Trainee personality: Factor C 'unaffected by feelings'	.519	.269	.034
6	Trainee personality: Factor I 'self-reliant'	.551	.304	.034
7	Trainer style: Factor I 'closed and incongruent'	.608	.369	.065
8	Trainee personality: Factor L 'self-opinionated'	.656	.430	.060

[a] Overall $F = 2.744$; $p = .022$

insignificant but also the amount of variance contributed by each additional variable (R^2 change) is very small.

Self/peer nominations of 'hurt' and 'helped'

We found among our sample that around 37 per cent of the participants were named at least once by themselves or other trainees as having been 'hurt' by the experience. Only 11 per cent, however, were named two or more times. On the other hand, over 75 per cent of the participants were named at least once as being 'helped' by experiential group training, with 61 per cent of all trainees nominated two or more times. There were, therefore, individuals who were obviously seen as having been both 'helped' and 'hurt' by their participation in groups.

Participants nominated as having been adversely affected.
Table 4.3 shows the group characteristic or process variables
that are linked to self/peer nominations of 'hurt'
participants. It can be seen from this table that the main
predictors (or process variables) of peer-determined
participant stress as a result of experiential groups are the
participants' personality predispositions and the behaviour or
style of the group leader during training. Participants who
are perceived by other trainees as having been 'hurt' by the
experience tend to be 'independent', 'self-assured', 'self-
reliant', 'unaffected by feelings', but also slightly 'tense and
overwrought'. These participants are likely to appear
dominant and more confident than they really are and as a
consequence are likely to attract attention and adverse
feedback. This tends to occur in groups with trainers who are
perceived as 'closed/incongruent/unreliable' and
'introverted and withdrawn', that is, group leaders who are
not very supportive of other group members because they
themselves may find it difficult to emerge and develop their
own 'person' or 'role' in the group. The data in Table 4.3
include participants who were nominated as 'hurt' and also
those judged as both 'hurt' and 'helped'. If we examine only
those participants judged as 'hurt' but not also judged as
'helped', we find that there are only two significant
predictors of adverse effect. They are the two perceived
trainer behaviour and style factors from above, 'closed and
incongruent' ($r = .77$) and 'introverted and withdrawn' ($r =
.98$), with the latter contributing most of the variance (R^2
change $= .964$).

*Participants nominated as having been 'helped' by group
training.* Table 4.4 shows the group characteristics or process
variables which are linked to self/peer nominations of
'helped' participants. It can be seen that the major predictors
(or process variables) of peer-determined participant *benefit*
were trainer and participant personality predisposition
factors, namely, self-sufficient participants with
psychologically relaxed, but guilt-prone trainers. It was felt

Table 4.4 Stepwise multiple regression analysis of peer nominations of 'helped' trainees with group characteristics and process variables[a]

Step	Process variable	Multiple R	R-square	R-square change
1	Trainer personality: Factor O 'apprehensive or guilt-prone'	.415	.172	.172
2	Trainee personality: Factor Q2 'self-sufficient'	.506	.256	.084
3	Trainer personality: Factor Q4 'relaxed'	.544	.296	.039

[a] Overall $F = 7.436$; $p < .001$.

Table 4.5 Stepwise multiple regression analysis of peer nominations of 'helped' but not 'hurt' trainees with group characteristics and process variables[a]

Step	Process variable	Multiple R	R-square	R-square change
1	Trainer personality: Factor Q1 'experimenting'	.365	.133	.133
2	Trainer personality: Factor Q4 'relaxed'	.505	.255	.122
3	Trainer style: Factor 5 'relaxed/tranquil'	.602	.363	.107
4	Trainee personality: Factor C 'affected by feelings'	.644	.415	.052
5	Trainee personality: Factor I 'self-sufficient'	.676	.457	.041

[a] Overall $F = 7.425$; $p < .001$.

that we might get a more 'rounded' picture of the learning processes for participants judged to have positively changed by examining only those participants judged as 'helped' but not also nominated as 'hurt'. The results from Table 4.5 provide a fuller and more consistent account of the learning precursors to positive change. From this we might infer that the conditions under which individuals are likely to be perceived as having benefited are those where there is a match of student-teacher needs and behaviour. That is, groups composed of individuals who are fairly 'realistic and self-sufficient' but also 'open to their own feelings', in an atmosphere with an 'experimenting' and 'relaxed/tranquil' trainer.

In addition to the specific results found above, there are a number of general points one should consider in the data on self/peer nominations of 'hurt' and 'helped' participants. First, that the *trainer personality and style* factors seem to be the main predictors or process variables related to participants identified as either 'hurt' or 'helped'. Second, that the next most important contributory factors are 'selected' participant personality predispositions. Third, that the group structure or observational variables (e.g., degree of confrontation, level of intimacy, etc.) and the trainees' conditions of participation are not significant predictors of perceived adverse effect or benefit.

Work colleague report on group participants

The work colleagues (e.g., boss, subordinates, and work peers) of each participant reported on the behaviour of returning group participants, six weeks and seven months after training. They assessed both the change in their work performance and relationships at work. On a five-point Likert-type scale ranging from (five) 'very important change' through (three) 'no change' to (one) 'very important negative change' in work performance and relationships separately, it was found that overall means were: work performance 3.54 at six weeks and 3.48 at seven months; work relationships 3.59 at six weeks and 3.52 at seven months. On balance, therefore, participants were seen to be changing in the positive direction, both shortly after training and in the longer term. Work colleague data were also collected on a control sample of thirty-nine managers who were on the waiting list for one of the small-group training programmes evaluated in this study. It was found that although there was no significant difference between the controls and group trainees on work colleague reports on change in work performance in the long term (at seven months) ($M_{controls}$ = 3.51, $M_{trainees}$ = 3.48, t = .24, p = n.s.), there was a significant difference between them in work relationships ($M_{controls}$ = 3.27, $M_{trainees}$ = 3.52, t = 2.19, p < .02). Trainees were seen by their work colleagues to have positively changed in their work relationships after training as compared to controls.

Change in work relationships. Tables 4.6 and 4.7 show the independent or group process variables that are linked to improved work relationships. It can be seen that in the short term (e.g., six weeks after training), there are a variety of process variables related to positive change at work: 'self-sufficient' participants in a group with an 'enthusiastic' and 'task competent' trainer who is 'open and sincere' but is not particularly 'comforting or supportive'. In addition, it was found that those participants who were *sent* by their organisations as opposed to opting for the group experience themselves were more likely to be seen subsequently as having positively changed in their work relationships. If we explore the seven-month data, we find, as in the more refined peer nomination data, that the participant personality characteristics are less important than are the trainer personality and style variables. In particular, we find that the most significant correlates of perceived positive change in participants' relationships at work are 'relaxed, unworried, and tranquil' and 'self-sufficient' trainers. And once again those participants who are sent by their organisation are perceived to gain most at work. Although this finding is contrary to normal expectation that those individuals forced to attend such training are likely to be the most 'at risk', it makes some sense in terms of the *Gestalt* of the data. That is, that the individuals who are being sent on such courses are the managers with 'human relations' problems; they are, for example, in terms of the psychometric data available, 'overly controlled', 'socially precise', and 'tend to prefer their own

Table 4.6 Stepwise multiple regression analysis of work colleague reports on relationships at work (six week) with group characteristics and process variables[a]

Step	Process variable	Multiple R	R-square	R-square change
1	Trainee personality: Factor Q2 'self-sufficient'	.264	.069	.069
2	Trainer personality: Factor F 'enthusiastic'	.335	.112	.043
3	Trainer style: Factor 2 'socially supportive'	.375	.141	.028
4	Reasons for attending: 'sent by organisation'	.419	.175	.034
5	Trainer style: Factor 6 'task competence'	.458	.210	.034

[a] Overall $F = 4.583$; $p = .001$.

decisions'. The potential for positive change for those types of individual in these types of social skill training programme, therefore, is great.

Change in work performance. Tables 4.8 and 4.9 show the relationships between positive change in work performance and the independent or process variables, six weeks and seven months after training. It was found, in the short term (i.e., six week data), that certain trainer-style characteristics acting upon participants sent on the group training programmes produced the most positive outcomes: that is, trainers who were seen to be relaxed/tranquil, with a low authority profile but who tend not to be supportive. Data from the seven-month follow-up period are more consistent with the results found earlier with peer-determined positive change: those participants who are seen to have gained the most in terms of their work performance are the ones who seem to be the most 'realistic' and self-sufficient; in groups with trainers whose personality predispositions lead them to be 'spontaneous', 'sensitive', and 'emotionally stable' and whose behaviour or style in the group is perceived by trainees to be 'open and

Table 4.7 Stepwise multiple regression analysis of work colleague reports on relationships at work (seven month) with group characteristics and process variables[a]

Step	Process variable	Multiple R	R-square	R-square change
1	Trainer personality: Factor Q4 'relaxed'	.247	.061	.061
2	Reasons for attending: 'sent by organisation'	.327	.107	.046
3	Trainer personality: Factor Q2 'self-sufficient'	.377	.142	.035

[a] Overall F = 4.262; p = .008.

congruent' and 'relaxed and unworried'. Once again we find that trainer personality and style variables are the best predictors of positive change in participants.

Discussion

Summary

In this section we will summarise the results of the study, draw attention to some additional general points of interest, and consider the implications of the research for the design and practice of experiential group training. There are several specific results worthy of note. First, that trainees attending small-group training programmes perceive participants 'at risk' or who may have been 'hurt' as dominant, self-assured, and not open to feelings in groups with closed, unreliable, and withdrawn trainers. Second, these trainees, on the other hand, perceive participants who have gained from their experience as realistic, self-sufficient, and open to their feelings in groups with relaxed, unworried, open and experimenting trainers. Third, that trainer personality and behaviour during training are very strongly linked to the most positive and the least negative change in subsequent work

Table 4.8 Stepwise multiple regression analysis of work colleague reports on work performance with group characteristics and process variables (six-week follow-up period).[a]

Step	Process variable	Multiple R	R-square	R-square change
1	Trainer style: Factor 3 'low-authority profile'	.273	.074	.074
2	Trainer style: Factor 2 'little social support'	.371	.137	.063
3	Trainer style: Factor 5 'relaxed'	.422	.178	.040
4	Reasons for attending: 'sent by organisation'	.447	.200	.021
5	Trainee personality: Factor O 'self-assured'	.476	.227	.027

[a] Overall $F = 5.065$; $p < .001$.

performance and relationships at work, particularly relaxed, self-sufficient, and tranquil trainers. Participant personality characteristics are not strongly related, however, to short- or long-term change back in the work environment. On the other hand, participants who are seen to gain the most, contrary to expectations, were those who were *sent* by their organisations on the training programmes (as opposed to self-selecting their own learning experience). Finally, one of the most consistent findings across all the outcome measures is that participants helped most and hurt least as judged by other trainees or who show the least negative and the most positive change in subsequent work performance and relationships (in the short and long term) are found in groups with trainers who tend to show low ergic tension (i.e., are relaxed and unworried) and are open to their own feelings (i.e., in Rogerian terms are congruent).

There are a number of more general points one might consider from the above results. First, that the success or failure of experiential group training seems strongly linked to the personality and style of the group trainer/s present. These

Table 4.9 Stepwise multiple regresson analysis of work colleague reports on work performance with group characteristics and process variables (seven-month follow-up period).[a]

Step	Process variable	Multiple R	R-square	R-square change
1	Trainer personality: Factor H 'spontaneous'	.207	.042	.042
2	Trainer personality: Factor C 'emotionally stable'	.278	.077	.034
3	Trainer style: Factor 1 'open and congruent'	.325	.105	.028
4	Trainer personality: Factor I 'sensitive'	.371	.137	.031
5	Trainee personality: Factor I 'realistic'	.407	.165	.028
6	Trainer style: Factor 5 'relaxed'	.445	.198	.032

[a] Overall $F = 3.053$; $p = .01$.

variables consistently appear as significant predictors of various outcome measures. The data above therefore confirm much of the speculation by Lieberman *et al.* (1973) and others on the significant impact of trainer behaviour on individual adverse and growth effects in groups. Indeed, Bolman (1976) recently summarised many writers' view of the effective group leader:

> '(1) The leader is able to empathize with the partici-pants, and communicates a consistent respect and caring for them. (2) The leader is sufficiently con-gruent and genuine that participants experience him as trustable. (3) The leader is willing to be open, to confront, and to provide feedback, and does not do it in a way which is punishing or which results in his completely dominating the group's activities.'

This caricature of the ideal group trainer/facilitator is, on balance, very similar to the composite picture which emerges of the effective leader from this study. This may not be surprising since much of the early T-group work stemmed from the conceptual foundation stones of Rogerian theory, which emphasised some of the change agent characteristics above.

Another interesting null result in our study was that adverse effect (either peer-determined or work-related) was not associated with trainers who were emotionally unstable or anxiety-prone (i.e., the second stratum 16PF anxiety-related factors). This is contrary to many views (e.g., Mann, 1970) that some experiential group trainers are involved in this form of training to meet their own neurotic needs. Indeed, Schein and Bennis (1965) have cautioned us to be aware of this: 'The possibilities for unconscious gratification in the trainer's role are enormous and because of their consequences (for the health of the client as well as the trainer) they must be examined.' Indeed, if we compare all the experiential group trainers in our study against the normative population data of the 16PF (see Table 4.10) we find that they are different from the norms on eight of the twelve scales (E, I, L, O, Q1, Q2, Q3, and Q4), and in a consistently positive direction. Experiential group trainers and facilitators are more tender-minded, more experimenting, more self-sufficient, more assertive, less suspicious, less apprehensive, less controlled, and less tense. So even when we found that certain negative trainer personality traits were associated with short-term distress, this may indicate only marginally negative or disruptive trainer behaviour.

Second, we found that the group structure and observational variables (e.g., degree of confrontation, level of intimacy, etc.) were not in any way significantly linked to either positive or negative outcome. This is contrary to numerous speculations (Gottschalk & Pattison, 1969) that the level of intimacy, individual as opposed to group focus, confrontation, etc., are central contributory factors to adverse effects from these group experiences. Indeed, Lieberman *et al.* (1973) found that certain group

Table 4.10 Mean trainer and participant sten scores on the 16PF[a]

16Pf factors	Trainer sten score	Participant sten score	Norm average
A	6	5-6	5-6
C	6	5-6	5-6
E	7	7	5-6
F	5-6	5-6	5-6
H	5-6	5	5-6
I	7	5-6	5-6
L	4-5	5-6	5-6
O	4	5-6	5-6
Q1	7	5-6	5-6
Q2	7-8	8	5-6
Q3	4-5	5	5-6
Q4	4-5	5	5-6

[a] Since raw scores are not whole numbers, approximate stens have been selected.

characteristics (e.g., group cohesiveness, involvement intensity, harmony, etc.) were related to positive change as a result of a group experience. Their work, however, was based on simple correlations between process and outcome variables and failed to explore the interrelationship of the process variables *vis-à-vis* the outcome measures, that is, the extent to which, in respect to one another, they contribute to change (i.e., obtain the best linear prediction equation).

Third, we found that participants' personality predispositions may be important in the short run, but not in the long term, as a precursor to positive or negative change from group training. This result may be accounted for by the fact that participants who are 'visible', that is, who are dominant, self-assured and apparently 'not open to their feelings', are likely to attract a great deal of the group's attention. As a consequence, other trainees may feel that these participants have been 'hurt or damaged' by the experience when in fact they have only attracted 'feedback'. It has not been established that the recipient of 'feedback' is necessarily a potential casualty; this will depend on the

coping style and defences of the participant and the
intervention skills of the group leader. In this study we found
that in the long term, the participant personality
characteristics described above, although associated with
peer-nominated 'hurt' in the short term, were not related to
either short- or long-term damage back in the work
environment.

In addition, it is very interesting to note that there was no
evidence that the participants who were identified as
suffering short-term (peer-nominated) distress as a result of
training were less emotionally stable or anxious than other
trainees (see Table 4.10). It has been suggested by Lakin
(1969) and others (Crawshaw, 1969) that experiential groups
attract people who are seeking and in need of therapy, i.e.,
individuals who are vulnerable, unstable, and capable of
being damaged. The research available to date is
inconclusive, however, in this area. Olch and Snow (1970),
for example, compared the California Personality Inventory
factors for university students who volunteered for a
sensitivity training ($n = 39$) group with those who did not ($n = 62$). The results suggest that students who volunteer for
participation in experiential groups see themselves as less
well-adjusted, less self-assured, less mature, and less skilled
socially than those who do not volunteer for such groups.
They conclude that experiential group participants are less
socially and emotionally adjusted than those not seeking such
experiences. On the other hand, Cooper and Bowles (1973)
found that university students who volunteered to take part
in an encounter group were not significantly different from
nonvolunteers on either the extraversion or neuroticism scales
of the EPI. Gilligan (1973) also found no differences between
sensitivity training participants and others on the social-
emotional adjustment index of the OPI. The participant
personality traits associated with emotional instability or
anxiety may not have linked up to identifiable short-term
distress in our study for at least two reasons. First, our
training population as a whole were relatively 'normal'.
When we compared our trainees with the normative

population data on the 16PF we found few differences between them (participants were more 'self-sufficient' and marginally more 'assertive') and no differences on any of the second stratum 16PF anxiety-related factors. Second, unlike Olch and Snow, who were running their experiential groups within a student counselling centre, our programmes were run as management training experiences and were not being advertised or marketed as 'personal growth' adventures.

And fourth, participants sent on group training programmes are more likely to be seen back in the work environment as having gained, particularly in terms of their work relationships. It was suggested that one of the possible variables contributing to adverse effects of experiential groups could be associated with the participant's reasons for attending the training. Managers who are forced to attend by their organisations without consultation, it is argued, may be more vulnerable since they have not self-selected themselves for (or out) of the training. The obverse of this seems to be the case. The explanation for this could be that industrial training officers are becoming more sophisticated and aware of the potential dangers of these forms of experiential learning method, and although they may send individuals who have various social skill difficulties, they 'screen out' those with deeper-level behavioural problems. Certainly the psychometric data available indicate that the experiential group participants are not significantly different from the normative population on most of the 16PF scales. If we examine those participants who indicate that they were obliged to attend the training by their organisation we found no significant differences between them and the other trainees on any of the second stratum anxiety-related factors of the 16PF. Since there is an indication that managers who are sent on group training may be gaining subsequently in the work environment, this may mean that the individuals responsible for training and development may be competently diagnosing managerial needs and effectively utilising the training resources available in the community.

Implications

Looking at some of the results and issues raised by this study on experiential group techniques, the question we must now ask ourselves is what can we do to minimise their risk and hopefully enhance their effectiveness? It has been suggested by many (Jaffe & Scherl, 1969; Gottschalk & Pattison, 1969; Mann, 1970) that the two most important areas for action are in participant selection or screening and in training and screening of group leaders. First, we examine the selection and screening of participants. Jaffe and Scherl (1969) have proposed a number of suggestions to minimise the possibility of psychological disturbance of these groups:

1. That participation be completely and truly voluntary.
2. That participation be based on informed consent with respect to purpose and goals. Each person should know clearly ahead of time what will occur, over how long a time, for what purposes, with what degree of confidentiality, and with what specific potential dangers. Participants should be warned that these groups are not intended for therapy nor are they intended for persons who consider themselves or fear they are 'sick' or in 'need of treatment'.
3. That participants be screened at least by questionnaire and preferably by interview.
4. That participants understand what types of behaviour are permissible during the group.
5. That follow-up for all participants be available to help deal with group termination.

Let us explore each of these in terms of this research and other work in the field. First, we have no evidence from our sample that forcing participants to attend such programmes is necessarily damaging, quite the reverse (in the case of our sample of managers). This may be because the large majority (roughly 75 per cent) came somewhat voluntarily but also perhaps because training and personnel officers in industry are more aware of the implications of 'forced attendance' and probably are very selective in the first instance.

Nevertheless, we must agree with the sentiments expressed by Jaffe and Scherl, primarily on the grounds that participant 'motivation to learn' must be greater under conditions of voluntary choice. Second, in principle we would agree with most of the second recommendation. Issue could be taken, however, about the suggestion of informing participants ahead of time about the potentially dangerous effects of training. This could, it might be argued, create the very conditions one is trying to avoid — that is, building up a normative expectation in the minds of participants that they are about to attend an 'intensive, quasi-therapy' experience (when this expectation might not have been there before). Indeed, this was one of the major criticisms of the Liebermann *et al.* (1973) study. It is obvious that participants should be provided with as much information as possible; if this is done, the likelihood is that the training programme will not attract individuals who are seeking therapy — this is firmly supported by a recent review of the literature (Cooper, 1975b). Their third suggestion has been given wide support by Lieberman *et al.,* Gottschalk and Pattison, and many others, but questions remain as to whether it is practical and on what criteria we decide to do the screening? In our study we did not find any anxiety-related or neurotic personality characteristics associated with short-term distressed participants but rather a 'dominant, self-assured, unaffected by feelings' profile. There are likely to be group experiences, however, which attract a larger number of less than stable trainees or participants who may find it difficult to cope with a higher than average 'affect level', in which case some screening procedure would be desirable. Stone and Tieger (1971) have demonstrated that this can work. They screened 105 applicants for a week-long T-group. Seventeen applicants were screened out and an additional six withdrew after the screening procedure. This procedure included not only the standard application form currently used by most training and consultancy organisations running these groups in the United Kingdom (e.g., what they hope to learn from the course, etc.), but also the MMPI and a small-group discussion. The screening eliminated about 25 per cent of applicants and in the end the group experience produced only one casualty, whereas participants in an unscreened programme produced four out of forty-one casualties. It is likely that Stone and Tieger's groups were higher risk ones in the first place but they at least demonstrated the usefulness of screening. In the management training field one has to weigh up the potential risk factor against the impracticality of such procedures, but there is evidence it can work. The fourth suggestion is also important and we touched on it earlier, that participants should have as much information as possible about the training situation they are likely to attend. It is not uncommon for trainers deliberately to provide a vague course description in the hope of attracting larger numbers of participants or in providing claims of 'interpersonal transformation'. This can only increase the risk of attracting those seeking therapy or counselling. And finally, Jaffe and Scherl (1969) suggest that we should provide follow-up facilities for ex-participants, to help short-term distressed trainees and those who manifest disturbance later. Once again we can only support the principle of this suggestion but is it realistic in 'stranger group' training contexts? One would have thought this was possible; most training and management consultancy organisations which participated in this research, for instance, have on their staff trainers who are very skilled at individual as well as group counselling, and one would have thought it would be possible for them to organise an 'open-door' resource facility for ex-experiential group participants. This would have been carefully planned in respect to the trainee's sponsoring organisation but it could be done and would ensure not only a safeguard but also some continuity of the learning experience.

Another major concern about experiential groups has to do with the trainers or group leaders. Yalom and Lieberman (1971) suggest that one of the major findings in their study is that the number and severity of casualties are almost a direct result of a particular leadership style; indeed, they say: 'The casualties seemed truly *caused* not merely hastened or facilitated, by the leader style, and is thereby preventable by a change in leader style.' In our view one should consider very carefully the skills that experiential group leaders should possess. Many of the group trainers currently involved in this form of training both in managment education and elsewhere in the United Kingdom possess some minimal level of insight into group and individual phenomena, obviously, some more than others. But there are two skills many of these trainees could be encouraged to acquire to minimise potentially negative effects and indeed enhance the possibility of greater success in their groups. Ross *et al.* (1971) have suggested one of these, albeit with wording a bit extreme, written from the clinician's point of view:

> 'The training of the group leader in some clinical setting becomes mandatory if he is to perceive subtle reactions of disorganization before they become full-blown. In addition, he should have sufficient clinical experience to be beyond the use of affective discharge and catharsis for its sake alone... The leader must be alert to step in and protect members of the group from promiscuous attack.'

In part we would concur with this recommendation, particularly that experiential group leaders, even in the field of management education, should attempt to obtain some training in being able to recognise and cope with participants 'at risk'. This would ensure not only a lower level of casualty but also that the group leader has the skills to deal with it when it occurs. At the moment no such training programme is available in the United Kingdom. Another important aspect has to do with the group trainer's understanding of his own behaviour and how this might lead to adverse or successful effects. Each group leader behaves in ways, as we have seen in this study, that create conditions for both psychological success and failure, which is related in no small measure to his own needs and psychological makeup (Argyris, 1966). The trainer can exploit his role in the pursuance of his own needs, particularly in his desire to be liked or to exercise power. It is essential that training programmes be developed that focus on the trainer's motives and how these may enable or prevent the participant from learning in his own way. In addition to trainer development programmes, it is important that group leaders in these types of learning experience have extensive group experience prior to 'solo training', where they can receive feedback, try out different behavioural styles and approaches, and generally learn to cope with the variety of phenomena that take place in different groups with different populations and compositions. In Britain at the moment there are very few opportunities for the *comprehensive* training of group leaders, whereas in Holland, the United States, and Australia there are more well-designed, thoroughly conceived programmes, which at the very least are likely to be providing fewer unskilled and potentially disruptive group trainers.

References

Argyris, C., *Exploration and issues in laboratory education,* Washington, DC: National Training Laboratory, 1966.

Back, K.W., Intervention techniques: small groups, *Annual Review of Psychology,* 1974, 25, 367-38.

Batchelder, R.L., & Hardy, J.M., *Using sensitivity training and the laboratory method,* New York: Association Press, 1968.

Bolman, L.G., Some effects of trainers on their T-groups, *Journal of Applied Behavioral Science,* 1971, 7, 309-326.

Bolman, L.G., Group leader effectiveness. In Cary L. Cooper (Ed.), *Developing social skills in managers,* London: Macmillan, 1976, pp. 37-51.

Bunker, D.R., Individual applications of laboratory training, *Journal of Applied Behavioral Science,* 1965, 1, 131-148.

Cattell, R.B., Eber, H.W., & Tatsuoka, M.M., *Handbook for the 16PF questionnaire,* Champaign, Illinois: Institute of Personality and Ability Testing, 1970.

Cooper, C.L., The influence of the trainer on participant change in T-groups, *Human Relations,* 1969, 22, 515-530.

Cooper, C.L., *Group training for individual and organizational development,* Basel: S. Karger, 1973.

Cooper, C.L., How psychologically dangerous are T-groups and encounter groups?, *Human Relations,* 1975, 28(3), 337-341. (b)

Cooper, C.L., *Theories of group processes,* London: John Wiley, 1975. (c)

Cooper, C.L., & Bowles, D., Physical encounter and self-disclosure, *Psychological Reports,* 1973, 33, 451-455.

Cooper, C.L., & Mangham, I.L., T-group training: Before and after, *Journal of Management Studies,* 1970, 7, 224-239.

Crawshaw, R., How sensitive is sensitivity training?, *American Journal of Psychiatry,* 1969, 126, 870-873.

Culbert, S.A., Trainer self-disclosure and member growth in two T-groups, *Journal of Applied Behavioral Science,* 1968, 4, 47-74.

Gilligan, J.F., Personality characteristics of selectors and nonselectors of sensitivity training, *Journal of Counseling Psychology,* 1973, 20, 265-268.

Gottschalk, L.., Psychoanalytic notes on T-groups at the human relations laboratory, Bethel, Maine, *Comprehensive Psychiatry,* 1966, 7, 474-487.

Gottschalk, L.A., & Pattison, E.M., Psychiatric perspective on T-groups and the laboratory movement: An overview, *American Journal of Psychiatry,* 1969, 126, 823-839.

Jaffe, S.L., & Scherl, D.J., Acute psychosis precipitated by T-group experiences, *Archives of General Psychiatry,* 1969, 21, 443-448.

Kerlinger, F.N., & Padhazer, E., *Multiple regression in behavioral research,* New York: Holt, Rinehart & Winston, 1973.

Lakin, M., Some ethical issues in sensitivity training, *American Psychologist,* 1969, 24, 923-928.

Lieberman, L.A., Yalom, I.D., & Miles, M.B., *Encounter groups: first facts,* New York: Basic Books, 1973.

Mann, E.K., Sensitivity training: Should we use it?, *Training*

Development Journal, 1970, 24, 44-48.

Moscow, D., T-group training in the Netherlands: An evaluation and cross-cultural comparison, *Journal of Applied Behavioral Science,* 1971, 7, 427-448.

National Training Laboratory (NTL), *News and Reports,* 1969, 3, 4.

Nie, N.H., Hull, C.H., Jenkins, J.G., Steinbrenner, K., & Bent, D.H., *Statistical package for the social sciences,* New York: McGraw-Hill, 1975.

Olch, D., & Snow, D.L., Personality characteristics of sensitivity group volunteers. *Personnel and Guidance Journal,* 1970, 48, 848-850.

Ross, W.D., Kligfeld, M., & Whitman, R.W., Psychiatrists, patients and sensitivity groups, *Archives of General Psychiatry,* 1971, 25, 178-180.

Schein, E.H., & Bennis, W.G., *Personal learning and organizational change through group methods,* New York: John Wiley, 1965.

Smith, P.B., Are there adverse effects of sensitivity training?' *Journal of Humanistic Psychology,* 1975, 15(2), 29-47.

Stone, W.N., & Tieger, M.E., Screening for T-groups: The myth of healthy candidates, *American Journal of Psychiatry,* 1971, 127, 1485-1490.

Weiss, J.H., Effect of professional training and amount and accuracy of information on behavioral predictions, *Journal of Consulting Psychology,* 1963, 27, 257-262.

Yalom, I.D., & Lieberman, M.A., A study of encounter group casualties, *Archives of General Psychiatry,* 1971, 25, 16-30.

5 The influence of the trainer on participant change in T-groups[1]

Much research evidence (Cooper & Mangham, 1971; Cooper, 1975; Smith, 1975) supports the use of the T-group as a highly important method of human relations or social skill training. Very little is known, however, about how or why it is effective. In particular, a better understanding is needed of the trainer's contribution to the participant's learning. Some progress has been made in measuring the trainer's personality needs and his behaviour in the group (Deutsch, Pepitone & Zander, 1948; Reisel, 1959), his effect on the perceptions of participants (Lohmann, Zenger & Weschler, 1959; Vansina, 1961), and his contribution to the development of the group (Stermerding, 1961; Psathas & Hardert, 1966; Mann, 1966). Theoretical formulation and empirical investigation of the trainer's influence on participant learning is, however, in a primitive state, though some relevant doctoral work has been completed (Peters, 1967; Bolman, 1968).

1. This study is a product of a research programme on T-group training supported by the Social Science Research Council. I am grateful to Dr Peter B. Smith of the University of Sussex for his help in the preparation of this paper, and to Professor Vernon L. Allen of the Department of Psychology of the University of Wisconsin for his comments on earlier drafts of this paper.

Theory

The present study is an attempt to test a theory of trainer influence on participants' change. Predictions of trainer influence on participants' change were derived from Kelman's (1961; 1963) theory of social influence. He distinguished three processes of social influence: compliance, identification, and internalisation, each characterised by distinct antecedent and consequent conditions. It is proposed that the participant's perception of trainer characteristics will determine which process of social influence is likely to result. Thus, compliance is likely to result if the trainer is seen as a *means controller,* that is, if he is seen 'to possess the ability to supply or withhold material or psychological resources on which the participant's goal achievement depends'. Identification is likely to result if the trainer is seen as *attractive,* that is, if he is seen 'to possess attributes that the participant desires for himself'. Internalisation is likely to result if the trainer is seen as credible or *self-congruent,* that is, if he is seen to be honest, direct and sincere in what he conveys.

It is proposed that the changes produced by each of the three processes will be different. In compliance, a participant will change by saying and doing the expected thing in the particular situation — he will express attitudes or display overt behaviours that he thinks the trainer expects. Change is an instrumental response for the purpose of achieving a favourable reaction from the trainer. In identification, the trainer 'serves as a model whom the participant wishes to resemble'. Here, the participant will change in the direction of saying and doing what the trainer says and does. In internalisation, the participant will involve himself in an active and idiosyncratic process of change which is independent of the trainer. Change produced through internalisation becomes part of the participant's *internal personal system* (i.e. self-concept). These changes will tend to occur in the direction of providing the individual with a more consistent self-concept.

The difference in the nature of the change between the three processes is due to the participant's motivation to accept the trainer's influence. In compliance, the participant expresses a certain attitude or displays a certain overt behaviour because he regards it as a condition for the trainer's favour, that is, to gain a reward or approval or to avoid punishment or disapproval. In identification, the participant accepts influence because the trainer is important or salient for him in the T-group. Thus, by doing what the trainer does and believing what he believes, the participant gains the satisfaction that goes with defining himself as identical with this salient figure. In internalisation, the participant accepts influence from the trainer because he regards him as a credible or trustworthy source of information. The key point for the participant is that he sees the trainer behaving in a way that he regards as consistent with the goals of the T-group, that is, to be genuine, direct, and sincere in expressing one's feelings about oneself and others.

As Kelman suggests, these types of influence process are by no means mutually exclusive. Frequently an influence relationship involves aspects of each. These processes are, therefore, intended as analytic devices rather than rigid or compartmentalised categories.

In this study, predictions were based only on the processes of identification and internalisation. Compliant-orientated influence was not examined since its relevance to the T-group was considered to be minimal (Harrison, 1966). The T-group environment tends to stress more non-directive sources of influence. This is not to say this form of influence does not take place, but rather that its presence is less strongly felt.

Hypotheses

Identification-based trainer influence

Hypothesis 1.   A participant will change in his *attitudes* toward being more like the trainer if the trainer is attractive to him.

Hypothesis 2.   A participant will change in his *behaviours* toward being more like the trainer if the trainer is attractive to him.

Aspects of the trainer behaviour and attitudes that the participant incorporates depend on the particular characteristics of the trainer that he finds attractive. The three characteristics that appear most central to the life of a T-group are *power* or control within the group, *affection* or intimacy within the group, and the *task* toward which the group must orient itself. In small-group research, Hare (1962) has distinguished these characteristics, on the basis of an extensive survey of research, as the three principal dimensions of small-group behaviour. Trainer attractiveness will be examined in terms of this differentiation.

The following sub-hypotheses with respect to an identification-based trainer influence process are distinguished:

1a.   If the trainer is attractive to the participant in terms of power, then the participant will become more like the trainer in his attitudes toward power.

1b.   If the trainer is attractive to the participant in terms of affection, then the participant will become more like the trainer in his attitudes toward affection.

1c.   If the trainer is attractive to the participant in terms of task, then the participant will become more like the trainer in his attitudes toward task.

2a.   If the trainer is attractive to the participant in terms of power, then the participant will become more like the trainer in his behaviour with respect to power.

2b.   If the trainer is attractive to the participant in terms of affection, then the participant will become more like the trainer in his behaviour with respect to affection.

2c.   If the trainer is attractive to the participant in terms of task, then the participant will become more like the trainer in his behaviour with respect to task.

In order to support the specific relationship between trainer-attractiveness and change toward being more like the trainer, it is necessary to show that the kind of change which occurs does not involve changes in self-concept. This must be established if we are to accept the proposition that the consequent changes produced by each process are different. Therefore, the following hypothesis is added:

Hypothesis 3. A participant will not necessarily show an increased consistency in his self-concept if the trainer is attractive to him.

Internalisation-based trainer influence

Hypothesis 4. A participant will show an increased consistency in his self-concept if the trainer is seen by him as congruent.

The self-concept may be thought of as an organised configuration of perceptions of the self (Rogers, 1961). When we speak of an individual increasing consistency in his self-concept we mean that he gains an insight into himself that helps him to realign these perceptions. Three operational measures that have been frequently used in this regard, particularly in client-centred therapy (Rogers, 1951) and in self-concept research (Wylie, 1961), are: (1) discrepancies between a person's self-percept and his ideal-percept, (2) his self-percept and others' perception of him, and (3) his self-percept and his actual behaviour. Characteristically, an increase in the consistency of one's self-concept involves a decrease in these discrepancies.

The following sub-hypotheses are distinguished:

4a.   If the participant sees the trainer as self-congruent then he will change toward an increased consistency in his self-concept, as shown by an increased match between his self-percept and ideal-percept.

4b.   If the participant sees the trainer as self-congruent, then he will change toward an increased consistency in his self-concept, as shown by an increased match between his self-percept and others' perception of him.

4c.   If the participant sees the trainer as self-congruent, then he will change toward an increased consistency in his self-concept, as shown by an increased match between his self-percept and actual behaviour.

Since the salience of the trainer for the participant is minimal in internalisation, any change which occurs in the participant is not expected to be in the direction of the trainer. Rather, the content of the change is expected to be idiosyncratic to each participant and related to movement toward greater self-congruence. Thus, some participants may increase the expression of certain attitudes and behaviours, decrease others, and do nothing to others in acquiring a more consistent self-concept. Therefore the following hypothesis is added:

Hypothesis 5.   Participants who see the trainer as congruent will show attitudinal and behavioural changes which are not consistently in the direction of being more like the trainer.

Method

Subjects.   The subjects of the study were 107 participant-members and sixteen trainers of twelve English T-groups, with several groups containing two trainers. The T-groups comprised three different populations and were conducted between 1965 and 1967. Analysis of these populations is found in Table 5.1

Measure of trainer attractiveness.   The Perceptual Inventory[2] was used to measure trainer attractiveness. It consists of twelve descriptive statements: four pertaining to power, four to affection, and four to task. In different versions the participant is asked to describe himself and

2. The Perceptual Inventory was designed by M.L. Berger (University of Sussex) and the author. Data on the test-retest reliability is given in Cooper (1968).

Table 5.1 Subject populations

Cate-gory*	No. of groups	Details of membership	Duration**	Trainers
A	4	36 senior-level industrial managers. Age range 30-50. All men.	10 days; residential	2 trainers per group
B	4	28 middle-level industrial managers and administrators. Age range 30-50. All men.	5 days; residential	1 trainer per group
C	4	43 university students. Age range 19-25. 13 women.	5 days; non-residential	1 trainer per group

* The designations A, B, and C will be used hereafter in referring to the various subject populations. The data from these groups will be analysed separately.
** Approximately 3 two-hour T-group sessions per day.

others by indicating to what extent (on a six-point scale) each item is true of the person being described. Data relevant to trainer attractiveness are each participant's description of his ideal self and of the trainer. By measuring the degree of similarity between these two descriptions, the trainer's attractiveness for each participant can be assessed with respect to power, affection, and task. The Perceptual Inventory was administered in an early and late session of the group. The trainers' attractiveness scores were computed on the basis of data from the early administration, in order to justify inferring that participant change was a consequence of trainer attractiveness.

Measure of trainer congruence. A trainer is considered congruent if perceived by the participant as genuine, direct, honest and sincere. An adaptation of the Relationship Inventory-Congruence Scale constructed by Barrett-Lennard (1962) was used. The adapted scale consists of sixteen items referring to various aspects of congruence. The participant is asked to describe his trainer by indicating to what extent (on a six-point scale) each item is true of the trainer. Scores for each item were summated to yield a single score for trainer congruence for the participant. The Relationship Inventory was administered early and late in the group. The trainer congruence score was calculated on the basis of the early administration.[3]

Measure of behaviour change. Behaviour change was assessed by an analysis of tape recordings of T-group sessions. All sessions were divided into thirds. 50 per cent of the sessions were randomly selected from the first and last third for analysis. These sessions were then randomised for coding in a sequence unknown to the raters. The unit of analysis was each participant's uninterrupted verbal communication, whether one word or three sentences. Two independent raters placed each unit of speech into one of fourteen major behavioural categories and several miscellaneous categories.[4] The fourteen major categories were adapted from the Behaviour Rating System (Whitaker & Lieberman, 1964). Raters combined their ratings, which provided a set of behavioural scores for each participant and trainer. In a single session these behaviours were expressed as a proportion of the total observed behaviours. A change score for each participant on each of the behavioural categories was obtained, consisting of the mean difference for each category between the first third and the last third of the group sessions.

In order to identify which of the categories in the coding system were 'power-, affection-, and task-orientated, for purposes of testing Hypothesis 2, a sorting procedure was used. Four independent judges (social psychologists familiar with small-group behaviour) were asked to examine the list of behaviours and to estimate which of these were related to the exercise of power in groups, to the expression of affection or intimacy in groups, and to the performance of the group's

---

3. The attractiveness and congruence scores were inter-correlated with the result that their usefulness as independent variables was substantiated.
4. Data on inter-rater reliability is given in Cooper (1968).

task. For each of these categories a number of behaviours, on which the judges had the greatest consensus, were selected as indicators. The behaviours judged to be related to the exercise of power in groups were: 'initiates' (five), 'asks for information or opinions' (one), 'projected defence' (eleven), and 'acknowledges' (four). Behaviours judged to be related to the expression of affection or intimacy in groups were: 'individual support' (eight), 'shares expressiveness' (fifteen), 'asks for expressiveness' (fourteen), 'facilitation of feelings' (thirteen), 'introjected defence' (ten), and 'provides information and opinions' (two). Behaviours judged to be related to the performance of the group's task were: 'asks for analysis' (six), 'analysis' (seven), 'group support' (nine), 'facilitation of content' (twelve), 'clarifies self' (sixteen), and 'asks for clarification' (seventeen).

Measure of attitude change. Schutz's (1958) FIRO-B questionnaire was used to measure participants' attitude change since it includes scales that deal with attitudes toward power and affection which provides measures relevant to the testing of Hypotheses 1a and 1b.[5] The FIRO-B is made up of four Guttman scales concerning attitudes toward control behaviour (power) and affection behaviour (close personal relations). For each dimension there is an 'expressed' and 'wanted' scale. The difference between the two is referred to as the originator score, which provides a measure for each behaviour of the relationship between the individual's wish to express (control or affection) and his wish for others to express it toward him. Each participant and the trainer completed the FIRO-B questionnaire near the beginning and again near the end of the T-group, which provided a measure of change (using the originator scores) of attitudes toward control and affection. No comparable attitude questionnaire was available to provide a measure of attitude toward task. Hypothesis 1c was therefore not tested.

---

5. Inclusion scales were omitted since they yield scores which show highly significant positive correlations with affection scales. (See Smith, 1967).

Measure of self-concept. A change toward greater consistency in the self-concept is considered to have occurred if (a) the participant shows greater similarity between his self-percept and his ideal-percept at the end of the T-group as compared with the beginning; (b) the participant shows greater similarity between self-percept and other participants' perception of him at the end of the T-group as compared with the beginning; and (c) the participant shows greater similarity between his self-percept and his actual behaviour at the end of the T-group as compared with the beginning.[6]

The Perceptual Inventory and the Behaviour Rating System were employed to assess self-concept change. The data relevant to (a) above, is the participant's description of self and ideal self. The data relevant to (b) is the participant's description of self and the combined description of the same participant produced by four randomly selected fellow-participants. The data relevant to (c) is the participant's description of self and the behaviour ratings of that participant. In every case, degree of relationship between the two measurements was determined at the beginning and at the end of the T-group, and the degree of change toward greater similarity between the two measures was taken to indicate change toward greater self-consistency.[7]

Results

Hypotheses 1a and 1b

1a.   If the trainer is attractive to the participant in terms of power, then the participant will become more like the trainer in his attitudes toward power.

6. For purposes of simplification the measures relevant to (a), (b) and (c) above will be symbolised as S—I, S—O and S—B respectively.
7. The S—I, S—O, and S—B scores were inter-correlated to assess their usefulness as independent variables. It is obvious, since each discrepancy score contains the self-percept, that the self-concept measures are not entirely independent of each other, nevertheless, the correlation coefficients were small enough to warrant their separate use.

Table 5.2 Relationship between trainer attractiveness and participant change toward the trainer's attitudes toward control and affection (Mann-Whitney 'U')

Trainer attractiveness	Control	Affection
Type A groups (N = 36)		
Power	92**	141
Affection	167	70***
Task	148	132
Type B groups (N = 14)		
Power	7**	20
Affection	23	10*
Task	18	17

*	indicates P ≤ .050
**	indicates P ≤ .025
***	indicates P ≤ .010

1b. If the trainer is attractive to the participant in terms of affection, then the participant will become more like the trainer in his attitudes toward affection.

Participants were divided between those persons who showed change in the direction of the trainer's early attitude, and those who did not. The latter category included those who showed no change as well as those who showed change away from the trainer's attitude. The trainer's early attitude scores were used, since this corresponds to the time at which trainer attractiveness for the participant is measured. The attitude change scores were assigned to the two categories regardless of degree of change. Attitude change data were available for six groups, four Type A groups and two Type B groups. In two-trainer groups, the attitude change scores were analysed with respect to the senior trainer only. The results of Hypotheses 1a and 1b are summarised in Table 5.2. Mann-Whitney 'U' tests (Siegel, 1956) were used to compare rank on trainer attractiveness with change in attitudes.

In both Type A and B groups, participants with higher trainer attractiveness scores in terms of power showed significantly (P < .025) more change in attitudes toward control in the direction of the trainer than did participants with low trainer attractiveness scores. In contrast, participants with higher trainer attractiveness scores in terms of affection and task did not show these changes. Hypothesis 1a is thus supported.

In Type A groups, participants with higher trainer attractiveness scores in terms of affection showed significantly (P < .01) more change in their attitudes toward affection in the direction of the trainer than did participants with low trainer attractiveness scores in terms of affection. Although the same high level significance was not found in the Type B groups, the associated probability was less than .05. In contrast, participants with higher trainer attractiveness scores in terms of power and task did not show these changes. Hypothesis 1b also received support.

Hypotheses 2a, 2b and 2c.

2a.   If the trainer is attractive to the participant in terms of power, then the participant will become more like the trainer in his behaviour with respect to power.
2b.   If the trainer is attractive to the participant in terms of affection, then the participant will become more like the trainer in his behaviour with respect to affection.
2c.   If the trainer is attractive to the participant in terms of task, then the participant will become more like the trainer in his behaviour with respect to task.

Participants were divided between those who showed behaviour change in the direction of the trainer's early behaviour and those who did not. The latter group included those who showed no change as well as those who showed change away from the trainer's behaviour. The trainer's early behaviour scores were means from the sample of sessions in the first third of the group. Behaviour change data were available for participants in all the groups except that a technical error in the recording of one group made analysis impossible.

Table 5.3 Relationship between trainer attractiveness and participant behaviour change toward the trainer's power behaviours (Mann-Whitney 'U')

Trainer attractiveness	Power behaviours§			
	1	4	5	11
Power attractiveness				
Group-types A	88**	107*	97**	92**
B	29*	35	24**	30*
C	159*	160*	124***	130
Affection-attractiveness				
A	146	162	151	146
B	30*	60	51	43
C	197	210	183	162
Task-attractiveness				
A	153	139	147	153
B	49	35	61	52
C	223	232	209	110*

*   indicates $P \leqslant .050$
** indicates $P \leqslant .025$
*** indicates $P \leqslant .010$
§   the power behaviours are outlined on page 119.

To test Hypothesis 2 scores for trainer attractiveness and participant change in the direction of the trainer's behaviours were compared. Mann-Whitney 'U' tests were again employed. Tables 5.3, 5.4 and 5.5 show the results for power-, affection-, and task-related behaviours respectively.

Table 5.3 shows that participants with higher trainer attractiveness scores in terms of power changed their power behaviours in the direction of the trainer. There were significant U-values at $P < .05$ across group types (with two exceptions of $P < .10$) for each of the four power behaviours. In contrast, participants with higher trainer attractiveness scores in terms of affection and task did not show change in their power behaviours in the direction of the trainer. Although there were two significant U-values in the latter cases, no trend was discernible in the data that would suggest

Table 5.4 Relationship between trainer attractiveness and participant behaviour change toward the trainer's affection behaviours (Mann-Whitney 'U')

Trainer attractiveness	Affection behaviours§					
	2	8	10	13	14	15
Power-attractiveness						
Group-types A	161	139	141	149	127	117
B	49	51	47	53	28*	38
C	202	213	217	179	218	186
Affection-attractiveness						
A	107	84**	110	101*	102*	72**
B	30*	23*	30	26**	29	14**
C	147**	148*	142	124*	141*	108***
Task-attractiveness						
A	152	143	162	153	148	124
B	59	44	27*	50	34	46
C	191	161	160	184	224	191

*	indicates P ≤ .050
**	indicates P ≤ .025
***	indicates P ≤ .010
§	the affection behaviours are outlined on page 119.

any generalisable association. The conclusion is that the data support the hypothesis.

Table 5.4 shows that participants with higher trainer attractiveness scores in terms of affection changed their affection behaviours in the direction of the trainer. There were significant U-values at P < .05 across group-types (with two exceptions of P < .10) for five of the six affection behaviours. Although there were no significant U-values in the predicted direction for 'introjected defence' behaviour (ten) the associated probability was less than .10 in each group-type. Changes in the direction of the trainer's affection behaviours were not consistently noted for participants with higher trainer attractiveness scores in terms of power and task.

Table 5.5 shows that participants with higher trainer

Table 5.5 Relationship between trainer attractiveness and participant behaviour change towards the trainer's task behaviours (Mann-Whitney 'U')

Trainer attractiveness	Task behaviours§					
	6	7	9	12	16	17
Power-attractiveness						
Group-types A	83*	140	137	148	117	141
B	47	41	45	28	26*	60
C	152	226	189	142	140*	142
Affection-attractiveness						
A	141	123	139	163	166	152
B	38	43	42	48	56	39
C	197	201	216	183	203	119
Task-attractiveness						
A	82*	94*	85**	104*	120	86**
B	25	22*	23*	19*	38	28*
C	125*	135**	143*	126*	153	105

* indicates P ≤ .050
** indicates P ≤ .025
*** indicates P ≤ .010
§ the task behaviours are outlined on page 119.

attractiveness scores in terms of task changed their task behaviour in the direction of the trainer. There were significant U-values at P ≥ .05 across group-types (with two exceptions of P ≤ .15) for five of the six task behaviours. There were no significant U-values in the predicted direction for 'clarifies self' behaviour (sixteen). Participants with higher trainer attractiveness scores in terms of power, however, showed significant changes in 'clarifies self' behaviour in the direction of the trainer. It may be that 'clarifies self' behaviour is more of a power-orientated than a task-orientated behaviour. With the exception of 'clarifies self' behaviour, participants with higher trainer attractiveness scores in terms of power and affection did not show changes in their task-related behaviours in the direction of the trainer. The data are thus in accord with Hypothesis 2c.

In conclusion, results from Hypotheses 1 and 2 provide considerable support for the predicted linkage between identification-based trainer influence and participant change. On balance, participants did show changes in the direction of the trainer's behaviour and attitudes. In addition, all three sample populations showed similar effects of identification-based trainer influence. This supports Kelman's contention that changes linked to identification are different in different influence situations only in so far as the goals of the situation are different.

Hypothesis 3

3. A participant will not necessarily show an increased consistency in his self-concept if the trainer is attractive to him.

To test the hypothesis, the power-, affection-, and task-attractiveness scores were ranked and correlated, using the Kendall tau rank correlation (Siegel, 1956), against the three self-concept scores ranked from high to low change. (See Table 5.6.)

No significant correlations between trainer attractiveness and change toward increased self-consistency were found. These findings are consistent with our expectations, and thus Hypothesis 3 is upheld.

Hypotheses 4a, 4b and 4c

4a. If the participant sees the trainer as self-congruent, then he will change toward an increased consistency in his self-concept, as shown by an increased match between his self-percept and ideal-percept.
4b. If the participant sees the trainer as self-congruent then he will change toward an increased consistency in his self-concept, as shown by an increased match between his self-percept and others' perception of him.
4c. If the participant sees the trainer as self-congruent then

Table 5.6 Relationship between trainer attractiveness and increase in similarity between self-ideal (S-I), self-others (S-O) and self-behaviour change (S-B) (Kendall tau)

Trainer attractiveness	*S-I*	*S-O*	*S-B*§
Type A groups (N = 36)			
Power	.08	-.09	.00
Affection	-.02	-.04	.07
Task	-.09	-.02	-.04
Type B groups (N = 28)			
Power	.03	.07	-.12
Affection	-.12	-.14	.01
Task	.01	-.04	.16
Type C groups (N = 43)			
Power	-.03	-.04	.01
Affection	-.06	.15	-.09
Task	.17*	-.10	.00

* indicates P ≤ .05
§ the N in Type B groups was 21.

he will change toward an increased consistency in his self-concept, as shown by an increased match between his self-percept and actual behaviour.

In testing these hypotheses the trainer congruence scores were ranked and correlated, using the Kendall tau, against the S—I, S—O, and S—B scores ranked from high to low change.

It can be seen from Table 5.7 that all three of the change predictions were confirmed at P ≤.05, with one exception at P ≤.10. These findings provide strong support for the hypothesised relationship between trainer congruence and the participant's change in the consistency of his self-concept.

Hypothesis 5

5. Participants who see the trainer as congruent will show attitudinal and behavioural changes which are not

consistently in the direction of being more like the trainer.

The Mann-Whitney U test was employed to test whether more high-scorers on trainer congruence change their behaviour and attitudes in the direction of the trainer's behaviour and attitudes than do low-scorers.

Table 5.8 shows that there was little direct relationship between trainer congruence and participant behaviour change in the direction of the trainer. There were only four significant U-values out of fifty-one possible and these did not fall into a discernible, consistent pattern. An examination of Table 5.9 reveals that there was no apparent relationship between trainer congruence and participant attitude change in the direction of the trainer.

The meaning of a lack of significant correlation is, of course, always ambiguous. But the data in Tables 5.8 and 5.9 are consistent with the expectation that participants who see the trainer as congruent do not consistently change their behaviour or attitudes in the direction of being more like the trainer.

Conclusion

An analysis of two influence processes involved in T-group training has been presented and their impact on participant change has been assessed. It cannot be claimed that this study has investigated all the factors in trainer influence based on identification and internalisation. Nevertheless an interesting and consistent pattern emerges relating the perceived characteristics of the trainer to the changes found in participants in T-groups. Stated simply, when the trainer is seen as attractive, participants identify with him and become more like him in attitude and behaviour; when the trainer is seen as self-congruent, participants change in ways that foster their own congruence.

The study was based on Kelman's theoretical framework for the study of social influence in general. In using this

Table 5.7 Relationship between trainer congruence and S-I, S-O, and S-B change (Kendall tau)

Trainer congruence	S-I	S-O	S-B
Type A groups (N = 36)	.32**	.22**	.24*
Type B groups (N = 28)	.25*	.20	.27*
Type C groups (N = 43)	.30**	.19*	.26**

* indicates $P \leqslant .05$
** indicates $P \leqslant .01$

Table 5.8 Relationship between trainer congruence and participant change toward the trainer's behaviour (Mann-Whitney 'U')

Trainer congruence (by group-type)				Behaviours§				
	1	2	3	4	5	6	7	8	9
A	142	158	70	148	100*	121	132	146	138
B	47	74	28	42	50	39	22*	23*	39
C	200	193	98	219	189	172	198	208	191
	10	11	12	13	14	15	16	17	
A	119	141	160	141	126	108	143	122	
B	46	51	32	42	74	46	41	56	
C	159	160	125*	184	162	182	139	154	

* indicates $P \leqslant .05$
** indicates $P \leqslant .01$
§ these behaviours are outlined on page 119.

Table 5.9 Relationship between trainer congruence and participant change toward the trainer's attitudes toward control and affection (Mann-Whitney 'U')

Trainer congruence	Control	Affection
Type A groups	141 (n.s.)	128 (n.s.)
Type B groups	26 (n.s.)	23 (n.s.)

model we have moved in the direction of creating a systematic basis for identifying types of trainer influence. In this respect the findings seemed to support and render more precise some of Kelman's conceptualisation to the special circumstances of T-groups. An assumption throughout was that the trainer is the principal source of influence. At the same time, we must consider whether factors other than the trainer — such as participant personality characteristics, group composition, and group format — may be determinants of participant change. In future research we must examine each of these factors by introducing them into the analysis and investigating how the relationship between trainer behaviour and participant change is affected by them.

A second aspect of the data was that it involved an assessment of the participant's perception of the trainer's behaviour and not the attributes of the trainer's actual behaviour. This stems from the presumption that it is the participant's experiences that affect him directly even though this may not represent with complete accuracy the way the trainer actually behaves (Rogers, 1957). There is, for instance, some indication that the patient's perception of the therapist in group psychotherapy is a stronger predictor of patient outcome than either the therapist's perception of the patient (Barrett-Lennard, 1962) or the actual behaviour of the therapist (van der Veen, 1965). The participant's view of the trainer therefore seemed a logical starting point in assessing participant change. It should be remembered that comparisons of participants' perception of the trainer were made 'within groups'. It is probable, as Bolman (1968) suggests, that the trainer's actual behaviour is responsible for 'differences between groups'. An analysis of these differences may generate findings which are relevant to the type of trainer behaviour which is most effective in promoting change in T-groups.

And finally, in an effort to establish a causal link between perceived trainer characteristics and participant change, an assumption was made that changes in participants and the trainer during the group are minimal. Given sufficient change in participants and/or the trainer, it may be that the influence processes of identification and internalisation do not retain their basic character over the course of the group. Further research should be undertaken to assess these processes over time.

Numerous theories have been offered in explanation of what occurs in the trainer-participant relationship within the T-group, but few have been subjected to any form of test. This study provides a basis for investigating this relationship and the beginning of a framework for its analysis.

References

Barrett-Lennard, G.T., Dimensions of therapist response as causal factors in therapeutic change, *Psychological Monographs,* 1962, 76, 43 (Whole Number 562).

Bolman, L., The effects of variations in educator behavior on the learning process in laboratory human relations education, University of Yale: unpublished Ph.D. thesis, 1968.

Bradford, L.P., Gibb, J.R. & Benne, K.D., *T-group theory and laboratory method: innovation in re-education,* New York: John Wiley & Sons, 1964.

Bunker, D.R., Individual application of laboratory training, *Journal of Applied Behavioral Science,* 1965, 1, 131-49.

Cooper, C.L., *Theories of group processes,* London & New York: John Wiley & Sons, 1975.

Cooper, C.L. & Mangham, I.L., *T-groups: a survey of research,* New York: John Wiley & Sons, 1971.

Deutsch, M. Pepitone, A. & Zander, A., Leadership in the small group, *Journal of Social Issues,* 4, 31—40.

Hare, A.P., *Handbook of small group research,* New York: John Wiley, 1962.

Harrison, R., A conceptual framework for laboratory training, University of Yale: unpublished manuscript, 1966.

House, R.J., T-group education and leadership effectiveness, *Personnel Psychology,* 1967, 20, 1—32.

Kelman, H.C., Processes of opinion change, *Public Opinion*

Quarterly, 1961, **25,** 57—78.

Kelman, H.C., The role of the group in the induction of therapeutic change, *International Journal of Group Psychotherapy,* 1963, **13,** 399—452.

Lohmann, K., Zenger, J.H. & Weschler, I.R., *Journal of Educational Research,* 1959, Some perceptual changes during sensitivity training, **53,** 28—31.

Mangham, I.L. & Cooper, C.L., The impact of T-groups on managerial behaviour, *Journal of Management Studies,* 1969, **6,** 53—72.

Mann, R.D., The development of the member-trainer relations in self-analytic groups, *Human Relations,* 1966, **19,** 85—119.

Peters, D.R., Identification and personal change in laboratory training groups, Massachusetts Institute of Technology: unpublished Ph.D. thesis, 1967.

Psathas, G. & Hardert, R., Trainer interventions and normative patterns in the T-group, *Journal of Applied Behavioral Science,* 1966, **2,** 149—70.

Reisel, J., The trainer role in human relations training, San Diego, Calif.: paper delivered to the Western Psychological Association, 1959.

Rogers, C.R., *Client-centered therapy,* Boston, Mass.: Houghton Mifflin, 1951.

Rogers, C.C., The necessary and sufficient conditions of therapeutic personality change, *Journal of Consulting Psychology,* 1957, **21,** 95-103.

Rogers, C.R., *On becoming a person,* Boston, Mass.: Houghton Mifflin, 1961.

Schutz, W.C., *FIRO: a theory of interpersonal relations,* New York: Rinehart, 1958.

Siegel, S., *Nonparametric statistics for the behavioral sciences,* New York: McGraw Hill, 1956.

Smith, P.B., Attitude change associated with training in human relations, *British Journal of Social and Clinical Psychology,* 1964, **2,** 104—12.

Smith, P.B., T-group climate and some tests of learning, University of Sussex: unpublished manuscript, 1967.

Smith, P.B., Are there adverse effects of sensitivity training? *Journal of Humanistic Psychology,* 1975, *15 (27,* 29—47.

Stermerding, A.H., Evaluation research in the field of sensitivity training, Netherlands Institute of Preventive Medicine, Leiden: unpublished manuscript, 1961.

Van Der Veen, F., Dimensions of client and therapist behavior in relation to outcome, *Proceedings of the 1965 Annual Convention of the American Psychological Association,* Washington, DC, American Psychological Association, 279—80.

Vansina, L., Research concerning the influence of the T-group method on the formation of the participant social values and opinions, *Evaluation of supervisory and management training methods,* Paris: Organization for Economic Co-operation and Development, 91—7, 1961.

Whitaker, D.S. & Lieberman, M.A., Assessing interpersonal behavior in group therapy, *Perceptual and Motor Skills,* 1964, **18,** 763—4.

Wylie, R.C., *The self-concept,* Lincoln, Nebr.: University of Nebraska Press, 1961.

6 Developing one's potential from West to East: the impact of experiential learning across cultures*

This study examines the impact of sensitivity training on participants' self-actualisation in the United Kingdom, Turkey, and Japan. Although the Japanese and Turkish participants showed less change than the English on the Personal Orientation Inventory, there is some evidence that sensitivity training can be applied to non-Western countries. The results suggest that as the economic and social conditions change and create a cultural environment more favourable to self-actualising tendencies, individuals will respond more positively to educational innovations such as experiential learning groups.

Experiential learning groups (e.g., sensitivity training, encounter groups, etc.) are being used extensively in industry, the social services, and hospitals as a method of training people to increase their self-awareness and to utilise their potential, i.e., to be more self-actualised (Cooper, 1973a). A great deal of research (Cooper & Mangham, 1971) has been

* Reproduced by special permission of John E. Jones and J. William Pfeiffer, University Associates and *Group and Organization Studies,* 1976, 1(1), 43-56.

done to evaluate the effects of experiential learning groups over the last ten years. These group experiences can be assessed in two ways — using measures related to the expected outcomes or using a wide variety of measures for the purpose of detecting whatever changes do in fact occur, expected or not (Smith, 1969). Most studies, until recently, used the second strategy because there were few measures available for assessing the kinds of attribute and outcome associated with these group approaches, particularly elements of self-actualisation.

Shostrom (1968) developed the Personal Orientation Inventory (POI), which provided measures of various aspects of self-actualising values and behaviour. Since then a large amount of evaluative research work has been carried out using the POI as an outcome measure in a variety of experiential learning contexts. An examination of these studies (Guinan & Foulds, 1970; Culbert, Clark, & Bobele, 1968; Cooper, 1971; Rueveni, Swift, & Bell, 1969) reveals a high degree of consistency in their findings. Participants who have attended experiential group activities have shown positive change on at least six of the POI scales: Scale I, independence and self-support; Scale Fr, sensitivity to their own needs and feelings; Scale Ex, flexibility in the application of self-actualising values; Scale S, spontaneity; Scale A, acceptance of aggression; and Scale C, capacity for intimate contact. These findings are not only consistent over a number of independent research studies but also consistent between the United States and Great Britain. It does seem, therefore, that, at least in Western countries, experiential learning groups are influencing people's attitudes and behaviour in the direction of greater self-actualisation. This research, however, has been restricted mainly to the West, although many of these learning experiences are now being used in the Middle and Far East (Cooper, 1973b).

Applicability of training groups to other cultures

This brings up a serious question, however, about the relevance of experiential learning groups and the kinds of insight gained within these groups to countries outside Western Europe and the United States. Training groups were developed in the United States and England at the beginning of the post-World War II expansion and tended to reflect the needs of a highly industrialised society and the middle-class orientation of its managers, businessmen, technocrats, professionals, and university teachers (Levine & Cooper, 1976). Although the movement early divided into a more practical 'organisational development' orientation and a more individual 'personal expression' orientation, the values inherent in the experiential learning group were related to those of Western society.

There is a question of whether non-Western societies develop the same conditions and are conducive to the same kinds of change. Undoubtedly, there is an increasing involvement of developing countires in the international economic arena — both capitalist and socialist — and many of the same kinds of internal economic change that occurred in the West in the nineteenth century are evident (the creation of market economies, transformation of agricultural relationships, urbanisation, and some industrialisation). These changes will in the long run produce a social environment that will be conducive to the kinds of learning that take place in experiential learning groups. However, developing countries differ a great deal among themselves and show greater or lesser degrees of industrialisation and involvement in the world economy. They also differ greatly in their exposure to so-called 'Western' ideological influences and their abilities to integrate such influences.

Thus, the purpose of this study was to explore whether the types of changes observed in participants in experiential learning groups in the United States and Great Britain would occur in group participants in two non-Western countries — Japan and Turkey. Japan is, of course, a highly industrialised country with a fairly high standard of living, although it has resisted until quite recently the impact of Western cultural and ideological influences (Benedict, 1946). Turkey, on the other hand, is a semi-industrialised country but ideologically more influenced by the West for a longer period (Mardin, 154; Lewis, 1968). We might expect, therefore, that if similarity in the economic sphere is the critical variable in supporting self-actualising changes, then Japanese participants in training groups would show changes similar to those of Western participants. However, if similarity in ideology is the critical variable, then Turkish participants would show more similarities to Western participants. The POI was used to compare the effects of experiential learning methods in these two countries with those found in the West.

Method

The subjects were sixty university students who were social science undergraduates in their third year of college: eighteen from the University of Manchester, twenty-four from Hacettepe University in Ankara, and eighteen from Toyo University in Tokyo. The groups were roughly matched in terms of age and sex. All the students took part in an experiential learning programme that consisted of T-groups (Golembiewski & Blumberg, 1970), and all groups were run along lines described by Tannenbaum, Wechsler, and Massarik (1961).

Students have taken part for a long time in experiential groups. While somewhat isolated from the society around them and protected from organisational and economic constraints, students are ideal participants in training groups (Levine, 1973a, p. 40-67); they are more open to self-experiences and tend to be more flexible about new behaviours than are fparticifpants from other segments of society. They also tend to be middle class in orientation and to come from relatively higher-income backgrounds. For the Japanese and Turkish groups, these students had been the most exposed to Western ideological influences and to the new institutions created by economic development. Thus, in this study, we were able roughly to estimate the extent to which students in non-Western societies are able to respond to the kinds of behaviour and value expressed in experiential learning groups — involvement, interdependence, and self-awareness (Levine, 1971) — compared to the extent to which such behaviours and values are either irrelevant or resisted by non-Western societies.

The Personal Orientation Inventory was administered to all students one week before and one week after the T-group session. The POI is self-administered and consists of 150 two-choice comparative value-judgement items reflecting values and behaviour seen to be of importance in the development of the self-actualising individual. As Knapp (1971) suggests, 'Such a person may be described as one who utilises his talents and capabilities more fully, lives in the present rather than dwelling on the past or the future, functions relatively autonomously, and tends to have a more benevolent outlook on life and on human nature than the average person.' The inventory consists of twelve scales:

Time-competence (Tc—living in the present).
Inner-directed (I—independent, self-supporting).
Self-actualising value (SAV—holds values of self-actualising people, e.g., 'I live in terms of my wants, likes, dislikes, and values').
Existentiality (Ex—flexibility of applying such values to one's life).
Feeling reactivity (Fr—sensitive to own needs and feelings).
Spontaneity (S—freely expresses feelings behaviourally).
Self-regard (Sr—has high self-worth).
Self-acceptance (Sa—accepting of self in spite of weaknesses).
Nature of man-constructive (Nc—sees man as essentially good).
Synergy (Sy—sees opposites of life meaningfully related).
Acceptance of aggression (A—accepts feeling of anger or

Table 6.1 Means, standard deviations and t values for significance of differences between pre-test POI scales for English and Turkish students

POI scales	English mean (n = 18)	S.D.	Turkish mean (n = 24)	S.D.	t*	p
Tc	15.50	3.25	15.96	2.53	0.49	
I	82.72	13.22	78.33	8.33	1.24	
SAV	18.67	3.46	17.57	3.12	1.05	
Ex	21.78	4.00	18.42	3.87	2.73	< .01
Fr	16.67	3.38	13.91	2.63	2.85	< .01
S	12.22	3.28	10.91	2.02	1.49	
Sr	10.39	3.30	11.61	2.23	1.35	
Sa	16.17	4.13	14.13	3.44	1.69	< .10
Nc	10.39	1.20	10.22	2.30	0.31	
Sy	6.50	1.21	6.09	1.78	0.88	
A	15.22	3.27	14.96	2.87	0.27	
C	18.33	3.42	15.43	2.76	2.93	< .01

* = two-tailed test

aggression).
Capacity for intimate contact (C—has warm interpersonal relationships).

Test-retest reliabiliy and validation studies for the POI can be found in Klavetter and Mogar (1967) and Shostrom (1968), respectively. The POI was translated into Japanese and Turkish for purposes of this investigation. Because the test-retest reliability coefficients for the POI scales were very high, ranging from .71 to .84, it was decided that an untrained control group was not needed.

Before examining the differential effects of experiential methods in the different groups, it was felt that we should examine the initial differences in the POI scales among the three populations. (See Tables 6.1, 6.2, and 6.3.)

Differences between the pre-test POI scores were calculated by t-tests for independent samples (two-tailed). It can be seen that there are a number of important differences between the various populations on the POI scales, mainly between the English sample and the other two. The English students' results were significantly different from the Japanese and Turkish subjects' results in the following respects: the English students were more flexible in applying their self-actualising values to their own lives (Ex), more sensitive to their own needs and feelings (Fr), more accepting of their 'self' in spite of weaknesses (Sa), and had a greater capacity for intimate contact (C). In addition, the English were significantly different from the Japanese students on two further dimensions: they were more independent and self-supporting (I) and more self-accepting of their own feelings of anger and aggression (A). There was only one scale on which the Japanese and Turkish subjects differed from each other — on Factor S, where the Japanese showed more spontaneity than the Turkish students.

This complex pattern of characteristics in the English group that differentiates it from the other two groups reflects a number of factors. First, the psychological sciences and the human potential movement have a long and deep-rooted history in the West. Over the years, this has encouraged greater self-exploration, which has led to greater sensitivity to individual needs and behaviour and, as a consequence, has led people in the West to accept and change various aspects of their personalities (Phillips, Watkins, & Noll, 1974). Second, the obverse of some of the dimensions (rigid adherence to principles and values, Ex; insensitivity to their own feelings and needs, Fr; less acceptance of 'self', Sa; and less ability to develop intimate relationships with others, C) that characterise the Japanese and Turkish students reflects cultural and social differences. In both Japan and Turkey a very strong emphasis is placed on loyalty and obligation to family relationships. In Japan, this obligation is explicityly termed *giri-ninjo* and extends not only to the family but into all aspects of human contact (Benedict, 1946; Lifton, 1970, p. 551-62). As Lifton (1970) suggests, there is an unspoken understanding that one will be loved, nourished, or at least taken care of by the family and that all feelings of intimacy, anger, of selfhood should be inhibited outside the context of familial relationships. In Turkey, such obligations are less

Table 6.2 Means, standard deviations and t values for significance of differences between pre-test POI scales for Japanese and English students

POI scales	Japanese mean (n = 18)	S.D.	English mean (n = 18)	S.D. t*	t*	p
Tc	14.39	3.16	15.50	3.25	1.86	< .10
I	76.44	11.18	82.72	13.22	5.40	< .01
SAV	17.94	3.01	18.67	3.41	1.22	
Ex	19.00	3.35	21.78	4.00	4.34	< .01
Fr	14.83	3.67	16.67	3.38	2.94	< .01
S	13.06	2.70	12.22	3.28	1.45	
Sr	10.72	2.71	10.39	3.30	0.57	
Sa	14.83	3.50	16.17	4.13	2.06	< .05
Nc	10.39	1.60	10.39	1.20	0.00	
Sy	6.78	1.17	6.50	1.21	0.77	
A	13.89	3.23	15.22	3.27	2.22	< .05
C	14.78	3.32	18.33	3.42	5.79	< .01

* = two-tailed test

Table 6.3 Means, standard deviations and t values for significance of differences between pre-test POI scales for Turkish and Japanese students

POI scales	Turkish mean (n = 24)	S.D.	Japanese mean (n = 18)	S.D.	t*	P
Tc	15.96	2.53	14.39	3.16	1.72	< .10
I	78.30	8.33	76.44	11.18	0.59	
SAV	17.57	3.12	17.94	3.01	0.38	
Ex	18.42	3.87	19.00	3.35	0.52	
Fr	13.91	2.63	14.83	3.67	0.90	
S	10.91	2.02	13.06	2.70	2.81	< .01
Sr	1.61	2.23	10.72	2.71	1.13	
Sa	14.13	3.44	14.83	3.50	0.64	
Nc	10.22	2.30	10.39	1.60	0.28	
Sy	6.09	1.78	6.78	1.17	1.49	
A	14.96	2.87	13.89	3.23	1.11	
C	15.43	2.76	14.78	3.32	0.67	

* = two-tailed test

explicit but understood, for the family intervenes in almost all areas of social life. In addition, the continual lack of social security, reflecting lack of employment, low incomes, and vulnerability in old age, forces a continual interdependency on individuals and their families (Karay & Hinderink, 1968; Levine, 1973b). Although both Japan and Turkey started their development processes in the mid-nineteenth century, instigated by economic and political pressures from the West, changes in both these countries have been mediated by tight social networks involving immediate family, relatives, and friends (Ward & Rustow, 1964). Power, income, and ideology tend to be expressed in small social networks, and impersonal institutions are limited in their indirect effect on individuals.

A third reason for the differences between the English groups and the Japanese and Turkish groups reflects the different social contexts in which such behaviour becomes meaningful. As has been argued elsewhere (Levine & Cooper, 1976), training groups emerged in the West as a response to affluence. For the first time, professionals and people in industrial organisations and service occupations felt secure enough economically to be able to subject their social interaction to scrutiny in order to asses whether experiencing new feelings and behaviours or doing things differently would improve one person's social interaction with others. Economic security thus becomes a necessary condition underlying self-actualising behaviour, for without it such behaviour is meaningless (Maslow, 1954). Until recently, however, in both Japan and Turkey, per capita incomes have been very low, even for the middle class. Only now are middle-class individuals starting to ask serious questions about their social interaction, their dependency on their families, and their sense of 'being' in the world, whereas in the West widespread high standards of living have existed since the end of World War II. Thus, for the first time, chances to 'self-actualise' are opening up to individuals. Although the number of persons involved is still small, such tendencies will slowly increase. However, the majority of individuals are still bound to 'dependent social relations', thus the differences we observe with the POI provide at least some degree of face validity for the test, since many of these differences would be expected.

Results

The basic question asked for this experiment, however, was whether an experiential training-group experience would produce changes toward more self-actualisation. In Table 6.4, the means and standard deviations for the pre-and post-POI scores of the English, Turkish, and Japanese students are presented. T-tests were calculated on the differences between the pre- and post-POI scores for individuals; as the direction of the changes had been expected, one-tailed tests were used.

The English students showed significant changes on seven of the twelve scales. These included significant increases in independence and self-support (I), in flexibility of values (Ex), in sensitivity to own needs and feelings (Fr), in spontaneity (S), in accpetance of self in spite of weaknesses (Sa), in acceptance of aggression (A), and in capacity for intimate contact (C). In addition, the English students showed a movement in the direction (p < .10) of being present orientated (as opposed to past orientated) in their relationships (Tc). These changes were consistent with the earlier research on the POI in the United States and Britain.

The Turkish students showed some of the same changes. They were found to change significantly on two of the same scales — greater acceptance of self in spite of weaknesses (Sa) and increased capacity for intimate contact (C) — and, in addition, to change in a positive direction in their view that man is essentially good (Nc). Also, the Turkish students moved in the direction (p < .10) of becoming more time competent/living in the present (Tc) and more synergistic (Sy).

The Japanese students, on the other hand, showed change

on only one scale of the POI (Factor Fr), in the direction of increasing their sensitivity to their own needs and feelings. In addition, they did show a slight movement ($p < .10$) in the direction of accepting their own aggression (Factor A), but on all other scales there was no significant change.

Discussion

We, therefore, found some evidence of change among both the Turkish and Japanese students consistent with the changes observed in the English students. However, the changes for both Turkish and Japanese groups were much more attenuated compared to the English groups and indicated a greater resistance to the experiential process. It would be unrealistic to over-generalise these results, however, since we have compared only two training groups from each country from among a fairly specialised and privileged population — university students. Nonetheless, the results are fairly consistent with our expectations and indicate certain cautions about using training groups uncritically in societies that may not be able to utilise the kind of information generated in such groups.

We can suggest several reasons why the Turkish and Japanese students showed smaller changes than the English students. First, the experiential group methods — essentially Western techniques — are more appropriate to Western culture, hence the differential change rate between the English and Japanese/Turkish groups. Although both Japan and Turkey have been exposed to Western ideological influences since the nineteenth century, changes in these countries have been adapted to internal structures and have not used Western culture as a model. Turkey, in fact, has had greater ideological impact from the West, being on the edge of Europe, and has made a more intense political effort to 'Westernise' than Japan has. Japan, while adopting industrial technology and 'Western' techniques, resisted Western ideological penetration until the end of World War

Table 6.4 Means and t values for significance of differences between pre- and post-test POI scales for English, Turkish and Japanese students

POI scales	English (N = 18)				Turkish (N = 24)				Japanese (N = 18)			
	M pre	M post	T*	p	M pre	M post	t	p	M pre	M post	t	p
Tc	15.50	16.11	2.08	<.10	17.42	18.29	1.73	<.10	14.39	15.06	1.51	
I	82.72	92.72	5.76	<.01	83.29	84.08	.49		76.44	79.17	1.66	
SAV	18.67	19.06	.98		17.92	17.83	.15		17.94	18.78	1.71	
Ex	21.78	24.78	5.25	<.01	18.42	18.71	.45		19.00	19.06	.09	
Fr	16.67	17.94	3.64	<.01	13.67	14.38	1.40		14.83	16.11	2.29	<.05
S	17.22	13.72	3.93	<.01	10.42	10.88	1.05		13.06	13.33	.56	
Sr	10.39	11.06	1.35		10.63	10.92	.29		10.72	10.89	.32	
Sa	16.17	17.44	2.89	<.01	16.29	17.25	2.44	<.025	14.83	15.28	.65	
Nc	10.39	11.00	1.48		10.63	11.58	2.26	<.05	10.39	10.67	.77	
Sy	6.50	6.94	1.41		5.92	6.42	1.81	<.10	6.78	7.11	1.19	
A	15.22	17.67	4.03	<.01	14.25	14.75	1.04		13.89	14.94	2.03	<.10
C	18.33	20.61	3.83	<.01	14.71	16.38	2.75	<.02	14.78	15.78	1.58	

* = one-tailed test

II. We thus found that the Turkish students showed greater changes on the POI than the Japanese students, consistent with the expected effect of these influences. However, ideological exposure by itself is insufficient to lead to change, but must be accompanied by congruent processes of industrialisation, where Turkey has lagged well behind Japan. Only when both these changes occur is a social environment created that is open to self-actualising behaviour.

A second possible reason that the Japanese and Turkish students show less change than the English students is that this basically Western form of training has been transplanted virtually without variation into Japanese and Turkish cultures. It is less effective than it could be if it were adapted in important ways to fit into the normative structures of these societies. For example, the learning mechanism of interpersonal behaviour *feedback* may be too difficult for the Japanese and Turkish participants to incorporate easily into an effective learning style because of severe cultural prohibitions on the 'free expression of feelings' (see Factor S). In both the Japanese and Turkish groups, we observed a continual resistance by participants toward giving feedback. Generally, the idea of *feedback* was equated with criticism and anger, and it took participants a long time to grasp the difference. Thus, if training groups are to be applicable in non-Western societies, they must be adapted to fit into the norms of these societies. For example, an emphasis on helping behaviour, co-operation, and the manner in which groups make decisions might be more effective as a learning theme than an emphasis on feedback and individual expression. The former goals are more consistent with the social life of tight-knit, interdependent social relations.

Another possible explanation is that sensitivity training groups do indeed have an impact on participants in Japan and Turkey, but not on values and behaviour associated with self-actualisation; that is, different criteria measures might have produced different results. However, the POI should have provided very good criteria scales in view of the probably underlying purpose of these groups in countries like Japan and Turkey (Levine & Cooper, 1976), namely helping individuals to cope with increasing industrialisation in a way that makes them more flexible and more independent and self-supporting, and helps them to live more in the present than in the past — all characteristics associated with self-actualisation.

Conclusion

The study did show evidence of some change among the participants of the Turkish and Japanese groups and did support the idea that training groups can be applied to non-Western countries. We can expect that in the future, as the economic and social changes unfolding in these countries create a social environment more favourable to self-actualising tendencies, individuals will respond more positively to educational innovations such as experiential learning groups. As the experiential methods are used more and more in a variety of cultures, they should be adapted to the needs and themes of their individual societies. In this way, they will become a useful educational tool aiding the social and economic development of the societies, allowing individuals to adapt better to the new situations and institutions that are emerging. In this sense, they will also fulfill Maslow's (1954) hope that individuals will utilise their talents and capabilities more fully, live in the present rather than dwell in the past or future, function more autonomously, and have a more constructive view of life and human nature.

References

Benedict, R., *The chrysanthemum and the sword,* Boston: Houghton Mifflin, 1946.
Cooper, C.L., T-group training and self-actualization,

Psychological Reports. 1971, 28, 391-394.

Cooper, C.L., (Ed.), *Group training for individual organizational development,* Basel, Switzerland: S. Karger, 1973. (a)

Cooper, C.L., Sensitivity training in Japan, *Self and Society: British Journal of Humanistic Psychology,* 1973, 3, 2-4. (b)

Cooper, C.L., & Mangham, I.L., *T-groups: A survey of research,* New York: John Wiley, 1971.

Culbert, S.A., Clark, J.V., & Bobele, H.K., Measures of change toward self-actualization in two sensitivity training groups, *Journal of Counseling Psychology,* 1968, 15, 53-57.

Golembiewski, R.T., & Blumberg, A., *Sensitivity training and the laboratory approach: Readings about concepts and applications,* Itasca, Ill.: F.E. Peacock, 1970.

Guinan, J.F., & Foulds, M.L. Marathon group: Facilitator of personal growth?, *Journal of Counseling Psychology,* 1970, 17, 145-149.

Kiray, M.B., & Hinderink, J., Interdependencies between agroeconomic development and social change: A comparative study conducted in the Cukurova region of southern Turkey, *Journal of Development Studies,* 1968, 4, 497-528.

Klavetter, R.E., & Mogar, R.E., Stability and internal consistency of a measure of self-actualization, *Psychological Reports,* 1967, 21, 422-424.

Knapp, R.R., *The measurement of self-actualization and its theoretical implications,* San Diego, Calif.: Educational and Industrial Testing Service, 1971.

Levine, N., Emotional factors in group development, *Human Relations,* 1971, 24, 65-89.

Levine, N., Group training with students in higher education. In C.L. Cooper (Ed.), *Group training for individual and organizational development,* Basel, Switzerland: S. Karger, 1973. (a)

Levine, N., Old culture-new culture: A study of migrants in Ankara, Turkey, *Social Forces,* 1973, 51, 355-368. (b)

Levine, N., & Cooper, C.L., T-groups, a prophecy: Twenty years on, *Human Relations,* 1976, 29, 1-23.

Lewis, B., *The emergence of modern Turkey,* Oxford:

Oxford University Press, 1968.

Lifton, R.J., Personal identity: Individual patterns in historical change, imagery of Japanese youth. In N.J. Smelser & W.T. Smelser (Eds.), *Personality and social systems,* New York: John Wiley, 1970.

Mardin, S., *The genesis of young Ottoman thought,* New York: Harper & Row, 1954.

Maslow, A., *Motivation and personality,* New York: Harper & Row, 1954.

Phillips, W., Watkins, J., & Noll, G., Self-actualization, self-transcendence, and personal philosophy, *Journal of Humanistic Psychology,* 1974, 14, 53-74.

Rueveni, U., Swift, M., & Bell, A.A., Sensitivity training: Its impact on mental health workers, *Journal of Applied Behavioural Science,* 1969, 5, 600-601.

Shostrom, E.;., *Personal orientation inventory,* San Diego, Calif.: Educational and Industrial Testing Service, 1968.

ßsmith, P.B., *Improving skills in working with people: T-groups,* London: Department of Employment, 1969.

Tannenbaum, R., Wechsler, I.R., & Massarik, F., *Leadership and organization: A behavioural science approach,* New York: McGraw-Hill, 1961.

Ward, R.E., & Rustow, D.A., *Political modernization in Japan and Turkey,* Princeton, N.J.: Princeton University Press, 1964.

Section C
The impact of group work in different environments

This section of the book will look at the use of groups in four different contexts: in developing more effective and coherent relations between executives on the board of a company; in cementing better relationships between teachers and students; in changing the work and outside behaviour of social workers; and in developing the social skills of personnel working in the restaurant industry.

Section C
The impact of group work in different environments

7 Developing executive relationships: six characters in search of a management style*

In the form of a condensed scenario or playlet, a case study is presented, showing the process of team-building and group-formation in a management setting in England. Personal, interpersonal, group and organisational processes are illustrated as we follow the re-experiences of a plant director, two joint deputy plant directors, the works engineer, and the commercial manager, together with consultants, in their search for improved personal and organisational functioning.

As teachers of management it often falls to us to present case studies to illustrate our teaching; as practitioners in the area of sensitivity training we are frequently asked to explain what happens in a T-group. Both situations present peculiar difficulties. Most case studies and virtually all descriptions of sensitivity groups fail to capture a realistic sense of *organisational* life or the dynamics of team-building in company settings.

In this chapter we try to convey something of the flavour of an in-company sensitivity training group. It seems to us that the format adopted by dramatists could be employed to

---

* Written with Iain Mangham and John Hayes, and published in *Interpersonal Development*.

provide the reader with a vicarious experience. Naturally, we could not present transcripts of some thirty hours of work so, again following dramatic precedent, we have selected highlights and linked them with descriptive narrative.

Setting

The action takes place in a large, heavy industrial plant somewhere in the North of England. Although part of a giant international group, the plant is relatively isolated from major centres; it is the major source of employment in the area and dominates the small town that surrounds it. It is dark, dirty and festooned with pipes, divided by boilers and suffocated with barrack-like offices. Part dates back to the turn of the century whilst other parts are in early stages of construction. The time is the late Sixties.

Cast

Eric (Plant Director), a man in his early forties; thin, energetic with rimless spectacles which create an almost teutonic appearance. He is relatively new to the works but a man with considerable experience in the company as a whole. He has a quiet yet authoritative, almost steely, voice and is used to getting his own way; he gives the impression that there are only two approaches to problems: his and the wrong one. He is reputed to be a schemer, an archplotter, a fixer, a setter-up, a Machiavelli, a manipulator. His characteristic approach is to explain in very great detail, and with great rationality and infinite patience, why others' perceptions of himself are wrong and ill-informed.

John (Joint Deputy Plant Director), a man in his late forties; plump, greying hair, rather avuncular, gives the appearance of being a somewhat vague country doctor. A man of high technical skill and a marked degree of ambition both of which he feels have been overlooked by the company. He is seen to be a strong supporter of Eric and, as he is also a relative newcomer, this does not add to his popularity. He is keen, in an antiseptic sort of way, on the possibilities of developing more teamwork, but is not remarkable for his own emotional repertoire or his skills in discussion. He is considered by all to be ready for promotion; in the meantime he runs the plant with Eric.

Bill (Joint Deputy Plant Manager), a man in his middle fifties, of average build with thinning hair. Almost totally obsessed with technical production problems and almost totally bewildered by managerial concepts. Has spent his entire life in the plant, though only recently has he been promoted after twelve years as a departmental head. His strong name is not reinforced by his behaviour which — at least at top management level — is seen to be that of a man 'who bends with the wind'; the problem is that it takes him some time to realise that there is a wind blowing.

Nicholas (Works Engineer), a man in his late thirties; slight, studious, neat and precise, he hardly looks like an engineer though he has the reputation of being a very good one. He often seems ill at ease and somewhat out of place amongst the top management, an impression which is not mitigated by the light tenor of his voice and the diffidence of his overall approach. He is a confidante of Harry as well as of John, which often places him in difficulties within the management meetings since these two are frequently opposing each other.

Harry (Commercial Manager), a man in his late forties; tall, masculine and rather debonair. He has been at the plant virtually all of his working life and is, like Bill, a relatively new member of the management team. He is often sarcastic, sometimes caustic, and nearly always opposed (irrespective of the issue). He sees himself as a necessary corrective to the enthusiasms of others, a sort of devil's advocate to the world at large. He is seen by others as critical, bigoted, old-fashioned and destructive. His devil-may-care, rather flip approach is not appreciated by either Eric or John.

Consultant, a university lecturer in early thirties with considerable experience of working with managers at all levels within the company. Average height and weight with a confident, warm and supportive approach to in-company training. Inclined to dominate proceedings with a penchant for blunt speaking which he is attempting to modify but not to obliterate. He sees himself as attempting to help the rest of the cast identify blocks to their effective performance as a team. Theoretically at least, he hopes to do this by: (1) encouraging the actors to talk about common problems and interrelationships; (2) by observing and writing comments upon immediate incidents and interactions; (3) by promoting effective listening, and (4) by promoting a climate where comment can be made clearly and unequivocally with the maximum effect and the minimum fear to all parties involved. In many ways — to mix metaphors — he sees himself as both the father and the midwife of the group; he guides, prods, provokes, observes as well as encourages the group to give birth to its own procedures and processes. He frequently makes mistakes, chases the wrong hares, blazes false trails. Occasionally he is willing to listen to comment on his shortcomings.

Observer, a university lecturer in his late twenties. Some experience in in-company training but rather nervous about working at senior levels. Competent, sensitive, unobtrusive and somewhat distant. He sees himself as helper to the consultant and recorder of the minutiae of the group discussions and procedures.

The story so far

The team had operated at irregular intervals over the last eighteen months; when it had been convened it was at the initiative of Eric. All members, including Eric, report dissatisfaction with its operation. The consultant was called in at the initiative of John whose overall brief for management development had led him to books on group dynamics and organisation development. A preliminary discussion led to the scenes below.

Act 1

Eric's office

A room within and overlooking the plant. Cast, with the exception of Eric, seated round a large table. Introductions are made. There is speculation among the cast as to whether Eric is absent accidentally or on purpose; there is further speculation as to whether or not he is behind the curtains, under the table or in the cloakroom.

The meeting formally opened with an examination of how members felt about the group. This was facilitated by each of them filling out a 'McGregor scale' reflecting their feelings among a number of dimensions such as degree of mutual trust, degree of mutual support, openness of communications, listening, clarity of team objectives and the handling of conflict.

Members were surprised at the discrepancies in scoring on these items. The first area of concern was whether the group objectives were clearly understood. After some desultory conversation, Harry jumped in and sketched a history of the group as he saw it: essentially, he said, it was one of disintegration, especially over the past six months, to a situation in which effectively two groups existed. Harry believed that Bill and he were in one group, largely concerned with day-to-day matters ('realities') whilst Eric, John and Nicholas were in the other group, concerned with policy and rather vague future plans.

Nicholas, whilst not accepting that he was in the camp, supported Harry's opinion that the group was disintegrating; he said he felt that Eric was responsible for the disintegrations:

'I do not feel Eric is committed to this group at all. I think be believes its activities are irrelevant.'

John replied by saying that he 'thought that Eric might be letting the group disintegrate deliberately', to which Nicholas responded quickly:

'If this is Eric's policy it is one which creates a great deal of frustration and confusion.'

Bill appeared to support both Nicholas and Harry when he crystallised his feelings about the group. He said that whilst he was not totally alien to group work he had become increasingly alien to this particular group. He felt that it had not been working effectively. He recalled a recent meeting where Eric had opened the proceedings by suggesting that the group should experiment with what he called 'joint problem-solving'. Eric has presented the group with a problem and then had proceeded to destroy every possible solution advanced by the group.

'It was just like bloody clay pigeon shooting, we fired them up and he shot them down.'

Bill concluded that Eric's motives in this case must have been to show how unsuccessful joint problem-solving could be and what an absolute waste of time it was. The results as far as Bill was concerned had been to create not only confusion but intense frustration.

This example seemed to be one with which most of the group were in sympathy, and they devoted some considerable time in discussing Eric's motives and his behaviour in the group. John supported Eric or attempted to interpret his behaviour generously most of the time. The morning concluded with the consultant asking what they were going to do, if anything, about confronting Eric with these issues if and when he turned up at the group meetings. There was no agreement as to what could or should be done.

In the afternoon all were present, including Eric. John quickly assumed the role of spokesman and said the group was uncertain of Eric's feelings towards the group and that this matter had been discussed in the morning. It was felt, John said, that Eric wanted the group to be effective, but it was possible that one method of achieving this was to let the old group disintegrate.

At this point Nicholas broke in and accused John of presenting a highly personalised and biased account of the group proceedings to Eric and suggested in no uncertain tems that John should 'shut up'.

Harry and Nicholas then continued to relay the events of the morning to Eric, with Harry finally concluding that the reality of the situation was that the group had broken up.

> 'The question that bothered most of us this morning was whether or not you, Eric, had deliberately engineered the situation.'

Eric's response was to deal calmly and logically with all the points raised. He accepted the essence of the group analysis, and explained in a quiet, authoritative voice, that his policy was one of initiating a change from a 'bureaucratic' to an 'organic' system of values.

> 'Unfortunately, the tempo of development of certain projects in the plant has led me to doubt my ability to take the group along with me. I was able to draw John and later Nicholas in with me, and I decided to leave you Bill, and you Harry to look after the works on a day-to-day basis. I realised that in the short term this would inevitably create an in-group and an out-group, and I have always anticipated a time when it would be necessary to re-integrate the team. The alternative was to take the whole group along with me, but I felt it would be impossible to progress fast enough to handle the new developments in the plant at the same time.'

Nicholas questioned the refusal of the alternative policy (taking all along together) to which Eric replied:

'Take Bill's position; he has an established relationship with this factory of seventeen years' standing.
It has been difficult enough for him to integrate
with top management at all. I thought it unfair to
expect him to take a new set of values, different to
anything he has experienced over the past seventeen
years, at the same time as changing his role within
the works.

'In the past the Plant Manager has been very
authoritarian, the Works Engineer has enjoyed an
especially strong position and the Commercial
Manager has been very much a third-class citizen:
my aim is to create *a group of equals*. I do not know
if this is how Harry and Bill view the works group
yet, but it is certainly my aim that at some time
they should view it in this way.'

Nicholas queried what this group would actually do when it
came together in the form that Eric was suggesting. Eric
replied that he wanted the group to develop a problem-
solving approach.

'We were talking about problem-solving this
morning, in particular your suggestion at a recent
meeting that we should experiment with problem-
solving.'

The consultant intervened to ask Eric what he thought this
experience had done for the group. Eric talked for quite some
time, rationalising why he had done what he had done and
how he saw his role in the group, which was as a devil's
advocate. Finally, however, he concluded that he did not
really know what effect his strategy had had on the group. He
felt, however, that John appreciated his efforts and he was,
therefore, satisfied. The consultant invited the other
members to say what they had in fact felt about the meeting:
Eric was visibly shaken by the feedback he received,
particularly so when he found that John had not, as he had

anticipated, appreciated the problem, its implications or Eric's motives in the situation.

Act 2

Some weeks later

A windowless room somewhere on the site

The second session followed closely on a working session where John had presented a paper to the team for consideration and was, at the time of the consultant's arrival, busily engaged in conducting a brain-storming session. At one point Nicholas suggested a point and John, acting in the role of scribe, looked very sceptical; in fact he turned towards Eric who said that he thought it was a pertinent point, so John wrote it up. Nicholas then suggested a further point. John looked sceptical again, but said:

'I'll put it down anyway to keep Nicholas quiet.'

The consultant asked how the group had evolved this procedure for dealing with problems, because it would appear to him, having watched for some time, that the person who was always turned to was Eric. The consultant also drew attention to John's differential response towards Eric and Nicholas. Eric explained:

'This is maybe because John and I "hand-clasp" to some extent, we are both relatively new men in the works, and we have worked together previously.'

Harry came in to say he found it difficult to follow Eric and John.

'I am not on the same wavelength as these blokes.'

He was particularly keen to get back, as he said, to some of the issues raised at the previous meeting. One thing that puzzled him he said was the notion of involvement; he was particularly puzzled by Eric's attitude towards involvement:

'You have involved me in standardisation by saying "this is your pigeon, but now this is what you are going to do". It seems to me that perhaps you are engineering deception by letting people *think* that they are involved, without letting them *really* be involved. Now this is one of the issues we were talking about early yesterday, you as a manipulator.'

Eric did not run away from this issue and some general discussion followed around whether or not he was manipulating the group to meet his own ends.

John: 'I feel Eric's objectives are not always quite clear to the group.'

Nicholas: 'Eric pushes so deep into a problem that he loses everybody. Sometimes I think he does it deliberately. In fact I'm sure he often complicates the picture. He might get something out of it, I certainly don't.'

Bill: 'Well, I get the uneasy feeling that Eric knows where he wants to go, and that despite all the involvement we usually arrive at the answer Eric wanted.'

Eric: 'My objectives may be different from those of the group in one particular area. I have always to bear in mind that whatever comes out of this meeting must be sold to the boys upstairs who think in totally different terms, therefore I often get the group to help me explore some of the problems I think that I will have to answer. This makes it appear devious to you and perhaps it would be better if I told you precisely what I was about; sometimes I don't even know myself.'

John: 'I still find it difficult to criticise Eric because I believe *he* does a lot of homework and feeds in more ideas to these groups than most of us.'

Support of John's point was general and led to some comments about Eric's superior ability and about how he could 'think more rapidly than most of us', and how this could possibly be one of the reasons why he tended to complicate problems.

> *Eric:* 'One of the problems that appears is how does the group control me?'

> *John:* (not responding to Eric's question): 'Another problem, Eric, is your reluctance to share information, if we don't get the information we have a great deal of difficulty in controlling you. Or even helping you.'

Eric then launched into a long talk about the group, about the value of the feedback he had got about being seen as a manipulator, how he had not realised this was the image he was presenting — indeed he thought he was giving much more information to the group:

> 'The group has *problems,* I'm one of them, I know, but our attitudes toward the group are different. For instance, it's very difficult to get you, Harry, to do homework on the same level as John — this may be a matter of time, pressure of other work, or social life, but it produces a reaction within the group and certainly it affects me and my relationship with you. For example, Harry, when you come in and say "I couldn't do the work last night because I had a golf match", it immediately sets four people against you.'

> *Bill* (very quickly): 'Three — not me, I'm not against him.'

> *Eric* (continuing): 'What about the recent occasion when you refused to come to a meeting because of your bowling match. These sort of statements hang in the air, you know. I don't know whether John thinks they hand in the air.'

John (coming to his support): 'Yes, yes I have very much the same impression.'

Harry: 'I believe Eric and John select items from what I say which are anti-Harry — you may well remember that on that particular bowling match occasion I said I would come any other time, that engagement was a very long-standing one. It's my impression you two look for excuses to duck out of day-to-day matters and to take things out on me. You only concern yourselves with the long term, and this is an excuse to duck out of the day-to-day matters we're here to consider. On that particular occasion when you wanted yet another meeting about long-term problems, I thought you would be unlikely to discuss my problems, so I thought "bugger you". I took my bat home.'

Consultant: 'You, Harry, feel that Eric and John select points to support their own view. What is their view — how do you think they see you?'

Harry: 'I'm firmly convinced that whatever I would have said at that particular time they would not have let us proceed to look at the problems we were supposed to look at — short-term plant affairs. They don't want to look at those problems, they don't want to look at the problems I want to look at. I know John thinks I'm not interested in the development of the organisation. Maybe that is how I come through to him, but John comes through to me as not giving a bugger about production because he has too much on his plate as it is.'

John: 'Though I have tried, I don't feel a bit sympathetic towards your problems. At times, mind you, I don't know whether you don't understand or whether you don't wish to understand. I think you're committed only to sit on the sidelines, to prod and to needle, not to do anything constructive.'

Harry: 'I'm surprised that you and Eric see me as sitting on the sidelines. I see myself as being more prepared than you to implement change. On occasions when I have wanted to do thinks that impinged on other areas I have come to you and you have told me not to do it, because it will affect this and it will affect that. I would have thought you would have seen me as being prepared to initiate change, not to sit on the sidelines.'

Eric: 'What you have not started to do is to think through the whole development picture — my concept of the group is one that would do just that, we would sit around together thinking about the implications of any individual item, working them through. I feel that you are only prepared to criticise, not to initiate or become involved in such thinking.'

John: 'Not wanting to hand-clasp with Eric, I also think that all you do is knock things down. Instead of thinking what to put in its place you just go and knock some more. You could make a more constructive contribution; a critical contribution is useful, but a new approach would be welcome.'

Eric: 'If I can summarise the group as I see it at the moment there are two of us in the group who are fairly committed to major change and are prepared to sit back and really think through what we should be doing. There is a third member who is prepared to go along with that — Nicholas. But I haven't a clue what you other two think really and basically. I have an impression of you, Bill, an impression of what you think but I don't really know because you never said. My impression is that you are prepared to go along with whatever we say, so to speak, you bend with the wind. You, Harry, I get the impression you are only prepared to prod and poke and see what you don't like, but what you really think and what you really want I have no idea, so this makes building a really good team bloody difficult. It's a sort of spectrum. At one end you, Harry, who says: "Don't let me stick my neck out unless I have some pretty good idea where I'm going." At the other end I see John who has a pretty clear idea where he's going and is prepared to examine things and get on with it. This creates a different willingness to move forward. I think you two, for example, are waiting to be spoon-fed, you're waiting to be spoon-fed from someone like John, fed in ideas'. — (Long silence.)

Consultant: 'Does this go any deeper than the three who think through long-term issues and the two who run the works. Is there not a basic value conflict here? What do Bill and Harry think about the kind of activity you are indulging in? What do you expect from them?'

Eric: 'Look, I don't think it's commitment in the sense that they wouldn't be prepared to come along with the other stuff. I think it's a question of at what rate they're prepared to come along. It's been my experience that to think around this problem you have to read a lot, and there's such a lot of literature that it probably takes one day each weekend over a period of several years — it also takes a lot of talking in the evenings and occasionally on the weekend.'

Harry: 'Look, I will make it quite clear here and now that I am not prepared to do that, I already put six hours in this weekend; I cannot in my order of priorities fit in that much extra time. My wife tells me I'm putting too much time in already, if you are doing this amount of work at home then all I can say is that you must be a bloody twit.'

Eric: 'My wife tells me the same thing, but this kind of commitment is necessary.'

Harry: 'I don't think that's a measure of commitment. I think it's a form of showing off: look how hard I work, folks!'

John: 'That's rather a rough comment, Harry. I think we can get by without making statements like that!' — (Long silence.)

Consultant: 'What sort of norm has been established? Are you saying, Eric, that if we're to be committed we're to be committed in terms of hours, days?'

Eric: 'In my opinion you can either have leaders and followers, or five equals, but I find it difficult to operate five equals because of the different levels of understanding, not just levels of willingness to give up time.'

Harry: 'Right, so I have another problem here, it's not just the time — there is an intellectual gap, no matter how much time I put in I couldn't work or think at your level.'

Eric and John go on to emphasise further that in order to think at their level, time needs to be spent.

Harry: 'The way you said that implies we haven't given up any social commitments, any sort of time.'

John: 'Well, that's your interpretation of what I said.'

Harry: 'All this has arisen from one thing — after eight years in the bowling club I get into the bloody final, therefore I said I was going to play in it. Eric seemed to resent it; he's referred to it several times

during this meeting, but let me tell you this, I would
do exactly the same thing again. Nonetheless, there
have been a lot of other things I have given up,
many of them for no point at all, including today.'

The meeting the following morning was opened by Bill who
said that he would like to recap a little on what Eric had been
saying the previous evening about the working group. He
went on to say that prior to dinner last night he had perceived
the group as being composed of various individuals who were
experts in their respective fields. He saw Harry, himself, and
to a lesser extent Nicholas as technical men with technical
responsibilities. As he now saw it, however, Eric was trying to
give him the impression that all members of the group should
be experts in general management and should increasingly
abandon their technical role. Harry followed on from Bill
and explained that his major concern was indeed with group
membership. He was clear, after last night, about Eric's
requirements for group membership. He was equally clear, he
said, that Eric did not feel that he, Harry, measured up to
these requirements; he was sorry about this, but that was the
way things were.

Eric then recapped and explained the ideas he had for the
group once more without directly commenting on either Bill's
or Harry's statements. The recap was met with silence. John
then suggested that since the consultant was leaving that day,
he might assist the group in developing procedural skills
which would be useful in forging a cohesive work group. The
consultant said that he was reluctant to concentrate on
procedural skills at this moment since he felt there were basic
issues still to be resolved:

'The problem of a value gap between ourselves is
still very evident.'

Harry returned once more to the issue of the previous day,
which evidently disturbed him. On reflection, he said, he was
extremely disturbed by the outcome of his interventions
because it appeared to him that neither John nor Eric were

prepared to be helpful when he tried to clarify issues that he did not understand.

The consultant asked Harry if he had ever directly requested help. Harry replied that yesterday was, as he saw it, an example of one such occasion. After a moment's pause he admitted that he would find it very difficult to say 'I need help'.

John stated quite categorically once more that he was unsympathetic toward Harry as a working colleague, but stressed that this was his attitude toward him as a 'working colleague' and not 'as a person'. He said that while he did not try to be unhelpful, it was always difficult to know where the initiative should come from in developing a working relationship. It could be that it was indeed difficult for Harry actually to ask for help, partly because of his, John's, admittedly unsympathetic attitude:

> 'Maybe I should be a little more open and receptive, make you feel that you would get a good response if you did ask for help.'

He went on to say that he did think that Harry played a useful role within the group, but, as he had said yesterday, one which tended to be performed in a very negative way:

> 'This was probably why I find it very difficult to display any sympathy towards you.'

> *Eric:* 'I feel much the same way, I think you can be of some use; I think you often are of some use, but I get very irritated when you're actually trying to be of some use.'

Eric then went on to say that he and John had to be very careful about the amount of pressure they put on Harry because they felt he was very much of a worrier. As an example, Eric cited a comment that Harry had made earlier that morning; he had mentioned in passing, partly as a joke to Bill, that he had got up at five o'clock. Eric said that this concerned him, that he would not like to think that what had been said the previous evening had caused Harry a sleepless night.

Bill attempted to explain the lack of sympathy between John and Harry; he said that because of their past experience, Eric and John could communicate very easily, in effect they had a common way of thinking.

> 'John and Harry, on the other hand', said *Bill.* 'think on different wavelengths — therefore they find communication between each other very difficult indeed.'

At this point Nicholas came in and questioned the hypothesis.

> 'You (Bill) say that John and Eric are on the beam all the time, I'm not too sure, I wonder if John really does think like Eric, often John seems to agree with Eric a little too readily — so quickly that he cannot really have thought about it at all.'

> *Eric:* 'No, that's quite unfair, I don't see the relationship with John in the same way you do, Nicholas. I feel that *I* sometimes follow *John.* Often when I reflect at the end of the day I realise that it's John who has got his way and not the other way around, not a case of him coming in too early, a case of him leading me along.'

> *Consultant:* 'What is that you are saying, Eric? Are you explaining that what Nicholas feels is not the way it is? If I were a full-time member of this group I'd be a little concerned about the relationship between you two.'

> *John:* 'Yes, it's a good point that Nicholas brought up. He sees the role I play opposite Eric as being different from the role I play opposite other people. Sometimes in the short run I might appear to go along with Eric — that's while I think it

through, in the long run you know I sometimes disagree.'

Nicholas: 'This may be so but on occasions I have felt that you have gone along with Eric even when you didn't agree. In short I feel that Eric can control this group; the two of you together are a formidable force.'

John: 'I do feel more sympathetic to Eric than to others; Harry would come at the bottom of any hierarchy of sympathy, in between is Bill and you, Nicholas. I have sympathy with Eric because he works bloody hard. I have a sense of values and this is damned important to me — working hard, but secondly he's an effective thinker, therefore I listen to him, I try to understand, whereas with Harry, after listening for a long time I certainly can't understand him.'

Nicholas: 'However, with me, occasionally you have been jocular and sort of down-putting, and this bloody irritates me.'

John: 'Well, why don't you say so at the time?'

Nicholas: 'Because I feel blocked out, by you two sitting up there smiling at each other, in the know, in each other's pockets all the time. It's bloody difficult for anyone else to get a point of view across. It does surprise me sometimes, that you had been putting pressure on Harry. I remember two or three weeks ago I got bloody angry toward you, John, about some issue but basically it was because I saw you as putting a hell of a lot of pressure on Harry.'

John: 'Well, you seeing that sort of thing upsets me because I honestly didn't know we were putting that much pressure on Harry, really I didn't, Eric might have noticed it but I did not.'

Eric (returning to the issue of the special relationships): 'I can't quite see how this special relationship that John and I are supposed to have can cause problems for the rest of the group. It might be useful to have a look at other people's relationships with me in the group, as I see them anyway. Maybe they'd like to say something about it after I've finished. Bill — you see, I'm really very neutral towards you, Bill — this could be one of the problems that's facing this group. As I see it, you don't appear to have built any relationships within the group — you have some sort of relationships outside. There's no meaningful relationship within the group. Harry, well, we've said a lot about that relationship. You, Nicholas, well, there have been a few problems, not many. You're learning you know. You've made a few mistakes, for example, with the shop stewards. You made me mad on occasions but you're doing alright, you're coming along.'

Consultant: 'How do you feel about that?'

Nicholas: 'Like a schoolboy being patted on the head by the headmaster. It's as if Eric is saying to me "you're an up and coming young lad, not yet in the same league as John but you're doing alright".'

Eric: 'Well, that's the way it is, I'm sorry — you know in my opinion, Nicholas, you have done well, in my opinion you aren't yet dealing with the same issues, thinking in the same way as John and I. If it's a question of you being in this group though I'm one hundred per cent for it.'

John: 'And this is really what we're still discussing, whether or not we want this group to exist at all, and if so, who's to be in.'

Consultant: 'Well, it seems to me that the two people you are very uncertain about, and who are uncertain about their own position in all of this are Bill and Harry. Before you try to gain their full commitment to the group, or to imply their rejection it might be useful if you could spell out the pros and cons of their commitment. What's in it for them?'

Eric: 'I said before and I'm going to repeat it now, that really the only way forward is to make a frank assessment and I expect the same and am willing to accept the same being done on me. As I see it, Bill and Harry have little to gain in terms of promotion so this group isn't going to be a stepping stone to anything else. The only reward can be intrinsic, neither Bill nor Harry have a future outside this plant as far as I know, unless they leave the company altogether. For John — I would say he is the company's next Plant Director, and there's no doubt about that. He's very intelligent, a very capable man and he's just about the right sort of age. He's got all the energy, all the drive, everything that's necessary to make a plant director. He'd make a hell of a lot better manager here than I do. Nicholas, well again, very unsure: young enough, has got enough ability, but the whole role of the engineer, and whole company structure is, as you know, currently in turmoil. Could be that this group will be very useful for him, to help him move into the area of general management, so it can make the transition to assistant plant director, or even to plant director at some stage much easier for him. So for two of the people, Bill and Harry, the group holds no attractions in terms of extrinsic rewards, it hold the attraction of being in something that makes the decisions, that implements them, that looks ahead, and that works in the very ambiguous area of general management. But the reward must essentially be inside themselves. Is this the sort of thing they really want to be doing with their time? For the other two it can clearly be of intrinsic and extrinsic use — it can give them satisfaction, it can also provide a platform for moving on. Now I can understand how many pressures there are, especially as you get older; when you're young your wife doesn't mind so much the long hours. They're expected if you're going to get on, but remember they become less sympathetic when you've reached your career ceiling. When that happens it is time to make the decision. I see this group as being one that has to meet frequently, one that has to make big decisions, one that has to take time, one which has to check out, one which has really got to learn to work together. Make no mistake about it, I basically want to work together, you see people are one of my problems. I have accused John earlier of being unemotional but I feel that really the most unemotional one is me. I have to work with lots of people and I keep getting in the same sort of problems we've been talking about these last two or three days. I just keep getting in these problems and I want to get out of them, and this group can help me do that. They can help me understand me, and they can help me become a better plant director.'

Consultant: 'Well, you've said something about what might be in it for other people, Eric, what's in it for you?'

Nicholas: 'That's the question I was just about to ask.'

Eric: 'Well, what's in it for me. I'm not viewing the success of this group as some sort of vehicle for promotion, no, I'm well past that sort of position, I'm not even sure that if it were offered to me I would want to take it. In some ways this group idea runs counter to what the company thinks about the way to work. In general, the boys upstairs think we should just tell people what to do. We shouldn't discuss things with them, we shouldn't try to talk things through, so I don't think they would look very favourably on it. Even if I were in the position to be promoted, anyway — and I am at the point of not really wanting to go further, not wanting to do anything else, other than just be a good plant director here — team work would not be viewed favourably. What will it do to me in other ways? I think it will make life a hell of a lot easier, because being at the top in an organisation like this is — it's a cliché, I know, but it's a bloody lonely job, and I just want to be able to talk to people to get things sorted out, to be able to get good and honest advice. That's what I want out of it, to be part of something, not trapped in a cold image of the boss, somebody who tells you to do things. You see, I think that at the top it should be a sort of "we" thing, not an "I". *We* should want to do something, *we* should agree to it, not *I* want *you* to do something for *me*.'

Over lunch Bill and Harry continued to explore issues and made it quite clear that they wanted to be full members of the group, and accepted the required commitment. In the afternoon the consultant opened the discussion by asking the rest of the group how they saw their positions.

John replied that on the basis of past experience, and before this two-day meeting, he would see himself as being in the most important relationship with Eric, and he would have been inclined to say that the group should have been restricted to Eric and John with the possible inclusion of Nicholas. One thing had struck him, however, over the past couple of days, and that was how different views within the group were, in fact, a desirable thing:

> 'I think we've got to learn how to use the differences that Harry, Nicholas, and to a lesser extent Bill present us with, I think they've also got to learn to use our skills. I would think that past experience is not going to be easy to shake off, I don't think past attitudes are going to be wiped out by these past forty-eight hours but, on the other hand, I don't think they should necessarily characterise our future experiences. What I think should happen is that we should have some sort of experimentation, like a probationary period, although that sounds wrong, in which we should all try to integrate to make a better group.'

> *Nicholas:* 'I want to be in this group, I want to be involved in the things it's going to be involved with, and I want to include Bill and Harry and John.'

> *Eric:* 'Well, we've got to make a decision one way or the other about this group, whether or not it should exist. Experimenting is out, we cannot go messing about, and we've got to make a decision here and now. It's either that we adopt this organic group approach and try to work it, or we continue with the old structure.'

In some further discussion it was agreed that the group was valuable, was one which everyone was interested in, one which needed to spend some further time to sort out its total objectives, as well as its relationships. The session concluded with the consultant pointing out the need to continue working on process issues, e.g. when Nicholas felt shut out by John and Eric, perhaps he ought to have said so; when John felt irritated by Harry's points perhaps he ought to have said so and tried to explore what was behind his criticisms, and when Eric felt the urge to explain away the comments directed towards him perhaps he ought to have stopped and tried to listen to them. It was concluded that some sort of temporary structure should be built whereby Bill and Harry could be helped both in their day-to-day work and in their adjustment to the longer-term problems of general management.

Act 3

Three months later

A windowless training room, somewhere on the site. All cast present.

The meeting opened with the observer providing detailed feedback with supporting data and descriptive comment on the previous acts. In effect he presented a running commentary on how he, as a relatively uninvolved observer had seen the dynamics of the interaction and the utilisation of resources within the group. He said that he saw John and Bill as the least eager to explore the interpersonal issues at any time throughout the sessions together. He felt that John frequently steered the group away from a consideration of interpersonal problems, and seemed more concerned to develop within the group a better understanding of *procedural techniques.* A characteristic trait displayed throughout the session was a tendency to identify with Eric, the boss. When Eric was absent from the group, John interpreted and defended his behaviour; he also supported arguments advanced by Eric, often without thought, and frequently sought Eric's approval for his own behaviour. While he accepted most of what Eric said, he tended to question and devalue the contributions made by others.

He appeared to be relatively insensitive to the feelings of others and did not readily display his own emotions. He was, for example, completely unaware of the pressures, recognised by both Eric and Nicholas, that he was imposing on one of his colleagues, Harry. Indeed, relationships between Harry and John were particularly strained. John believed that Harry had a negative attitude toward the group; nevertheless he could not bring himself to adopt any sort of positive attitude when handling this problem with Harry. John was also markedly negative toward Nicholas, notably in the early stages of the group discussions. He appeared to have made some real progress during the meetings and there was strong evidence that he was willing to be more critical of Eric and more supportive toward Harry. While he was visibly disturbed by Harry's comments about his relationship with Eric, he refused to accept them as valid.

Perhaps, said the observer, it was John who stood to lose most in the 'group of equals' envisaged by Eric. He recognised that his 'special relationship' would disappear. This could, at least in part, explain some of his behaviour, especially toward Nicholas.

The observer commented that Bill appeared at a superficial level to experience few serious problems interacting with others. Eric described Bill as being a 'neutral' member of the group. Perhaps this was a problem. Bill rarely involved himself and when he did, he was seen by others as being willing to 'bend with the wind'.

Harry, said the observer, had displayed throughout a style of behaviour within the group which irritated some of the others. Harry's considered view was that the group was too ready to follow Eric and that for healthy development it was necessary to confront the group fairly frequently with an opposing point of view. Unfortunately, his attempts to take this positive line were interpreted by others as being symptomatic of a basically negative and destructive attitude toward the group as a whole. He was seen by nearly all the members as an 'obstructionist'. Even when he explained his behaviour as being 'for the good of the group' the situation was not greatly improved, because no one knew when to believe him. The members were of the opinion that it was impossible to determine whether he was sincerely committed to an opinion or whether he was advancing it merely as a point of principle. The role of devil's advocate seemed to fit him well.

Eric and John were particularly critical of Harry because they felt that he negated the ideas of others without ever advancing contributions of his own. They also felt that he was not prepared to put in any time outside normal working hours, and this was a major issue in itself.

Harry, on the other hand, felt that Eric and John pursued a deliberate policy of 'misinterpreting my behaviour'. For every occasion he refused to attend an evening meeting he felt he had offered a reasonable explanation. He also felt that they devalued his commitment to the organisation because he did not spend any extra time on those tasks which 'they though most appropriate'. Harry believed that Eric and John were generally unsympathetic toward him, and that they made little attempt to disguise their view that he was a second-class member of the group. He had raised examples of when they criticised a paper he prepared on the grounds that it did not represent his own feelings, whereas a later discussion made it evident there was little consensus about the form such papers should take anyway. He claimed that they had also criticised him for playing the role of devil's advocate, yet this, he had claimed, was precisely the role Eric himself had assumed at a meeting on problem-solving, much to the consternation of the rest of the group. Harry also thought that their accusation that he was 'sitting on the sideline' and unwilling to change was 'grossly unjustified'. He thought of himself as not only being willing to change, but as an initiator of change.

During the course of the meetings, the observer noted, Eric, and to a lesser extent John, recognised the positive contribution Harry was able to make; they were also very much alerted to the antagonism they displayed to many of the points advanced by him, often irrespective of their value. Harry listened to and repeated much of the feedback he received, but still appeared to feel that the role of devil's advocate was a legitimate one, though he did appear to accept that the way he performed the role was one which did not make it effective.

The group interaction with Harry highlighted a general unwillingness to face problems and work them through. People were reluctant to confront Harry and ask him what he was doing and why — whether or not he was being sincere.

Nicholas, the observer said, appeared to occupy a no-man's land within the group. Harry apparently confided in him outside the group, but within the group identified him as being closely associated with Eric and John. Neither Eric nor John saw this as being the case. Nicholas' contributions were frequently devalued by them, and Eric tended to regard him somewhat patronisingly as 'an up and coming lad', but not yet quite one of the boys (meaning Eric and John).

While Nicholas certainly appeared to find Eric patronising at times, he seemed to experience a great deal more difficulty with John. This may have been because John recognised, consciously or otherwise, that Nicholas was the greatest threat to his 'special relationship' with Eric.

Eric as plant director, said the observer, occupied a powerful position within the group. His position was greatly reinforced by his manner. It was his quiet, authoritative, discursive style which led the group to look upon him as a 'manipulator', 'master planner', a 'Machiavelli'.

At times he appeared to be quite insensitive to the impact his behaviour had on the group, for example, in the much-discussed group problem-solving exercise reported by Bill. On a number of occasions he also refused to accept feedback about his behaviour, going into long and confusing arguments about why things *were* the way he had stated them to be. Indeed, his characteristic response was to explain how the group feelings about him were totally unrealistic and had no basis in fact. He failed to communicate his ideas and blamed any subsequent misunderstanding on members of the group.

The observer next raised the issue of the utilisation of resources within the group. Harry, he said, frequently opened the way for the group to explore various issues. He was, for example, one of the first to suggest that the group was disintegrating, an issue which was taken up and developed by the group as a whole, and he was the first to confront Eric with the suggestion that he might be a manipulator, another point which was taken up and developed by the group. He also introduced into the group a divergent point of view, which was eventually recognised by Eric and Nicholas as being potentially useful. Harry's potential contribution to the group was not fully realised because of the various problems he experienced in relating with others.

It was noted that Nicholas also was an extremely useful resource within the group, but was largely unrecognised as such by the rest. He played an effective role opposite Eric, being willing to criticise him when he thought it appropriate, seeking elaboration and further explanation from him when it seemed necessary. He displayed considerable insight into what the group was doing and he offered to John constructive feedback on his relationships with Harry and Eric. He also developed skills in the area of drawing others out and had a particularly constructive relationship with Harry, offering him considerable support and useful criticism.

Though it was recognised that much of the material contributed by the observer was repetitive of issues previously faced and somewhat evaluative of individual members, nonetheless, it provided a good base from which the group could review its progress.

For the next couple of hours the group considered how it had developed over the past eight months and came to the conclusion, with qualifications and reservations, that they were much more effective:

John: 'You know, I even listen to Harry now — really listen, not just wait for something I can zap him with! What's more he has some ideas worth listening to.'

Nicholas: 'He listens to some of mine as well!'

Eric: 'Lest you go away with the idea that everything in the garden is lovely let me hasten to add that we still have our problems. Yesterday, for example, we got into one hell of a bind over something that was relatively trivial — it really was of very little importance but we managed to argue over it for close on two hours.'

John: 'Yes, it was strange conversation, that.'

Nicholas: 'Funny thing was, everyone thought it was trivial and not worth arguing about yet we went on arguing.'

Eric: 'On thinking about it last night I realised it was largely my fault — I kept the thing going but no one stopped me. In short, they still haven't learned how to shut me up.'

Consultant: 'What responsibility have you got for yourself, Eric?'

Eric: 'OK. I suppose I should say *we,* including me, haven't learned how to shut me up.'

Consultant: 'I'm not sure what it is that you are saying, Eric. Are you disappointed with progress since the training sessions?'

Eric: 'Oh no. No. I'm very pleased, it's just that it's not in my nature to go over the top about anything. No, no ... the meetings have been a great deal better. I'm getting ordered to cut over operating costs by an astronomical figure. The boys upstairs have decided and we must obey. That's participation for you ... in the past I would have sweated over the figures and then dished out the cuts much to everyone's dissatisfaction. This time the team got together and we all sweated — I've still got to carry the can, but the feeling of support, of understanding and of willingness to put into effect the agreed plan is ... well it's something to be experienced. You know it's no longer that I'm the meat in the sandwich. Them upstairs, me, and them downstairs. We are all in this together. This way we all lose our heads.' — (Laughter.)

(Curtain)

8 The impact of marathon encounters on teacher — student relationships

This study examined the hypothesis that an intensive encounter group experience between teacher and students can improve their relationship. The Barrett-Lennard Relationship Inventory, which measures the degree of level of regard, empathy, unconditionality and congruence in relationships, was given to two classes of students at the beginning and end of their academic term. One class (n = 36) participated with their faculty member in a twenty-four-hour marathon encounter group near the beginning of the course, whereas the other (n = 24) did not (although they were provided with additional group seminars to control for absolute contact time). Students attending the encounter group with their teacher showed significant increases in their perceptions of their teacher on his level of regard and congruence, and a movement in the direction of significance on his empathy. In contrast, no change was observed on any of the RI scales for the control students. The implications of these results are discussed in detail.

Increasingly various participation-based methods of small group training (i.e, T-group, encounter groups, etc.) are being used in industry, the civil service, hospitals, the social services, and in schools and universities (Cooper, 1973). The initial thrust of these developments was aimed at providing *individuals* within these setting the opportunity of enhancing their own self-awareness and potential. More recently there have been attempts to adapt these techniques to improve the *institutional environment* within which these individuals function, on the assumption that this will, in addition to promoting organisational development, provide in the longer run, greater opportunities for individual personal growth (Appley and Winter, 1973). In higher education, in particular, there has been a significant movement in this direction. Levine (1973), for example, suggested that there should be more involvement and interdependency in the learning process within educational institutions, and strongly advocated the expanded use of experiential group techniques in these contexts. Rogers (1970) in his book *Encounter Groups* summed up the position for further innovation in the use of encounter groups and related methods in enhancing the teacher—student relationship: 'in our schools, colleges, and universities, there is a most desperate need for more participation on the part of learners in the whole program, and for better communication between faculty and students, administrators and faculty, administrators and students. There have been enough experiments along this line so that we know it is perfectly feasible to improve communication in all these relationships, and it is nothing short of tragic that education has been so slow to make use of this new social invention.'

Although the number of group work innovations in educational institutions is on the increase, very little empirical evidence is available to support these methods in these contexts. The research questions which need to be answered are: do encounter groups run for teachers and students improve communication and help develop a meaningful relationship between them? And if so, does this improved relationship create a better and more effective learning environment? It is the purpose of this study to attempt to provide some tentative answers to these questions.

Methods

Subjects and procedure

The subjects (Ss) were sixty university undergraduates. They were social science students, aged between nineteen and twenty-two. All Ss were enrolled in a course in social and organisational psychology, thirty-six in course A and twenty-four in course B. Both courses were taught by the same faculty member and contained the same content material. In A, the beginning of the course was organised so that the students and teacher spent a twenty-four-hour period together in a marathon encounter group while course B had no such experience. In order to provide the teacher and his students with an intensive group experience, which it was hoped would enable them to develop a closer working relationship, it was decided that the training should be *massed* as opposed to *spaced*. That is, that the group experience should be held over a short but intensive period of time (i.e., twenty-four hours) as opposed to one-hour weekly meetings, since research (Mitchell, 1970; Simmons, 1972) seems to indicate that massed sessions are more effective than spaced. In addition, it was felt that the encounter group would then not be seen as just another course but an effort at team-relationship building. Course B was extended in class contact time to include additional group seminars, to compensate for the increased teacher-student time of course A due to the marathon encounter group. The teacher and students of both courses therefore had roughly an equal amount of actual contact time.

The encounter group employed in course A emphasised the development and improvement of interpersonal communication and relationship between the teacher and students through experiential processes, i.e., by using planned exercises to focus on helping and improving relationships, by emphasising a here-and-now interpersonal process, by creating a climate of behavioural experimentation, and by sharing personal perceptions and experiences (Rogers, 1970). It should be noted that the encounter group was run by the teacher himself who was a trained group counsellor.

The Relationship Inventory

The Relationship Inventory (RI) (Barrett-Lennard, 1962) was selected as the instrument for securing study data on the nature of the relationship between the teacher and student. The Inventory is comprised of sixty-four items broken down into four scales; level of regard, empathy, unconditionality and congruence. The RI was given to course A and B students to assess their perception of their relationship with their teacher at the beginning and the end of the term of lectures. The RI was given to all students at the end of the third week of term and the encounter group was run several days later. In addition, the RI was adapted (third-person-plural form) to obtain the teacher's perception of his students.

The *level of regard* scale measures the degree to which the students experience the teacher as expressing a warm, positive and acceptant attitude toward him, e.g., 'he respects me as a person', 'I feel appreciated by him', 'he cares for me'. The *empathy* scales measures the extent to which the students perceive the teacher as sensing the feelings and personal meanings which the student himself is experiencing and trying to communicate, e.g., 'he nearly always knows what I mean', 'he realises what I mean even when I have difficulty saying it', 'he understands me'. The *unconditionality* scale measures the degree to which the teacher not only accepts the student but does so without reservations, without evaluations, that is, the degree of unconditional positive regard, e.g., 'I don't think that anything I say or do really changes the way he feels towards me', 'how much he likes or dislikes me is not altered by anything that I tell him about myself', 'his feeling toward me doesn't depend on how I feel toward him'. And finally, the *congruence* scale assesses the degree to which the student perceives the teacher as genuine and without facade in his relationship to him/her, e.g., 'I feel he is real and genuine with me', 'he is willing to express whatever is actually in his mind with me, including any feelings about himself or about me', 'I have not felt that he tried to hide anything from himself that he feels with me.' Each scale contains sixteen items, half of which are expressed positively and the other half expressed negatively in order to minimise acquiescence response set. A six-point Likert-type rating scale is used for each item. Theoretically, negative items are reversed and summated with positive ones and each S is assigned a single score for each scale. A constant of 48 was added to change the theoretical scoring limits from -48 to +48 to 0 to 96. Split-half and test-retest reliabilities for the RI scales are very high (Barrett-Lennard, 1962) and the RI has been extensively validated in a wide range of differing contexts (Blumberg, 1968; Caracena and Vicory, 1969; Hollenbeck, 1965).

Results

Differences between pre (beginning of academic term) and post (end of term) test scores on each scale of the RI were tested by t tests for correlated means for the marathon encounter and control Ss. The data are represented in Table 8.1.

First, it can be seen that there is no significant pre-test difference on the RI scale scores between the marathon and control group Ss, so that any significant change observed is not a function of initial score bias between experimental and controls. Second, it can be seen that the students who attended the marathon encounter group showed significant increases in their perceptions of their teacher on the *level of regard* (LR) and *congruence* (C) scales, and a movement in the direction of significance on the *empathy* (E) scale. No change was found on the *unconditionality* (U) scale. In contrast, no change for students' perception of their teacher was found on any of the RI scales for the control Ss.

If we examine the RI scale scores for the teacher, that is, his perceptions of his students on the four RI attributes, we

Table 8.1 Means and t values for significance of differences between pre and post test RI scores for students

Relationship Inventory scales	Marathon encounter group				Control group			
	M pre	M post	t	p	M pre	M post	t	p
Level of regard	71.69	80.94	2.14	<0.05	73.75	74.62	<1.00	—
Empathy	62.31	69.06	1.67	0.10	65.66	63.00	<1.00	—
Unconditionality	67.50	67.37	<1.00	—	65.30	66.22	<1.00	—
Congruence	71.56	83.94	2.44	<0.02	69.82	71.24	<1.00	—

find the same trend as in the student results for the marathon encounter group course, his pre- and post-test RI scores, respectively, were as follows: LR scale 64 and 85; E scale 58 and 70; U scale 61 and 59; C scale 57 and 67; for the control group: LR scale 65 and 67; E scale 60 and 61; U scale 58 and 54, and C scale 60 and 63. In summary, positive changes were observed on the LR, E, and C scales for the students in the marathon encounter group, but no improvement for the teacher in his relationship with the control group students on any of the RI scales.

Discussion

It seems from this evidence that there is some relationship between intensive encounter group experiences among teachers and students and an improvement in the teacher-student relationship. Obviously, shared personal experiences between staff and students is only one way in which a better relationship can be created but it seems noteworthy that the responsibility for enhancing the relational climate must go beyond the confines of traditional classroom behaviour and role relationships, as the control group results suggest. These results also help us partly to answer the second question posited at the beginning of this paper 'does an improved teacher-student relationship create a better learning environment'. From the voluminous data accumulated on the RI over the past twelve years, there is substantial evidence that an improvement in RI attributes can help to create a measurably more effective learning climate. For example, Scheuer (1971) found a significant gain in academic achievement level in disturbed and maladjusted pupils who saw their teachers as possessing a high degree of RI characteristics. Mason and Blumberg (1969) found that high-school students, who, judged by independent assessors to have *learned the most,* rated the perceived relational responses (RI) of their teachers significantly higher than those students judged to have *learned least.* Emmerling (1961) found among 600 pupils and twenty teachers that those teachers receiving high RI scores were also assessed as significantly more pupil-centred, more open to their experience, and more effective in the classroom as judged by the students themselves. These and other studies (Van der Veen and Novak, 1970) provide some rather convincing evidence of a link between the nature of the teacher-student relationship as measured by the RI and learning outcomes. While the results in this study are potentially useful, there are a number of points we should make about it. First, it seems fairly reasonable to expect that the more contact teachers and students have with one another the closer the relationship. We did to some extent control the gross amount of contact time between courses but it is obvious from the results that the quality of contact is likely to be more important. It might have been a better control, therefore, had we organised for course-B students to spend their additional teacher contact time in a 'social' as distinct from a 'class-room' setting. The impact of the encounter group experience could have been more clearly demonstrated. There is some evidence, however, that the relationship between frequency of 'social' contact between people, and closer personal relationships, is to some extent a function of the size of the group (Snortum and Myers, 1971), that is, the larger the size of the group, the weaker the relationship. There is no compelling reason to expect, therefore, that additional 'social' time in a group of twenty-four would have contributed significantly to RI attributes — it is open to investigation, however. Second, it is interesting to note that no change was found on the unconditionality scale. This might reflect the organisational reality that an 'evaluative' relationship does and will continue to exist between the faculty member and particular students, which indeed is imposed on both in their respective roles within the university. Mason and Blumberg (1969) also found that unconditionality was the only non-predictive RI variable within their study. Third, it would have been more useful to have obtained some objective data on subsequent student performance among the subject population in this study. Within the UK context this presents some practical difficulties, for in English universities there is, in the vast majority of cases, no examination or grading system for individual courses. Students are assessed by their performance in examinations taken at the very end of their final year, which is meant to cover their whole performance during their three years at university. If we could have instrumented a specially designed examination or attainment test it would have presented, considering English university norms, other methodological difficulties. Since there is a great deal of evidence of the predictive validity of the RI it was felt that we should concentrate on change in relational variables.

In conclusion, higher education is undergoing a new and exciting period of experimentation and exploration of teaching techniques and methods of enhancing the leaning community. Experiential group methods such as encounter and T-groups for teachers and students is only one small development and as Levine (1973) suggests 'a development toward a more relevant and active educational experience; and while they certainly do not constitute answers to all problems, they, nevertheless, represent a step forwards'.

References

Appley, D.G. and Winter, A.R., *T-groups and therapy groups in a changing society,* Jossey-Bass: San Francisco 1973.
Barrett-Lennard, G.T., Dimensions of therapist response as casual factors in therapeutic change, *Psychological Monographs,* 1962, 76 (43).
Blumberg, A., Supervisor behavior and interpersonal relations, *Educational Administration Quarterly,* 1968, 34-45, spring.
Caracena, P.F. and Vicory, J.R., Correlates of phenomenological and judged empathy, *Journal of Counselling Psychology,* 1969, 16: 510-515.
Cooper, C.L., *Group training for individual and organizational development,* pp. 40-67, Karger: Basel 1973.
Emmerling, F.A., A study of the relationship between personality characteristics of classroom teachers and pupil perceptions of these teachers. Unpublished PhD dissertation, Auburn University, 1961 (available University Microfilms, Ann Arbor, Mich.).
Hollenbeck, G.P., Conditions and outcomes in the student-parent relationship, Journal of Counselling Psychology, 1965, 29: 237-241.
Levine, N., Group training for students in higher education; in Cooper, *Group training for individual and organizational development,* pp. 40-67, Karger: Basel 1973.
Mason, J. and Blumberg, A., Perceived educational value of the classroom and teacher-pupil interpersonal relationships, *Journal of Secondary Education,* 1969, 44, 135-139.
Mitchell, R.R., An evaluation of the relative effectiveness of spaced, massed, and combined sensitivity training groups in promoting positive behaviour change, *Dissertation Abstracts,* 1970, 29, 4834.
Rogers, C., *Encounter groups,* Allen Lane: London 1970.
Scheuer, A.L., The relationship between personal attributes and effectiveness in teachers of the emotionally disturbed, *Exceptional Children,* 1971, 723-731.

Simmons, R.C., Intensity as a variable in programmed group interaction: the marathon, *Dissertation Abstracts,* 1972, 31: 2494.

Snortum, J.R. and Myers, H.F., Intensity of T-group relationships as a function of interaction, *International Journal of Group Psychotherapy,* 1971, 21: 190-201.

Van der Veen, F. and Novak, A.L., Perceived parental attitudes and family concepts of disturbed adolescents, normal siblings, and normal controls, *Institute of Juvenile Research Journal,* 1970, 7 (3).

9 The impact of experiential groups on social workers

Cries that sensitivity training and encounter groups are psychologically dangerous and in Gottschalk's (1966) opinion potentially 'psychiatrically disruptive to almost half of the delegates in a group' have not as yet been proved. Several case studies (Jaffe and Scherl, 1969) or anecdotal reports have been published (Gottschalk and Pattison, 1969) supporting this view. Recently, however, more empirical work has been carried out. On the negative side, Reddy (1970) found, using a paper-and-pencil personality inventory measuring psychological disturbance, that participants in two T-groups compared with control groups (one of which was a therapy group) increased their scores more in the direction of greater disturbance following training. This could merely indicate a greater willingness on the part of the T-group participants to admit more personally threatening material in the questionnaire, which may reflect greater openness or sensitivity to their symptoms and not disturbance. In a more comprehensive study involving eighteen different experiential groups, Yalom and Lieberman (1971) found some evidence of psychiatric casualties, that is, participants becoming more 'psychologically distressed or employing more maladaptive mechanisms'. They came to the conclusion, however, that this was more a function of the particular leadership style of the trainers or facilitators than the nature of the particular group experience (i.e. T-groups, encounter groups, psychodrama groups, etc.). On the positive side, there is some evidence that indicates that T-groups may be less stressful than university examinations (Lubin and Lubin, 1971) or perceptual isolation experiments of varying degrees of intensity (Lubin and Zuckerman, 1969). There is also some evidence that these groups may enable participants to cope better with sexual and aggressive stimuli (Pollack and Stanley, 1971) and with stressful periods in their life, for instance, with the pressures of university life (Cooper, 1972a, 1972b).

At present the one area that has not been given the attention it deserves in this context is the effect of this type of training on the family and close friends of participants. Do husbands, wives, children, close relatives and friends see the returning T-group participants as more or less disturbed, more or less able to communicate, more or less able to cope with personal and family problems? The purpose of this study was to answer this question. In addition, it was hoped that one could examine the relationship between a paper-and-pencil test measure of psychological disturbance (or neuroticism) before and after training and the family and friends report on aspects of the participants' behaviour judged to be associated with psychological distress. The answer to these questions is particularly important in the context of the helping professions, e.g. social workers, who are increasingly using these group techniques.

Method

Subjects and training programme

The T-group participants were members of the helping professions; social workers, psychiatrists, nurses, and probation officers. There were thirty trainees and six staff trainers, roughly half of whom were women and half men.

The participants were separated into three groups to make them as heterogeneous as possible (in terms of sex, age, and occupation), with two trainers in each group. The training consisted of a one-week residential T-group run along lines described by Tannenbaum, Weschler and Massarik (1961). First, the training was primarily 'process-orientated' rather than 'content-orientated'. That is, the primary stress was on the feeling level of communications rather than solely on the informational or conceptual level. This emphasis was accomplished by focusing on the here-and-now behaviour and themes in the group. Second, the training was not structured in a conventional manner. Opportunities were provided for the individuals to decide what they wanted to talk about, what kinds of problem they desired to deal with, and what means they wanted to use in reaching their goals. As they concerned themselves with the problems occasioned by this lack of direction, they began to act in characteristic ways: some people remained silent, some were aggressive, some tended to initiate discussions, some attempted to structure the proceedings. With the aid of the staff member, these approaches and developments became the focal points for discussion and analysis. The trainer drew attention to events and behaviour in the group by occasional interventions in the form of tentative interpretations, which he considered would provide useful data for study. Third, the value of the T-group was its restriction to small groups, allowing a high level of participation, involvement, and free communication.

Questionnaires

Eysenck Personality Inventory. The Eysenck Personality Inventory (EPI) was administered to all trainees just before the start of the first session of the training week and just after the final session. The EPI is self-administering and consists of fifty-seven statements, which comprise two scales, I-E (introversion/extraversion) and the N-scale (neuroticism). The N-scale of the EPI was used as an independent change measure of psychological disturbance, and in addition, as a measure to test the relationship between paper-and-pencil tests of disturbance and reports of behaviour by participants' closest family and friends. The EPI has been widely used as a measure of personality disturbance or neuroticism in recent years and has been extensively validated (Eysenck and Eysenck, 1969). Since the test-retest reliability coefficients for the N-scale are very high, ranging from 0.81 to 0.91, it was decided that an untrained control group was not necessary. The anonymity of each subject was maintained throughout the study by asking each one to choose a number at random and to use that number in place of their name on the EPI and on all other research questionnaires.

Behaviour Change questionnaire. The post-training behaviour change questionnaire was designed by the author with the help of a consultant psychiatrist (Dr R. Sandison, Director, Southampton Mental Health Centre) and a lecturer in social work with clinical casework experience (B. Hughes, University of Southampton). It consisted of eight statements with a five, six or seven choice Likert-type continuum for each one. Five of the questions were designed to assess behaviour patterns one might reasonably expect to reflect psychological disturbance. These questions were carefully constructed to be comprehensible to people unfamiliar with clinical-type questionnaires. The questions were: (1) Are you and he/she (T-group participant) communicating better or worse since the course (seven-point scale from *very much better* to *very much worse);* (2) Has he/she been emotionally affected by the course (seven-point scale from *very much disturbed* to *much more stable);* (3) Does he/she appear more or less happy as a result of the course (five-point scale from *much more happy* to *much less happy);* (4) Does he/she seem more or less able to cope with difficult personal or family or relationship problems since the course (five-point scale from *much more able* to *much less able);* (5) Has his/her relationship with his/her children or other significant person/s been affected by the course (seven-point scale from *very much better* to *very much worse).* Three additional questions were included, two at the beginning to lead into the main statements ('How well did he/she communicate his/her experience after returning from the training course' and 'How far do you feel he/she has excluded you from the experience') and one at the end to give closure to the questionnaire ('How would you feel about his/her attending a future similar course').

There were two forms to this questionnaire; a 'self' form, which the participant filled out (a modification of the above statements in the first person singular), and an 'other' form (stated as above), which was filled out by two or three of the participants' closest relatives and friends (i.e. husband, wife, older children, other close personal friends). At the conclusion of the T-group training week, each participant was given a sealed envelope which included one 'self' form and three 'others' forms and was told that it contained questionnaires which were to be completed by himself and three close relatives and friends two weeks after the training course, and that the envelope should be opened at that time. Instructions were included in the envelopes together with four self-addressed stamped envelopes so that each respondent could send them back to the researchers without showing them to the participant. The instructions indicated that the respondents were to complete the questionnaires within three days of receiving them, that is, between fourteen and sixteen days after the training course. In addition, to minimise the possibility of response inhibition or social desirability in responding each participant was asked to place the number used on the EPI form on all Behaviour Change questionnaires before distributing them. This allowed the researchers to compare different perceptions of a given person and to provide the anonymity that would encourage honesty in responding.

Behaviour Change forms were received from all thirty participants and seventy members of their family and friends. Since three 'other' forms were given to each participant, the response rate was 77 per cent. The 'real' response rate was, in fact, 88 per cent, since ten participants indicated to the researchers (on returning their own forms) that they had distributed only two forms. These participants indicated that they had only two close relatives or friends who would have enough contact with them in the two-week period following training to make the questionnaire meaningful. 27 per cent of the forms came from the wives and husbands, 30 per cent from the other close relatives and children, and 43 per cent from close friends of the participants.

Results and discussion

In analysing the results it was decided to examine the data in the following order. First, an assessment of participant change on the neuroticism scale of the EPI. Second, an investigation into the relationship between the N-scale and each of the five questions on the Behaviour Change measure relating to perceptions of participant behaviour reasonably expected to reflect psychological disturbance or distress. Third, an inspection of the post-course Behaviour Change questionnaire results.

Differences between pre-and post-test scores on the N-scale of the EPI were tested by a t test for correlated means (two-tailed). The data are represented in Table 9.1.

Table 9.1 Means and value for significance of differences between pre- and post-test N-scale (neuroticism) scores

	$M_{pre-test}$	$M_{post-test}$	t	p
Participants (N = 30)	10.53	11.73	2.12	< 0.05

It can be seen that T-group trainees show statistically significant change on the N-scale in the direction of increased neuroticism following training. These results are consistent with Reddy's (1970) findings which also indicated increased psychological disturbance following training using a different psychometric measure, the NDS (number of deviant signs) scale of the Tennessee Self-Concept Tests (Fitts, 1965). Once again, these results are not as straightforward as they might appear, that is, that T-group participants became more neurotic as a result of training. Although they confirm a previous finding, both measures are paper-and-pencil tests which require the subject to admit the presence of specific physiological, psychological, and behavioural symptoms. As argued previously, it is quite conceivable that the increase in scores on these measures might indicate a greater willingness on the part of the participant to admit these symptoms following training, reflecting an increase in self-disclosure or openness and not psychological disturbance. Or alternatively, the increase in these scores could indicate a greater sensitivity by participants to their own physiological, psychological and behavioural patterns or symptoms. In either case, this would reflect the achievement of T-group goals and not the opposite. An assessment of the Behaviour Change questionnaire might help to clarify this point, for if participants who show increases in neuroticism on the EPI also are seen by their family and friends as being much worse at communicating since the course, disturbed by the course, and less happy as a result of the course, etc., then we might have greater confidence in generalising from the results of the personality inventories. To examine this relationship, a change score for each participant was calculated for the N-scale (difference between before and after scores) and this was correlated, using a Pearson product-moment, with the mean scores of the perceptions of the trainee by his/her family and friends on each of the five questions judged to be related to psychological disturbance in the Behaviour Change questionnaire.

It can be seen from Table 9.2 that there appears to be no significant relationship between an increase in neuroticism and the perceptions of the trainees' closest family and friends on behaviour which should be associated with neuroticism; communicating worse, less happy, less able to cope with personal problems and relationships, emotionally disturbed by the course, and communicating worse with children or other significant person/s. There are a number of points that could be made about this set of results. First, that the

Table 9.2 Relationship between participant change in neuroticism and family friends perception of change as a result of T-group training (n = 30)

Pearson Product-Moment Correlation		
Questions	*Increase in N-Scale*	
	rho	p
Communication worse since the course	0.1914	n.s.
Emotionally disturbed by the course	−0.1196	n.s.
Less happy as a result of the course	0.1754	n.s.
Less able to cope with difficult personal or family or relationship problems	0.0117	n.s.
Worse relationship with children or other significant person/s	0.1912	n.s.

(p = 0.05 requires rho of 0.35)

Behaviour Change measure is not a good one and if it was there would be a positive relationship between these measures. Methodologically it could be that the family and friends of the participants were providing socially desirable responses, responses that would put the particular participant in a 'good light' or indicate that the participant was able to cope with the training. Although this may be possible, it is unlikely for two reasons. One, every effort was made to communicate to the respondents that their questionnaires would not be identifiable by name and that, in any case, the researchers were unaware of which number related to which participant. Two, if social desirability was present it should reflect itself in a skewed distribution on the positive end of the various scales, yet it was found that a sizeable minority of respondents utilised the negative end of the continuum on several questions, for instance, 25 per cent of the family/friends felt excluded from the experience, over 30 per cent felt that the participant had been emotionally disturbed by the course, etc. Second, and the most probably explanation, is that paper-and-pencil questionnaires attempting to measure psychological disturbance or neuroticism as a result of training may not be appropriate measures of change. The reason for this is that the line between a 'real' response (the expression of the onset of a symptom) and a response that indicated greater opennes or willingness to admit symptoms or, in fact, increased sensitivity to symptoms, is a very thin one indeed. In any case, participants who showed increases in neuroticism scores on the EPI were not seen by family and friends during the two weeks following the training to display various behaviours one might associate with psychological distress or disturbance.

And finally, some interesting results emerged from the Behaviour Change questionnaire (Table 9.3). There are two aspects of these data that will be examined; first, the overall responses of 'participants' and 'others' to each question, and second, the differences between 'participants' and 'others' perceptions of the effect of the training programme. In the first question it can be seen that both participants and close relatives and friends thought that they had adequately communicated their training experience. It is interesting to note that the family and friends had a slightly more positive view of the ability of the participant to communicate than the participant had himself. In the second question, on balance, both participants and the 'relevant others' felt *included* in the experience although there was a sizeable minority who did not (24 per cent). There seemed to be very little difference between the two groups. Question three seems to reveal something of a halo-effect, for although the participants themselves feel that they are communicating better since the course (62 per cent), a smaller proportion of their family/friends agree (38 per cent), in fact a majority see no change (58 per cent). This same phenomenon repeats itself in question four. Although a majority of participants felt *slightly* to *more stable* as a result of the course (53 per cent), a very large minority of family and friends felt that they were *unaffected* (42 per cent). Roughly the same number of 'participants' and 'others' (approximately 30 per cent) felt that the participants were slightly disturbed or disturbed by the T-group. Although a large minority of respondents, 'participants' and 'others', felt that the course was disturbing, a majority of participants (51 per cent) and a sizeable minority of family/friends (39 per cent) felt that the trainees were better able to cope with difficult personal, family, or relationship problems (question six), with virtually no respondents feeling that they were less able. This seemed to be the case with question seven as well, that a majority of participants (59 per cent) and a sizeable minority of 'others' (44 per cent) felt that the trainees' relationship with his/her children or other significant person/s had been very much better since the course, and virtually nobody felt that it had been worse. In addition, when the participants and their close relatives and friends were asked whether they appeared more or less happy as a result of the course, over 50 per cent of both groups felt they were more happy and only a very small minority felt they were less happy.

These results seem to indicate that although some social worker participants see themselves and are seen by others as disturbed by the experience, they also see themselves and are seen by their close family and friends as slightly better able to cope with problems, get on better in their relationships with their children and other significant people, are more happy and are slightly better able to communicate after the course. One must qualify this conclusion by making two points. First, it can be seen that participants seem to have a halo-effect as a result of the course, for on a number of questions they have responded more on the positive end of the continuum than the 'others'. Second, that there is still a sizeable group of participants and close family and friends who have used the categories labelled *no difference* or *the same,* that is, that no change was perceived. Nevertheless, the fears of many that this form of training may lead to 'acute pathological emotional responses' (Odiorne, 1963) has not been substantiated by close family and friends or the participants themselves. On the contrary, it appears that for a large number of trainees their familial and close relationships may have improved rather than become more maladaptive.

Table 9.3 Responses on Behaviour Change questionnaire by T-group participants and their family and friends

Percentages

1. How well did he/she communicate his/her experience after returning from the training course?

	Very well	Well	Fairly well	Fairly badly	Badly	Very badly
Participants	6	33	50	13	2	0
Family/friends	30	31	32	3	4	0

2. How far do you feel he/she has excluded you from the experience?

	Strongly excluded	Excluded	Slightly excluded	Slightly included	Included	Very included
Participants	0	9	20	23	40	8
Family/friends	1	7	16	25	36	15

3. Are you and he/she communicating better or worse since the course?

	Very much better	Better	Slightly better	The same	Slightly worse	Worse	Very much worse
Participants	0	27	35	38	3	0	0
Family/friends	4	12	22	58	4	0	0

4. Has he/she been emotionally affected by the course?

	Very much disturbed	Disturbed	Slightly disturbed	Unaffected	Slightly more stable	Stable	Much more stable
Participants	0	9	20	18	44	6	3
Family/friends	0	7	24	42	19	4	4

Table 9.3 continued

5. Does he/she appear more or less happy as a result of the course?

	Much more happy	More happy	No difference	Less happy	Much less happy
Participants	6	48	37	9	0
Family/friends	11	39	42	8	0

6. Does he/she seem more or less able to cope with difficult personal or family or relationship problems since the course?

	Much more able	More able	No difference	Less able	Much less able
Participants	2	49	49	0	0
Family/friends	4	35	57	4	0

7. Has his/her relationship with his/her children or other significant person/s been affected by the course?

	Very much better	Better	Slightly better	The same	Slightly worse	Worse	Very much worse
Participants	0	18	41	41	0	0	0
Family/friends	5	12	27	55	1	0	0

8. How would you feel about his/her attending a future similar course?

	Agreeable	Slightly agreeable	Neither agreeable or disagreeable	Slightly disagreeable	Disagreeable
Participants	74	9	11	6	0
Family/friends	68	9	19	4	0

Acknowledgement

I would like to thank all the participants of the Southampton Group Work Course 1973, their family and friends, and the staff of the course, particularly Brian Hughes and Dr Ronald Sandison for their co-operation and help in making this study possible.

References

Gottschalk, L.A., Psychoanalytic notes on T-groups at the human relations laboratory, Bethel, Maine, *Psychiatry,* 1966, 7, 472-87.

Jaffe, S.L. and Scherl, D.J., Acute psychosis precipitated by T-group experiences, *Archives of General Psychiatry,* 1969, 21, 443-8.

Gottschalk, L.A. and Pattison, E.M., Psychiatric perspectives on T-groups and the laboratory movement, *American Journal of Psychiatry,* 1969, 126, 823-39.

Reddy, W.B., Sensitivity training or group psychotherapy: the need for adequate screening, *International Journal of Group Psychotherapy,* 1970, 20, 366-71.

Yalom, I.D. and Lieberman, M.A., A study of encounter group casualties, *Archives of General Psychiatry,* 1971, 25, 16-30.

Lubin, B: and Lubin, A.W., Laboratory training stress compared with college examination stress, *Journal of Applied Behavioral Science,* 1971, 7, 502-7.

Lubin, B. and Zuckerman, M., Level of emotional arousal in laboratory training, *Journal of Applied Behavioral Science,* 1969, 5, 483-90.

Pollack, D. and Stanley, G., Coping and marathon sensitivity training, *Psychology Reports,* 1971, 29, 379-85.

Cooper, C.L., An attempt to assess the psychologically disturbing effects of T-group training, *British Journal of Social and Clinical Psychology,* 1972a, 11, 342-5.

Cooper, C.L., Coping with life stress after T-groups, *Psychology Reports,* 1972b, 31, 602.

Tannenbaum, R., Weschler, I., and Massarik, F., *Leadership and organizations,* McGraw-Hill, 1961.

Eysenck, H.J. and Eysenck, S.B.G., *Manual for the Eysenck personality inventory* (Educational and Industrial Testing Service, San Diego), 1969.

Fitts, W.H., *Manual: Tennessee self-concept scale,* Nashville, Tenn: Department of Mental Health, 1965.

Odiorne, G.S., The trouble with sensitivity training, *Journal of the American Society of Training Directors,* 1963, 9-20.

10   Toward the development of
social skills in restaurants

A social skill development programme, conducted with government support (UK) in the restaurant industry is reported. Related research is summarised and the programme's training approach and evaluative research concept are explicated.

Introduction

By statute, all firms in the United Kingdom employing over a minimum number of personnel in every industry are required to contribute a percentage of their corporate wage bill towards the organisation, development and administration of training within their particular industry. The actual amount levied is determined by levying bodies called Industrial Training Boards who are empowered to control and direct all training within their respective industries. The Hotel and Catering Industry Training Board (HCITB) is one such body and is responsible for training and research for all hotels, restaurants, cafeterias, snack bars and allied activities in the whole of the British Isles.

In late 1969, the HCITB contacted the authors asking them if they would examine the feasibility of providing training in social skills for food service operatives (i.e. waiters, waitresses, chefs, etc.). The HCITB recognised that customers in restaurants and cafeterias are sensitive to the way in which staff related to them in the course of their duties. Most trainers within the Board agreed that training in interpersonal relations or social skills was desirable. What was being requested, therefore, was guidance on the form and method of training. In addition, the HCITB felt that research should be carried out to evaluate the effect of this training so that the development of social skill training within the Industry might evolve in an orderly and efficient manner. The present chapter describes our effort at achieving these aims. Specifically the aims were (1) to design courses which represent different approaches to social skill training but whose objectives are in line with the needs of the Industry; and (2) to evaluate by means of a controlled study the relative usefulness of these approaches. It was hoped that the result of these efforts would be to provide a reservoir of experience in the day-to-day operation of social skill training courses for the HCITB that could be drawn on by the Catering Industry at large. In addition, it was hoped that it would be possible to monitor the reaction of the Industry (as represented by the host company) to social skill training and its effects.

The purpose of this chapter is to describe the social skill training courses devised for the Catering Industry and the research design and measures utilised to evaluate them.

Relevant research prior to the present project

Studies within the hotel and catering industry

Whyte (1948) pioneered the application of the 'human relations' approach to the Hotel and Catering Industry. He highlighted the 'crisis of authority' characteristic of the Industry and was the first to analyse customer/staff relations and describe potential 'flashpoints' within a typical restaurant work team. However, Whyte did not propose training programmes to help resolve the problems he had delineated, he was interested only in drawing attention to the dynamics of the restaurant as a social organisation.

Pickard *et al.* (1969) interested themselves in the application of social relations theory to training techniques in the Catering Industry. However, their study did not go much further than offering tentative suggestions concerning the general direction of the proposed training method. A much more determined approach was made by Damodaran (1967), who mounted a small action training and research programme consisting of lectures, seminars and practical exercises. The objectives of this training were stated: 'To train people (i.e. waiters, waitresses, etc.) to be more adaptable and more skilled in the customer contact area, and to improve job satisfaction and staff awareness of organisational problems.' Although the project had certain limitations — it was based on a single restaurant and the research worker conducting the evaluation was also administering the training programme — it did give promise of generally instructive outcomes. Unfortunately, the research programme had to be seriously curtailed and the final evaluation stage omitted.

It is clear that very little research into social skills has taken place within the Catering Industry and in particular there is a conspicuous absence of clearly designed social skill courses.

Studies in related fields

Outside the Hotel and Catering Industry there have been a number of studies concerned with organisation development and managerial improvement. Typical of such studies is that of Buchanan and Brunstetter (1959). It is clear from the outline of their programme goals that they were very much interested in developing *social skills* within an organisational context. The second of two major goals is described thus: 'Facilitate development of people . . . (a) perceptiveness of social situations and process, (b) skill and creativeness in problem solving, (c) flexibility of behaviour.' This study is important because it applies the philosophy and method of scientific research to social skill training. The researchers proceeded by first presenting their training goals and isolating the assumptions behind the change process in the organisational setting. They next related their goals to the context of the organisation for which the development programme was being instituted. The programme itself was conceived in research terms in that the design allowed for a controlled evaluation of training outcomes against stated goals.

Whilst Buchanan and Brunstetter (1959) and similar studies throughout the 1960s focused on organisational development, a parallel series concerned itself with the individual trainee (Miles, 1960; Bunker, 1965). However, training method and philosophy in all these studies were generally similar. All were primarily interested in the development of training techniques and in methods of evaluation in human relations, whether the research focused on the individual or on the organisation. Thus in one study, Valiquet (1968) looked specifically at individual changes in what was essentially a management (organisational) development programme.

The project reported here derives its basic rationale and evaluative techniques from these two traditions. It builds on the work already done by extending the application of training for interpersonal relations beyond the managerial and supervisory level to that of the operative and by essaying refinements of the evaluation tools developed by Bunker (1965), Harrison (1966) and van der Vegt (1970).

Two approaches to social skill training

Any survey of the literature of social skills training techniques and methods reveals an interesting dichotomy. The different approaches can nearly always be assigned to one of two categories, each based on a different underlying training philosophy. Essentially, one approach sees social skill training as primarily *skill* training, that is, social skills are acquired in much the same way as motor skills — one learns to get on better with customers and colleagues by similar methods as one learns to drive an automobile. This approach is based on Argyle's (1969) conception and model of interpersonal behaviour in terms of motor skills. The other approach (fostered by the National Training Laboratories — Institute for Applied Behavioural Science) stresses the *social* rather than the *skill* aspect of interpersonal interactions. Training, according to this approach, has to be 'process-orientated' rather than 'content-orientated' (Tannenbaum *et al.,* 1961) and people are seen to improve their social skills by studying their own behaviour through observing interaction and receiving direct feedback within an ongoing small group situation. The main distinction between the two approaches is that the latter is person-centred whereas the former asserts that social skill acquisition can occur without focusing on the trainee as a person. It is this dichotomy of training philosophies that form the basis of the training programmes utilised in this project.

The research design

The main features of the research design were as follows:

1. There would be two programmes of social skill training based on two different training methods.
2. *Programme 'A' (Skills* Course) would be developed out of an earlier HCITB course and would encompass essentially the teaching techniques and social skills that would be useful to participants in their work situations. The teaching methods employed would be 'traditional', that is, they would use 'learning by example', group discussion of work problems, role-playing, films and other audiovisual aids, lectures, and finally exercises and projects to be completed by participants. The development and running of this programme would be in the hands of the consultants who developed the earlier HCITB courses.

3. *Programme 'B' (Social* Course) would have a different starting point. It would be centred on the T-group approach to social skill training. The emphasis would be on learning by participating in and observing ongoing group interaction. The courses would be run by consultants experienced in and committed to this training technique.
4. Each programme would consist of seven one-week courses. All would take place over the same time period (two months) and at two independent training centres.
5. Evaluation would consist of four measurement samples. The first sample to be taken a few weeks prior to training; the second on the first day of each course; the third on the last day of each course; and the fourth and final sample would be taken three to four months after the training programme had ended.

Before going on to discuss the programmes in more detail there are two areas that need to be described. The first area is that of goals and assumptions of the training; the second is the specific context in which training was to take place.

Training goals

Many theorists have outlined a number of social skill training goals (Buchanan and Brunstetter, 1959; Schein and Bennis, 1965; Campbell and Dunnette, 1968). There will be no attempt to look at these in detail here but the reader will find a summary in Cooper (1973; 1975).

In the present study it was felt that a slavish adherence to any of the above lists of training goals would not be helpful, since (1) this was an industrial project and the training had to be related to the specific needs of the parent industry, (2) because the project was a field study sited with a specific company, the needs of this organisation had to be taken into account, (3) and finally, as the two programmes were to be run by two independent teams of consultants, it was felt that the teams should have a certain amount of freedom in formulating their own training programmes. This allowed differences between the methodologies to be accentuated, and it also maintained a high level of personal commitment to the respective programmes by the consultants — which helped to facilitate relations between the training and the research side of the project. In the main it amounted to letting the trainers 'do their own thing' within the bounds dictated by the Industry's and the company's training needs.

The company's needs were not formally stated but were generated by a number of liaison meetings involving research staff, HCITB officials, consultants, company training personnel and company site management. With the aid of HCITB officers, the Industry's needs were canvassed by the researchers prior to the project's commencement. The kinds of social skill training outcome deemed desirable by the Industry on the basis of our short survey included (1) increased perceptiveness of social cues, (2) increased understanding of inter- and intra-working group relations, (3) improved performance of behavioural skills related to social cues, (4) increased awareness and understanding of social norms operating in the work environment and (5) a general increase in the sensitivity of staff to their social environment. These proved useful guidelines to the training consultants and researchers.

The industrial context

For research purposes we required a host company that could provide a number of similar sites, to establish a research population from which a research sample could be extracted. Ideally, we wanted sites which (1) provided a variety of catering activities, (2) had a range of work-roles to create a wide base for generalisations of research findings, (3) would be typical of a broad section of the Industry, and (4) would provide organisations with sub-populations that would be relatively balanced with regard to function, structure, management/staff ratio, etc.

The sites

Four sites were chosen. All belonged to the Motorway Division of an international hotel and catering organisation. The four establishments were all situated along the UK's main North-South motorway or highway route (the M1). Since the M1 is the largest and longest UK motorway, restaurants and other activities along it have to comply to strict central government regulations. There are, therefore, both strong statutory and environmental pressures on motorway service areas to maintain organisational conformity.

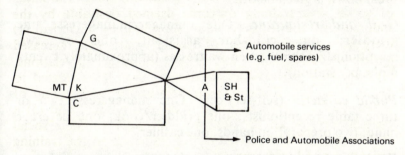

MT = Motor transport cafeteria; G = grill and restaurant; C = cafeteria;
K = kitchen; A = administration offices; Sh & St = shop and stores.

Figure 10.1

A typical service area consists of several interlocking service units. The sites we chose had the basic lay-out shown in Figure 10.1. As can be seen, the basic motorway site unit consists of a kitchen, motor transport cafeteria, public cafeteria, grill and restaurant, and a 'peripheral' service area (i.e. the fuel and spares services, shop, stores, motoring organisation offices, motorway personnel depots and police stations). Some of these peripheral site activities are not under the control of the operating company but, nevertheless, they have to be liaisoned with and, from time to time, they make demands on the organisation. For training and research purposes the authors were mainly concerned with the grill and restaurant and cafeteria areas.

Staffing

Because the sites are generally remote from urban areas, staff often must travel some distance to the work location. The company typically makes special transport arrangements in this connection. There are usually three shifts — two day shifts and a night shift — and staff tend to be permanently assigned to one particular shift. For training and research purposes, only day shifts were used. There were on average ten to twelve personnel per unit per shift; a typical breakdown is given below.

Grill and restaurant. One manager/manageress; one griddler; one cold-bar assistant; one or two receptionist/cashier; seven waitresses (approximately twenty tables per station).

Public cafeteria (self-service). One manageress; two or three table receptionists; one griddler/cook; one beverage hand; two preparation hands; one cashier.

Kitchen. One manager; one cook (assistant manager); one assistant cook; two preparation hands; one to three porters including wash-up.

The training programmes

The research sample

Courses were run at independent training centres so that the centres were completely outside company influence. Because most participants had heavy home commitments the courses were all non-residential. Special transport facilities were made available to all participants between their homes and the training centres. Participants were drawn from the staffs of the major units of grills and cafeterias. 106 persons participated in the training programme. Course membership was kept as heterogeneous (as the circumstances would allow) in terms of organisational roles. A typical course might consist of between seven to nine persons: a cashier, a table receptionist, a manageress, a counter assistant and three waitresses. Each programme consisted of seven consecutively run one-week courses.

The staff from the grills and cafeterias of two motorway sites underwent training along programme A lines and the trainees from two comparable sites were trained along programme B lines.

The course programmes and schedules

Schedule A: The 'Skills' Course.

Day 1	Introduction	Participants introduce themselves to each other.
	Motorway service	Discussion of what is involved in motorway service—the people—business.
	Social skill	Discussion: What is it? How socially skilled do participants consider themselves? How does social skill relate to job performance?
	Assignment	Short exercise for participants on motor service.
Day 2	Observing people	There's more to it than meets the eye! . . . seeing is not believing.
	Understanding people	Closer observation; the kinds of cues to look for.
	Assignment	'As I see it'-exercise on person perception.

Day 3	First impressions	The art of making friends . . . and getting on with the boss.
	Customer needs	Recognising and meeting needs.
	Assignment	Personal project work on getting on with customers and colleagues.
Day 4	Putting it over	How to give information.
	Dealing with customers	The awkward, the amorous or the merely complaining.
	Assignment	Project work.
Day 5	Practical sessions	Customer/waiter role-playing exercise—feedback from colleagues.
	Personal appearances	Dress, make-up . . . discussion of standards.
	Private sessions	What I do well . . . and not so well!
	Summing up	Discussion: What to do next.
	Assignment	Project work.

The programme was varied to suit individual course needs. Assignments were often begun in class and completed in the evening. Each participant was provided with a folder in which course notes could be stored together with 'hand-outs' from the instructor. Each participant was given a course schedule.

Schedule B: The 'Social' Course: T-group orientation

Day 1	Introductions; sharing and comparing perceptions of the participants' roles; exploring differences, looking at stereotypes and noticing how various role functions relate to each other.

Day 2	Looking at interpersonal problems within a restaurant context; exploring the similarities and differences of the problems faced by the members of different units.
Day 3	Direct focusing on the interpersonal behaviour of group members; exercises to facilitate giving and receiving personal feedback.
Day 4	Same as for day 3.
Day 5	Same as for day 3 but with an emphasis on the development of 'action plans' related to the back-home situation.

A brief description of the main teaching technique was given by the consultants concerned: '"Laboratory methods" are simply teaching techniques which utilise the data generated from the group of trainees. Thus the participants learn from their own experience as it is occurring . . . participants learn *by doing* rather than by a passive, purely cognitive learning process.'

As stressed earlier, the consultants played a major part in moulding training goals. The consultants for programme B explicitly stated their formulation of training goals.

1.   To improve participants' ability to work effectively with other members of his/her unit by: (a) facilitating more open communication between different roles and levels; (b) developing understanding of the functioning of work groups; (c) exploring differences in perception of the job situation and confronting role relationship problems.
2.   To increase participants' awareness of the impact of their own behaviour on others.
3.   To increase self and other-awareness by examining and testing their assumptions and perceptions about their own role and behaviour — and of other people to whom they relate.

Evaluation measures

A number of measures for assessing social skills have been described by researchers (Harrison, 1971; Cooper and Mangham, 1971). The basic approach of these researchers has been to sample the trainee's perception of himself and his associates' perception of his on-the-job behaviour. A similar approach was followed in the present study although certain refinements had been made in the measurement instruments. Measurements were taken at four points in time (as discussed earlier) in the following areas: (1) the trainee's perception of himself; (2) work associates' perception of the trainee's behaviour on the job; (3) the customer's perception of trainee service.

Perception measures.   Bi-polar adjectival scales similar to the measure of Osgood *et al.* (1957) were used, with the exception that the concepts were generated by the individual trainees using a modified form of Kelly's [1955] role repertory test.

Behaviour measures.   The open-ended behaviour change inventory of Bunker (1965) was used. This measure utilised reports of trainee behavioural change by his work associates and is now well-established as an evaluation tool (Valiquet, 1968; Moscow, 1969).

A further measure of behavioural change was obtained from a post-course questionnaire. This questionnaire asked trainees to outline planned behavioural change in the light of their training experience. They were questioned closely as to the practicability of their plans. There was also a later check on the implementation of trainees' plans.

The instructors had access to trainees requiring any help after the training period, and the researchers were also able to observe the trainees at a number of spaced intervals over the evaluation period.

Finally, information about labour turnover was available.

Customer measure. Customers' perception of trainee service before and after the training period was obtained at random points in time. This was done by asking customers to fill in a simplified form of the bi-polar adjectival scales described above.

Controls and comparisons

The trainees in both types of course were given the same questionnaires, which allowed for the direct comparison of change measures across types of training. In effect, each set of courses became the control for the other. In addition, it was decided to have the trainee act as his own control to examine changes over time. This was particularly feasible in connection with the perception measures and with some of the behavioural measures. Two measures were taken prior to training (four weeks before and just before training), so that later measures (just after, and four to six months after training) could be compared. The Bunker inventory was also administered in a similar fashion. In this way each trainee was uniquely controlled for a 'training' versus 'no training' effect.

Concluding remarks

The intention of this project was twofold. First, to design social skill training programmes to meet the needs of the Catering Industry. Second, to evaluate these programmes in a controlled way. It is intended that evaluation would provide answers to the following questions:

1. In what ways have the trainees changed as a result of the two training programmes?
2. How long-lasting are the effects of the training?
3. Does the training have any impact on the customer's view of service?
4. Does a trainee have a clearer understanding of his associates' work-roles as a result of training?

It is hoped that the research relating to this study will not only provide some answers to the above questions but also that it will highlight the process of learning itself — the unfolding of techniques used by the various trainer approaches and styles, and the transfer of learning to the work environment.

A review of the results of this evaluative inquiry can be found in Cooper (1973).

References

Argyle, M., *Social interaction,* Methuen: London 1969.

Buchanan, P.C. and Brunstetter, P.H., A research approach to management development. I and II, *Journal of the American Society of Training Directors,* 1959, 12: 18-27.

Bunker, D.R., Individual applications of laboratory training, *Journal of Applied Behavioral Science,* 1965, 1: 131-148.

Campbell, J.P. and Dunnette, M.D., Effectiveness of T-group experiences in managerial training and development, *Psychology Bulletin,* 1968, 70: 73-104.

Cooper, C.L. and Mangham, I.L., *T-groups: a survey of research,* Wiley: London 1971.

Cooper, C.L., *Group Training for Individual and Organizational Development,* S. Karger: Basel, Switzerland, 1973.

Cooper, C.L., *Theories of Group Processes,* Wiley: London, 1975.

Damodaran, L., Social skills in the hotel and catering industry. Unpublished manuscript, Brunel University: London 1967.

Harrison, R., Cognitive change and participation in a sensitivity training laboratory, *Journal of Consulting Psychology,* 1966, 30: 517-520.

Harrison, R., Problems in design and interpretation of research in human relations training, *Journal of Applied Behavioral Science,* 1971, 7: 71-87.

Kelly, G.A., *The psychology of personal constructs,* Norton: New York 1955

Miles, M., Human relations training: processes and outcomes, *Journal of Consulting Psychology,* 1960, 7: 301-306.

Moscow, D., *T-group training in the Netherlands: an evaluation and cross-cultural comparison,* Mens en Ondemening: Leiden 1969.

Osgood, C.E.; Suci, G.A., and Tannenbaum, P.H., *The measurement of meaning,* University of Illinois: Urbana 1957.

Pickard, O.G.; Thomas, L.F.; Snapes, A.W., and Clare, J.N., Research into training for skills in the hotel and catering industry. Unpublished manuscript, Ealing Technical College: London 1969.

Schein, E.H. and Bennis, W.G., *Personal and organizational change through group methods,* Wiley: New York 1965.

Tannenbaum, R.; Weschler, I.R., and Massarik, F., *Leadership and organization,* McGraw-Hill: New York 1961.

Valiquet, M.I., Individual change in a management development program, *Journal of Applied Behavioral Science,* 1968, 4: 313-325.

Vegt, R. van der, Personal communication regarding ongoing research, University of Utrecht: Utrecht 1970.

Whyte, W.F., *Human relations in the restaurant industry,* McGraw-Hill: New York 1948.

Section D
Characteristics of groups

This section will look at some research done on different aspects of the learning environment of experiential groups: examining the personality profiles of group participants and leaders; exploring the effect of physical contact on self-disclosure of participants; and isolating the impact of structured exercise-based groups and more unstructured experiential approaches and their impact on the psychological conditions of learning.

11 Personality profiles of experiential group participants and leaders

This study examined the differences in personality between experiential group participants and trainers and between each of these with the general population norms. It was found that trainees differed only slightly from the normative sample, while trainers were significantly different and in a positive direction (e.g., better adjusted, open, spontaneous). Trainers were also found to have more positive profiles than trainees.

There has been an enormous growth in the experiential learning group movement (e.g., T-groups, encounter groups, etc.) over the last decade (Levine and Cooper, 1976). As these human potential methods grow in popularity, so they tend to attract more and more ciriticsm, indeed, that they are disruptive to the well-being of individual participants (Crawshaw, 1969). It has been argued specifically that the two main reasons why these group experiences are potentially dangerous are because they attract (a) participants who are seeking and in need of therapy (i.e., individuals who are personally or psychometrically vulnerable) (Lakin, 1969), and (b) trainers who are less well adjusted and/or personality-wise unsuited to the role of group leader (Lieberman *et al.*, 1973). It was felt that it might be useful in this context briefly to examine these two contentions.

Methods

The subjects of our study were 227 male participants and thirty-two trainers in twelve management development training programmes using experiential small group methods. Each of these programmes was broken down into a number of small groups, so that participants were working generally in groups of between eight and twelve fellow trainees. The participants were middle to senior level UK managers, drawn from a variety of industrial organisations. All these experiential training groups were organised on a one-week residential basis and had a number of important characteristics in common, which Cooper (1975) suggests are essential to all experiential learning groups; 'process' as distinct from 'content' orientation, concerned with the development of human relations as opposed to technical skills, structure of the group to a large extent determined by the participants themselves, use of small group and inter-group techniques, etc.

In order to examine the notions implicit in the arguments put forward by Lakin (1969), Lieberman *et al.* (1973) and others about the personality predispositions of participants and trainers, we administered the 16PF Inventory (Cattell *et al.*, 1970) to our total sample of trainees and trainers just before the start of their training programme. The 16PF was chosen as our psychometric measure because it was felt to be one of the most comprehensive and widely validated of the personality inventories, it contains several subscales which seem to be reliably related to various aspects of anxiety or disturbance and it could be easily and quickly administered. Form C was used which is self-administering and consists of 105 three-alternative choice items, comprising sixteen scales (four scales were omitted in our study because of their low reliability with our sample). The following twelve source trait personality factors were used (the first of the bipolar traits mentioned for each factor represents the low score end of the continuum): factor A: the sizothymia versus affectothymia source trait, which corresponds most closely to reserved, detached, critical, aloof versus warm-hearted, outgoing, easygoing, participating, respectively; factor C: the higher ego strength versus emotional instability trait, which is one of dynamic integration and maturity as opposed to uncontrolled, disorganised, general emotionality; factor E: the submissiveness versus dominance trait, which can be dichotomised as obedience, docile, accommodating, as opposed to assertive, aggressive, and competitive; factor F: the trait of desurgency versus surgency, or the differentiation between the sober and serious personality and the enthusiastic, happy-go-lucky one; factor H: the threctia versus parmia source trait, the shy, timid, threat-sensitive, as opposed to the adventurous, socially bold personality; factor I: the harria versus premsia trait, which is comparable to Eysenck's (1954) tough-minded typology; factor L: the alaxia or 'trusting and free of jealousy' versus protension, or 'suspicious and hard to fool' trait; factor O: the untroubled adequacy versus guilt proneness trait, ranging from self-assured and confident to apprehensive and troubled; factor Q1: reflects the continuum of conservatism to radicalism, or from rigidity and upholding established ideas to experimenting and free thinking; factor Q2: assesses the dichotomous trait of being group adherent at one end of the continuum to self-sufficient at the other; factor Q3: low self-concept integration (undisciplined self-concept) to high self-concept control (following self-image); factor Q4: low ergic tension or relaxed and unfrustrated to high tension or frustrated and overwrought. Considering the goals (Miles, 1960) of experiential learning groups, one might think of the following as negative 16PF directions: A-, C-, E-, F-, H-, I-, L +, O-, Q1-, Q2-, Q3-, and Q4 +. Six of these scales make up the second stratum factor (QII) of anxiety/adjustment, they are: C-, H-, L +, O-, Q3- and Q4 +.

Results and discussion

Before examining how experiential group participants and trainers differ from the normative population on the various scales of the 16PF Inventory, we felt it might be useful to see, in the first instance, if, and how, participants differed significantly from the trainers. Table 11.1 provides the means for the total trainee and trainer populations on the twelve 16PF scales and the t values of the difference between them.

It can be seen that there are significant or approaching significant differences between the trainers and participants on *all* but factors E, F, and Q2 of the 16PF. Trainers tend to be significantly more 'outgoing', 'experimenting', 'venturesome' and 'tender-minded' than participants, while the latter tend to be more 'tense', 'apprehensive' 'suspicious' and 'controlled' than trainers.

In order more directly to test the specific contentions above, we compared our sample of trainees and trainers with the normative information available for the 16PF. We therefore converted our raw scores on the 16PF to sten scores and compared these to the 1969 norm average for form C of the 16PF (unfortunately, these norms are based on American data, since no British norms are yet available).

From Table 11.2, it can be noted that experiential group participants differed from the general population norms on only two factors of the 16PF (E and Q2). They tended to be more 'assertive', more 'tender-minded', more 'experimenting' and more 'self-sufficient' than the normative population and less 'suspicious', less 'apprehensive', less 'controlled' and less 'tense'. The psychometric *Gestalt* of the experiential group leader is a very positive one indeed, a picture of a more open, well-adjusted, flexible and supportive person than average.

In summary, the composite results above therefore do not seem to support the contention that experiential group participants or trainers represent the 'psychological fringes' of society. In respect of participants they are very similar to the psychometric profile of the wider community, while the trainers are significantly better adjusted, open and spontaneous than the norm.

Table 11.1 Mean trainer and participant scores on the 16PF and t-tests for differences between them

16PF factor	Mean trainer score (n = 32)	Mean participant score (n = 227)	t value	Probability
A	8.99	8.32	2.59	< 0.02
C	7.95	7.35	2.14	< 0.05
E	6.89	6.88	—	NS
F	6.70	6.79	—	NS
H	7.63	7.01	1.85	< 0.10
I	7.25	5.52	7.00	< 0.001
L	4.31	5.39	-4.03	< 0.001
O	3.95	5.46	-4.82	< 0.001
Q1	8.46	6.80	6.22	< 0.001
Q2	6.72	6.99	—	NS
Q3	6.65	7.92	-4.11	< 0.001
Q4	4.49	5.07	-1.94	< 0.05

NS = Not significant

Table 11.2 Mean trainer and participant sten scores on the 16PF

16PF factor	Trainer sten score	Participant sten score	Norm average
A	6	5-6	5-6
C	6	5-6	5-6
E	7	7	5-6
F	5-6	5-6	5-6
H	5-6	5	5-6
I	7	5-6	5-6
L	4-5	5-6	5-6
O	4	5-6	5-6
Q1	7	5-6	5-6
Q2	7-8	8	5-6
Q3	4-5	5	5-6
Q4	4-5	5	5-6

Since raw scores are not whole numbers, approximate stens have been selected.

References

Cooper, C.L., *Theories of group processes,* John Wiley & Sons: London 1975.

Crawshaw, R., How sensitive is sensitivity training?, *American Journal of Psychiatry,* 1969, 126, 870-3.

Lakin, M., Some ethical issues in sensitivity training, *American Psychology,* 1969, 24, 923-8.

Levine, N. and Cooper, C.L., T-groups twenty years on. A prophecy. *Human Relations,* 1976, 29, 1-23.

Lieberman, M.A., Yalom, I.D., and Miles, M.B., *Encounter groups: first facts,* Basic Books: New York, 1973.

Miles, M.B., *Human relations training: processes and outcomes, Journal of Counselling Psychology,* 1960, 7: 301-6.

12 Physical encounter and self-disclosure*

This study investigated the hypothesis that physical and body contact exercises within an encounter group reduce barriers between people and increase their willingness to self-disclose. Ss participating in these exercises (n = 18), in contrast to nine controls, showed a significant increase in self-disclosure following the group session.

It has been suggested by many advocates of the human potential movement, particularly those involved in encounter groups (Rogers, 1971), that the elimination of the taboos concerning physical contact between people may enable them to be more open and self-disclosing with one another. The growth in techniques such as body touching and exploration is very noticeable in current basic encounter and sensitivity training experiences (Boderman, 1972). In fact, a variety of new experiential methods based almost entirely on non-verbal forms of interaction has emerged within the last several years, such as sensory and body awareness groups, *Gestalt* groups and body movement groups.

As more people participate in such activities, one may ask

* Reprinted with permission of the publishers from: Cooper C.L. and Bowles D., 'Physical Encounter and Self-disclosure', *Psychological Reports*, 1973, 33, 451-4.

'do encounter groups with exercises designed to encourage physical and body contact between people lead to increased self-disclosure or the willingness to talk more openly to others?' The purpose of this study was to investigate the possibility of a relationship between physical contact and self-disclosure.

Method

Ss were 116 first-year social science undergraduates enrolled in the introductory course in psychology at the University of Southampton. Students were provided with a detailed handout describing an encounter group and were asked if they would like to attend a two-hour encounter session during their free time. It was made quite clear that it was not compulsory; this is consistent with the usual practice in encounter group activities of recruiting volunteers only. Twenty-seven students volunteered and were randomly assigned to two experimental groups and a control group ($ns = 9$).

A problem in empirical evaluation of such a group is that one is dealing with a self-selected population. In this study, for example, volunteers may be psychometrically different in some important way from non-volunteers, such differences might limit generalisation from the results. Jourard (1971) has suggested, for instance, that self-disclosure may be associated with certain personality traits generally characterised by an 'inability or unwillingness to establish close, confiding relationships with others'. Two such characteristics have been found to be related to self-disclosure: extraversion (Swenson, 1968) and neuroticism (Pederson & Breglio, 1968). It was necessary, therefore, to see if the volunteers differed significantly on these attributes from the non-volunteers. The Eysenck Personality Inventory, which provided measures of extraversion (E-scale) and neuroticism (N-scale), was administered to all first-year students.

The means and standard deviations for the volunteers on the E-scale and N-scale were 11.42 ± 4.48 and 11.32 ± 4.18 respectively; and for the non-volunteers 11.34 ± 3.14 and 11.69 ± 3.98 respectively. A two-way analysis of variance indicated no significant difference between encounter group volunteers (N = 27) and non-volunteers (N = 89) on the E-scale (F = 2.20, df = 1/114) or the N-scale (F < 1.00). Thus, with respect to extraversion and neuroticism (personality variables known to be related to self-disclosure), there were no measurable differences between these two groups.

Jourard's sixty-item Self-disclosure Scale was divided into two separate thirty-item forms, one consisting of odd items and the other of even items. Two forms were used to minimise the effect of Ss remembering previous responses. Odd-even reliability is reported at .85 (Jourard, 1971). Test-retest stability was .76 (N = 18). The statements included in the questionnaire ranged from relatively non-threatening ones such as 'my favourite beverages, and the ones I don't like' to 'what I think and feel about religion; my personal religious views', to highly personal topics such as 'the factors of my present sex life — including knowledge of how I get sexual gratification, problems that I might have, and with whom I have relations, if anybody'. The instructions on the questionnaire were adapted so that each S was asked to indicate which of the three following categories applied to each statement: (a) perfectly willing to talk to the group about; (b) less willing but still prepared to talk to the group about, and (c) unwilling to talk to the group about. In order to minimise social desirability bias, that is, a bias that might encourage Ss to say that they were 'perfectly willing to talk about all items,' it was made clear to them that they were likely to talk about these topics during or after the encounter group if the majority indicated a willingness to do so.

All Ss, both experimentals and controls, filled out the thirty odd-item self-disclosure form just before participating or listening to the encounter group and the thirty even-item form just after the group session.

The Encountertapes designed by Human Development

Institute of Bell & Howell, a self-learning programme (a leader is not required) of interpersonal exercises for groups of between eight and ten persons, were used. There are ten sessions and detailed instructions for each are presented on a set of audio-tape recordings. In this study the first session only was used, which included a basic encounter group of several exercises requiring extensive physical and body contact. There were three basic activities: the first was entitled *impressions* and this involved group members standing in a circle, with one member at a time going around the circle stopping in front of each person. Each S was asked to touch each person in turn, look directly at him, and give him/her their first impression. The second exercise was called *break-in.* Group members stood in a circle and one at a time each individual stepped outside and then tried to 'break in' the group. The other group members were instructed to link arms and to prevent the person from breaking in. The third session was entitled *rolling.* With the group standing in a circle, each individual in turn goes to the centre of the circle, relaxes as completely as he can, falls into the arms of the other group members, and allows himself to be passed around from member to member. After each of the three activities, a time-limited discussion period was provided in which participants are asked to discuss their feelings about what they had just done.

The eighteen experimental Ss were randomly divided into two groups of nine students each (five males and four females in each group); they did the exercises from the tapes without guidance from the authors or other trainers/facilitators. The nine control Ss did not engage in the physical and body contact activities but merely listened to the same Encounter-tape session. In addition, the controls were asked to discuss what they might have felt like had they participated in the exercises described on the Encountertape. This discussion took as long as the discussion for the experimental groups. Including a control group with a group discussion equivalent in duration to that of the experimental groups permitted separation of possible effects of physical and body contact.

Results and discussion

The means and standard deviations for the self-disclosure scores of the experimental (Encountertape participants) and control Ss (Encountertape listeners) are presented in Table 12.1.

Table 12.1 Pre- and post-test means and standard deviations of self-disclosure scores

Group		M*	SD
Experimental tape participants	pre	11.22	14.87
	post	6.00	12.07
Control tape listeners	pre	11.88	9.87
	post	12.00	10.24

*High score indicates low willingness to self-disclose.

t tests for correlated samples were calculated to assess the change in Ss' willingness to self-disclose before and after the Encountertapes. There was a significant difference between pre- and post-test scores in the direction of greater willingness to self-disclose for Ss who participated in the physical contact exercises t = 2.62, df = 17, p < .02, two-tailed test), but no significant difference for those who merely listened to the tapes but did not participate t = .26, df = 8). A t test for independent samples was used to calculate the significance of the difference between the change score means (difference score from pre- to post-test) between the experimental and control Ss. Experimental Ss moved significantly more in the direction of increased self-disclosure following participation in the Encountertapes than the control Ss (t = 1.97, df = 25, p = .05). No pre-score difference between these groups was found (t = .12, df = 25).

It seems from this evidence there is some relationship between encounter group exercises involving physical or body contact and the increased willingness for self-disclosure. This is interesting in view of the fact that encounter groups are generally held for periods longer than the two hours used here. There are, however, a number of points we would like to make about the present study. First, the study examined the change in one's willingness to self-disclose by a self-report measure as opposed to judges' assessment of actual self-disclosure. Many have argued that this is one of the weaknesses in Jourard's work although a number of validation studies support his methodology (Jourard, 1961). In this study, it was felt justifiable to use a self-report measure of self-disclosure as long as Ss had a reasonable expectation that the topics in the questionnaire might be used in an actual discussion. Subsequent interviews indicated that this was the case. Second, a better control condition might have been to require control Ss to watch a video-tape recording of one of the experimental groups performing the Encountertape session. Then either they could have listened to the experimental group during their discussion or discussed among themselves how they might have felt doing the exercises in their group. Although this control condition would have been better, it was decided not to use it because it was felt that the filming and recording (with attendant lights and cameramen) might have been inhibiting. Third, the study was limited in the sense that no attempt was made to assess the long-term effect of these physical contact exercises on self-disclosure. It may only be a temporary phenomenon which affects immediate willingness to self-disclose but dissipates over time. Encounter group advocates might argue, however, that this is sufficient consequence, since within the training situation, a willingness to disclose one's self helps to create an atmosphere in which the primary aim of the experience can be achieved, namely, enhanced self-awareness.

References

Boderman, A., Freed, D.W., & Kinnucan, M.T., Touch me, like me: testing an encounter group assumption, *Journal of Applied Behavioral Science,* 1972, 8, 527-533.

Jourard, S., Self-disclosure patterns in British and American college students, *Journal of Social Psychology,* 1961, 54, 315-320.
Jourard, S., *Self-disclosure,* New York: Wiley, 1971.
Pederson, D., & Breglio, U., Personality correlates of actual self-disclosure, *Psychological Reports,* 1968, 22, 495-501.
Rogers, C.R., *Encounter groups,* London: Allen Lane, Penguin Press, 1971.
Schutz, W.C., *Joy,* New York: Grove, 1967.
Stanley, G., & Bownes, A., Self-disclosure and neuroticism, *Psychological Reports,* 1966, 18, 350.
Swenson, C., Self-disclosure as a function of personality variables, *Proceedings of the American Psychological Association,* 1968, 3, 21-22.

13 Structured exercise-based groups and the psychological conditions of learning

This study investigated the hypothesis that unstructured experiential learning groups for managers produce more psychological disturbance than more structured exercise-based ones. Three unstructured/semistructured and three structured groups were compared, a total of 104 trainees. Two measures of disturbance were used: a personality inventory (16PF questionnaire) and peer/trainee ratings of disturbance. Although none of the six groups were found to change significantly in the direction of emotional instability or increased anxiety (scales C and QII from the 16PF questionnaire), all three structured exercise-based groups were found to have more negative changes on a variety of other personality dimensions and to have the highest number of peer-rated casualties. The relevance of these findings is discussed in relation to the theory of Argyris (1967) of psychological success and failure of experiential groups.

Introduction

It has been suggested (Gottschalk, 1966; Crawshaw, 1969; Mann, 1970) in recent years that experiential learning groups (e.g., sensitivity training or T-groups, encounter groups, etc.) are psychologically dangerous to an unacceptably high number of their participants. There are a number of case studies (Jaffe and Scherl, 1969) and anecdotal reports (Gottschalk and Pattison, 1969), together with some empirical studies (Reddy, 1970; Yalom and Lieberman, 1971), which purport to support this viewpoint. The Yalom and Lieberman ·study represents the most comprehensive empirical investigation to date, claiming approximately a 10 per cent casualty rate among its 170 subjects. There were, however, some serious methodological difficulties with this study which limit its usefulness. First, the source of data was undergraduate students and not managers, social workers, teachers or other professional people, toward whom the market for this type of group training is in the main directed. Second, the investigators assigned these students to ten different group experiences (sensitivity training, *Gestalt* therapy, psychodrama, psychoanalytic, transactional analysis, sensory awareness, marathon, synanon, personal growth and encounter tape groups) *on a random basis,* which may have increased the risk of disturbance or stress, since a large proportion of participants who normally attend these groups (in the wider community) self-select their own training programme, partly on the basis of its appropriateness and partly, it might be hypothesised, on their own assessment of their capacity to cope psychologically with the experience. And finally, it is arguable that informing experiential group participants about the possibility of 'considerable emotional upsets', as the investigators did, before the start of the experience minimises (as they suggested), the psychological risk to participants. Nevertheless, this study raised the most wide-ranging questions about the damaging effects of these groups and also highlighted some of the possible contributory factors.

It should be mentioned, however, that there is some evidence available which contradicts the direction of the results of the above study. For example, Ross *et al.* (1971) found that of an estimated 2900 experiential group participants in the city of Cincinnati, less than 1 per cent (forty-nine) were reported by 148 psychiatrists in the community as becoming acutely disturbed and needing psychiatric attention as a consequence of their experience (over a five-year period). It has also been found that experiential learning groups may be *less stressful* than university examinations (Lubin and Lubin, 1971) or perceptual isolation experiments of varying degrees of intensity (Lubin and Zuckerman, 1969) and may indeed allow people to cope better with family and friendship relationships (Cooper, 1974).

As we can see, a great deal of research is currently available (and in process) to assess the *extent* of the psychological cost of experiential learning groups. Very little is known, however, about the characteristics of the group experience that might be responsible for psychological disturbance. One variable that has recently been considered (Watson, 1972; Bradford and Eoyang, 1975) a possible contributory source of stress is the *unstructured* nature of some of these groups. It has been suggested that unstructured group experiences, as distinct from the structured exercise-based ones (Pfeiffer and Jones, 1972; Kolb *et al.,* 1971), are more tension-producing and anxiety-provoking and as a consequence more potentially damaging. Bradford and Eoyang (1975) argue that structured exercises can provide psychological safety because 'they are initiated by somebody else and have set rules and procedures, and are less threatening than having the individual take the initiative on his own'. This may be why there has been a movement in recent years toward exercise-based group training. The purpose of this study was to investigate the hypothesis that unstructured experiential learning groups are more likely to produce psychological disturbance than more structured exercise-based ones.

Methods

Subjects and training programmes

The experiential learning group participants were middle to senior level managers from a variety of industrial organisations. There were 104 trainees and fifteen staff group leaders (frequently referred to as trainers or facilitators). The participants were drawn from different group-training programmes organised by management consultancy organisations. All six groups were organised on a one-week residential basis and had a number of important characteristics in common, which Tannenbaum *et al.* (1961) suggest are essential to all experiential-learning groups. First, they were all primarily 'process-orientated' as distinct from 'content-orientated'. That is, the primary emphasis was on the feeling level of communications rather than solely on the informational or conceptual level. This is accomplished by focusing on the here-and-now behaviour and themes that develop in the group. And second, these programmes were designed so that learning took place primarily in *small groups,* allowing a high level of participation, involvement and free communications. One lab training programme (composed of three small groups) was run along traditional T-group lines as described by Tannenbaum *et al.* (1961), that is, unstructured and non-directive. Two other programmes were semi-structured, that is, they used experiential-based exercises on the model of Pfeiffer and Jones (1972) but within a flexible laboratory design. Participants were encouraged to identify their own learning objectives and to select those structured exercises that might meet these objectives. And finally, three programmes were based, in the main, on pre-determined learning goals and associated exercises, pre-planned for the training week. We therefore had gradations of learning environments from highly structured and pre-planned through semi-structured and non-directive.

Measures of psychological disturbance

Two criteria of psychological disturbance were used; negative changes on the 16PF Inventory and peer ratings of disturbance.

16PF inventory. The Sixteen Personality Factor Questionnaire (Cattell *et al.,* 1970) was administered to all trainees just before the start of the first session of the training week and just after the final session. The 16PF was chosen as one measure of possible disturbance because it was felt to be one of the most comprehensive and widely validated of the personality inventories, because it contains several subscales which seem to be reliably related to various aspects of anxiety or disturbance, and because it could be easily and quickly administered. Form C was used which is self-administering and consists of 105 three-alternative-choice items, comprising sixteen scales (four scales were omitted because of their low reliability). The following twelve source trait personality factors were used (the first of the bipolar traits mentioned for each factor represents the low score end of the continuum): Factor A: the sizothymia versus affectothymia source trait, which corresponds most closely to reserved, detached, critical, aloof versus warmhearted, outgoing, easygoing, participating, respectively; Factor C: the higher ego strength versus emotional instability trait, which is one of dynamic integration and maturity as opposed to uncontrolled, disorganised, general emotionality; Factor E: the submissiveness versus dominance trait, which can be dichotomized as obedience, docile, accommodating, as opposed to assertive, aggressive, and competitive; Factor F: the trait of desurgency versus surgency, or the differentiation between the sober and serious personality and the enthusiastic, happy-go-lucky one; Factor H: the threctia versus parmia source trait, the shy, timid, threat-sensitive, as opposed to the adventurous, socially bold personality; Factor I: the harria versus premsia trait, which is comparable to Eysenck's (1954) tough-minded versus tender-minded typology; Factor L: the alaxia or 'trusting and free of jealousy' versus protension, or 'suspicious and hard to fool' trait; Factor O; the untroubled adequacy versus guilt proneness trait, ranging from self-assured and confident to apprehensive and troubled; Factor Qi: reflects the continuum of conservatism to radicalism, or from rigidity and upholding established ideas to experimenting and free thinking; Factor Q2: assesses the dichotomous trait of being group adherent at one end of the continuum to self-sufficient at the other; Factor Q3: low self-concept integration (undisciplined self-concept) to high self-concept control (following self-image); Factor Q4: low ergic tension or relaxed and unfrustrated to high tension or frustrated and overwrought. In addition to these twelve factors a thirteen scale was included was developed by Cattell *et al.* (1970) as a second stratum scale of adjustment versus anxiety (QII) and was calculated by combining six of the original source traits (C − , H − , L + , O + , Q3 − , and Q4 +). This scale has been shown to rise with anxiety stimuli (Cattell and Scheier, 1960) and to be related to neuroticism (Cattell and Scheier, 1961). Considering the goals (Miles, 1960) of experiential learning groups one might consider the following 16PF shifts as indications of negative change; A − , C − , E − , F − , H − , I − , L + , O − , Q1 − , Q2 − , Q3 − , Q4 + , and QII + .

Peer ratings of disturbance. Yalom and Lieberman (1971) found in their study that one of the best indices of disturbance (from a large number utilised) was peer or trainee ratings of those who were 'hurt' as a direct result of their group experience. It was on the basis of their findings that it was decided to use a similar measure here. All participants in all six groups were asked the following question after the last session of their training programme:

> 'Can you think of people in your group who were hurt (made worse, became overly upset), by the experience? Please describe *what happened* and to *whom* it happened. Include yourself, if this question is appropriate to you.'

For each trainee, therefore, data was available on the number of times he was named as being hurt by the other trainees (and himself). In addition, we could calculate the proportion (and means) of peer rated casualties in each group.

Results and discussion

The means and standard deviations for the 16PF scores for the structured, semi-structured and unstructured groups are presented in Table 13.1; t tests for correlated means were calculated to assess the change on the 16PF traits before and after the experiential learning groups.

Groups 2 and 3 show the most significant (or in the direction of) negative change, based on our assumptions of experiential learning group goals and associated 16PF change discussed earlier. Group 2 shows a significant increase in desurgency (F) and threat-sensitivity (H). Group 3 shows two negative changes, and one significant increase in undisciplined self-conflict (Q3) and one in the direction of submissiveness (E). Group 1, on the other hand, shows mixed results with one significant positive change in self-confidence (O) and one in the direction of being relaxed and tranquil (Q4); and two negative changes in the direction of greater submissiveness (E) and undisciplined self-conflict (Q3). In contrast, group 4, the unstructured learning experience, shows a number of positive changes; two significant positive increases in emotional stability (C) and being more relaxed and unfrustrated (Q4); and one directional positive increase in greater trust in relationships (L). In terms of 16PF shifts, the semi-structured groups seem to have more positive changes than the structured but more negative ones than the unstructured groups. Group 5 shows one significant positive change on group dependency (Q2). Group 6 indicates mixed results as well with one significant increase in tenseness and frustration (Q4) and two findings, one positive and one negative, in the direction of significance (trusting, L; desurgency, F). Even though there is a trend in the results indicating more negative change the more structured the experience, it must be noted that there is no significantly negative change for any of the six groups on Factors C (emotional instability) or QII (anxiety) — two traits on which one might have expected psychological disturbance to have manifested itself.

The peer ratings, which Yalom and Lieberman (1971, p. 19) suggest is the most accurate mode of identifying casualties in experiential groups, may help to clarify the above trend. In the three structured groups the proportion of trainees named as being hurt by two or more fellow trainees was 13.6, 21.4 and 9.5 per cent; a mean of 14.8 per cent. On the other hand, no member of the unstructured group (group 4) was named as hurt. It the semi-structured groups (5 and 6) the proportions were 8.7 and 0.0 per cent, respectively. The number of trainees nominated as hurt increases, therefore, as the learning environment becomes more structured. If we calculate an overall mean (based on trainee hurt scores of 0, 1, 2 . . . times named) and standard deviation for all the structured groups (m = 0.616, SD = 0.916, n = 39) and the unstructured/semi-structured groups taken together (m = 0.237, SD = 0.510, n = 65), we find a significant difference (t = 2.373, df = 104, p = 0.02) between them on the average number of times trainees were named as hurt. Nevertheless, one should note that the proportion of participants named as hurt at least twice in the structured groups is still, some would argue, rather small. These results are rather illuminating, however, in view of the many suggestions that the recent development of structured exercise-based groups were in part a reaction to the potential danger of unstructured groups.

The most likely explanation of these findings is one suggested by Argyris (1967) in an article 'On the Future of Laboratory Education'. Drawing on the work of Lewin *et al.* (1944, pp. 333—78) he developed a theory which suggested that the necessary learning conditions for psychological success in laboratory education were: (1) that the participant should define his/her own learning goal; (2) that he/she should develop the path to this goal; (3) that he/she should control the centrality of the needs involved, and finally (4) that he/she should control the strength of the challenge. In other words, that the individual should be responsible for his/her own re-education as much as possible. The group leader/trainer/facilitator should help to create the conditions under which the 'individuals can define their own goals, the

Table 13.1 Mean (M) and t values for significance of differences between pre- and post-test 16PF scales

	Structured experiential learning groups								
	1 (n = 16)			2 (n = 10)			3 (n = 13)		
16PF scales	M_{pre}	M_{post}	t	M_{pre}	M_{post}	t	M_{pre}	M_{post}	t
A	8.87	9.12	0.67	8.20	8.00	-0.41	10.38	10.31	-0.23
C	7.37	8.19	1.68	7.40	7.70	0.67	8.23	8.08	-0.35
E	7.06	6.50	-2.06*	5.90	6.20	0.67	6.54	5.85	-2.00*
F	6.87	6.50	-0.90	6.40	5.40	-2.37**	6.30	6.61	0.57
H	7.50	7.50	0	7.50	5.90	-4.31***	6.69	6.46	-0.41
I	5.94	5.81	-0.49	6.30	6.40	0.17	5.85	6.38	1.10
L	5.75	5.25	-1.41	5.20	4.80	-0.80	4.85	5.46	1.34
O	7.56	5.87	-3.81***	5.40	5.70	0.54	6.15	6.31	0.33
Q1	6.62	6.87	0.75	6.80	5.90	-1.59	7.23	7.08	-0.22
Q2	4.94	5.06	0.18	7.70	8.10	0.80	5.15	5.38	0.27
Q3	8.50	7.75	-2.02*	6.80	7.20	0.80	7.54	7.08	-2.14**
Q4	7.56	6.56	-2.07*	6.10	7.00	0.95	5.00	5.00	0
QII	4.65	4.43	0.93	5.19	5.45	0.84	4.92	5.19	0.38

* p < .10; ** p < .05; *** p < .01

Table 13.1 (continued)

| 16PF scales | Unstructured experiential learning group (n = 35) | | | Semi-structured experiential learning groups | | | | | |
| | | | | 5 (n = 20) | | | 6 (n = 10) | | |
	M_{pre}	M_{post}	t	M_{pre}	M_{post}	t	M_{pre}	M_{post}	t
A	7.23	7.14	-0.45	6.85	7.90	2.33**	6.50	6.50	0
C	6.88	7.43	2.17**	6.75	6.6	-0.38	7.50	8.00	0.83
E	7.37	7.20	-0.59	6.35	5.85	-1.27	7.00	7.20	0.30
F	7.23	7.17	-0.19	7.65	7.05	-1.30	7.30	6.80	-1.86*
H	7.63	7.11	-1.53	7.45	6.70	-1.19	6.40	5.60	-1.56
I	3.88	3.97	0.38	5.80	6.50	1.42	3.10	3.30	0.29
L	6.00	5.51	-1.78*	5.35	4.90	-0.90	5.70	4.30	-1.80*
O	5.23	5.23	0	5.25	5.80	1.31	4.20	4.30	0.22
Q1	7.14	6.71	-1.69	6.30	6.80	1.17	6.70	6.10	-1.50
Q2	8.14	8.43	1.04	7.90	7.20	-1.73*	7.70	6.60	-1.67
Q3	8.03	8.23	0.89	7.10	6.50	-1.41	8.70	7.90	-0.78
Q4	4.48	3.78	-2.56***	4.20	4.70	1.14	3.40	4.30	2.59**
QII	4.83	4.64	1.21	4.93	5.27	1.90*	4.25	4.45	0.60

* p < .10; ** p < .05; *** p < .01

paths to their goals, and the strength of the behaviour that they wish to overcome' (Argyris, 1967, p. 359). Structured, exercise-based experiential learning groups simply do not allow this degree of freedom. The primary responsibility for the learning experience is in the hands of the group leader; it is he who 'defines the goal, the path to the goal, the strength of the challenge, and to some extent the centrality of the needs involved'. According to Argyris these are not the conditions for psychological success, essentiality, and confirmation, but rather of psychological failure. This approach forces individuals willy-nilly into circumstances which they may not be prepared for or, in fact, be able to cope with, at a time in their own personal development which may be inappropriate or undesirable. A possible outcome, therefore, of not allowing an individual control over his own learning, in a situation which may involve highly charged personal material, may be, at the very least, an uneventful learning experience and, at worst, a potentially psychologically disturbing one. We must seriously consider the degree of control of group leaders, as Schein and Bennis (1965) suggest 'the possibilities for unconscious gratification in the change agent's role are enormous and because of their consequences (for the health of the client as well as the change agent) they must be examined'.

There are several methodological points that need to be made about this study before concluding. First, it may be that the indices used in this study may over-represent the extent of psychological disturbance. It could be argued that an *immediate* post-course assessment by the trainee himself (as in the 16PF Inventory) and particularly by his fellow trainees (as in the peer ratings) might be influenced by a negative halo effect, that is, that incidents of conflict, or direct personal feedback, might be over-dramatised. This may particularly be the case with events occurring toward the end of training which may have remained unresolved. This argument seems a very plausible one indeed, even though Yalom and Lieberman (1971) found peer ratings to be the best predictors of clinically assessed psychological disturbance. Second, as the observations of Argyris (1967) suggest, the possible contributory sources of disturbance in experiential learning groups may be many and interrelated, it would be inappropriate and irresponsible, therefore, to draw the conclusion from this study that structured, exercise-based groups lead to psychological disturbance. Rather, one might argue that this may be one factor in conjunction with others that may create the conditions under which re-educative learning may not be fully achieved. To draw any firm conclusions about experiential group casualties, further work must inevitably include a consideration of the following: the trainee (the vulnerability the individual brings with him to the group, what usually happens to him in the group, what he expects to happen in the group, and what support he has back home); the group leader (will his personality needs create conditions for psychological failure, will his behaviour in the group encourage or prevent learning); group structure (will the design of the group experience, inhibit or encourage individual and group growth, etc.). The answers to these questions and others will bring us closer to understanding the potential dangers, as well as benefits of experiential learning groups.

References

Argyris, C., On the future of laboratory education, *Journal of Applied Behavioral Science,* 1967. 3 (2): 153-183.
Bradford, D. and Eoyang, C., On the use and misuse of structured exercises, in Cooper, C.L., *Developing social skills in managers,* Macmillan: London 1976.
Cattell, R.B. and Scheier, I.H., Stimuli related to stress, neuroticism, excitation, and anxiety response patterns, *Journal of Abnormal Social Psychology,* 1969, 60: 195-204.
Cattell, R.B. and Scheier, I.H., *The meaning and measurement of neuroticism and anxiety,* Ronald Press: New York 1961.

Cattell, R.B.; Eber, H.W., and Tatsuoka, M.M., *Handbook of the 16PF Questionnaire,* IPAT: Illinois 1970.

Cooper, C.L., Psychological disturbance following T-groups: relationship between Eysenck Personality Inventory and family/friends' judgements, *British Journal of Social Work,* 1974, 4 (1): 39-49.

Crawshaw, R., How sensitive is sensitivity training?' *American Journal of Psychiatry,* 1969, 126: 870-873.

Eysenck, H.J., *The psychology of politics,* Routledge: London 1954.

Gottschalk, L.A., Psychoanalytic notes on T-groups at the human relations laboratory, Bethel, Maine, *Comprehensive Psychiatry,* 1966, 71: 472-487.

Gottschalk, L.A. and Pattison, E.M., Psychiatric perspective on T-groups and the laboratory movement: an overview, *American Journal of Psychiatry,* 1969, 126: 823-839.

Jaffe, S.L. and Scherl, D.J., Acute psychosis precipitated by T-group experiences, *Archives of General Psychiatry,* 1969, 21: 443-448.

Kolb, D.; Rubin, I.M., and McIntyre, J.M., *Organizational psychology: an experiential approach,* Prentice Hall: Englewood Cliffs 1971.

Lewin, K.; Dembo, T.; Festinger, L., and Sears, P., Level of aspiration, in Hunt, *Personality and behaviour disorders,* Ronald Press: New York 1944.

Lubin, B. and Lubin, A.W., Laboratory training stress compared with college examination stress, *Journal of Applied Behavioral Science,* 1971, 7: 502-507.

Lubin, B. and Zuckerman, M., Level of emotional arousal in laboratory training, *Journal of Applied Behavioral Science,* 1969. 5: 483-490.

Mann, E.K., Sensitivity training: should we use it?, *Training Development Journal,* 1970, 24: 44-48.

Miles, M.B., Human relations training: processes and outcomes, *Journal of Counselling Psychology,* 1960, 7: 301-306.

Pfeiffer, W. and Jones, J., *The annual handbook for group facilitators,* University Associates: Iowa 1972.

Reddy, W.B., Sensitivity training or group psychotherapy: the need for adequate screening, *International Journal of Group Psychotherapy,* 1970, 20: 366-371.

Ross, W.D.; Kligfield, M., and Whitman, R.W., Psychiatrists, patients, and sensitivity groups, *Archives of General Psychiatry,* 1971, 25: 178-280.

Schein, E.H. and Bennis, W.G., *Personal and organizational change through group methods,* John Wiley: New York 1965.

Tannenbaum, R.; Wechsler, I., and Massarik, F., *Leadership and organization,* McGraw Hill: New York 1961.

Watson, G., Nonverbal activities: why? when? how? in Dyer, *Modern theory and method in group training,* Van Nostrand & Reinhold: New York 1972.

Yalom, I.D. and Lieberman, M.A., A study of encounter group casualties, *Archives of General Psychiatry,* 1971, 25: 16-30.

Section E
The future of group work

In this extended essay the author is attempting to provide a prognostication of the future of experiential learning techniques by a detailed examination of four socio-economic trends: Anglo-American orientation of the movement, production and growth trends of advanced capitalist economies, shifting age structure and the changes in the expression of middle-class needs.

14 T-groups—twenty years on: a prophecy

This article examines the development of experiential learning groups in terms of their social values and the socio-economic conditions leading to their growth. In addition, and more importantly, it will attempt to prophesy the future of the human relations/experiential movement by a detailed examination of four socio-economic trends: Anglo-American orientation of the movement, production and growth trends of advanced capitalist economies, shifting age structure, and the changes in the expression of middle-class needs. These issues are considered in the context of the developing and developed countries separately.

It is almost thirty years since the first T-groups were developed in the United States as a new form of educational technique. Since that time, T-groups have experienced an enormous expansion and have become institutionalised into many universities, business organisations, social service agencies, and a host of other places (Bradford, Gibb, & Benne, 1964; Cooper, 1972). There are literally thousands of groups run each year, representing a wide range of different social situations and different techniques (Siroka, Siroka, & Schloss, 1971). Further, many of the techniques developed within T-groups and laboratory training situations have been incorporated in a whole range of other educational techniques, so that one can conceive of the T-group movement as having represented one of the major educational developments over the last twenty-five years. Many claims have been made about what T-groups actually teach participants, some undoubtedly wide of the mark, but there is sufficient research to indicate that T-groups can change participants under certain circumstances (Cooper & Mangham, 1971). People *can* learn to be more open with others (Rubin, 1967), more sensitive to social situations (Bass, 1962), more understanding of how other people see them (Burke & Bennis, 1961), more insightful into human behaviour (Argyris, 1965), more aware of their own feelings (French, Sherwood, & Bradford, 1966), and more adaptable and flexible in social situations (Cooper, 1971). In short, T-groups can be meaningful experiences for people. At the same time, though, there have been an increasing number of criticisms levelled against T-groups (Back, 1967; Back, 1972; Lakin, 1969), all of which point to serious questions about the methods and values involved. T-group practitioners have been accused of being anti-scientific and unconcerned with the problems of society, of showing a lack of concern for ethical issues, and of not making careful selection of participants; and, further, critics speculate that T-groups are not particularly good places for people to become sensitive. While these critics have not empirically proven their points, and certainly have not stopped T-groups from operating, they have opened up a dialogue on T-group values which should sharpen future thinking and should in the long run make the human relations movement more realistic.

What we want to do in this chapter is to continue this discussion and analyse some of the major assumptions which underlie T-group learning. But we want to formulate this analysis in terms of the future, rather than the present: how T-groups might develop over the next years and what kind of predictions we can make about the future course of their development. A critical question at this point would be, why bother to make such a prophecy at all? T-groups have been, after all, only one of the many innovations in education and social science since the end of World War II. Predicting the future of T-groups should not really give us very much useful information, since a prediction is nothing more than an educated guess about what will happen. Yet we feel that such an exercise can be quite useful, in spite of all the inherent unknowns about the future. For one thing, such an elaboration forces us to reveal the underlying assumptions about the process. In order to talk about the future, we have to conceptualise those elements of the T-group process that are influenced by external elements, and to decide in which ways these external elements are liable to change. The fact that most T-group trainers have concerned themselves with the uniqueness of each group, and on the uniqueness of social experience in general, does not really mean that T-groups have no general process nor that they are not really a particular type of social formation. Conversely, the fact that T-groups emerged when they did and where they did really reveals something critical about this type of educational innovation.

Also, a prediction forces us to reveal our underlying social assumptions. For, if we argue that T-groups can be useful social experiences and that people can learn inside them, we are definitely making a number of specific social assumptions, both for the participants concerned and for the T-group trainers themselves. An elaboration of these assumptions and the manner in which they are liable to change really represents a formulation of our social values and the extent to which these may be moulded by social changes. The exercise, therefore, is a conceptual device for talking about the present, and by doing this we want to suggest some alternative directions that T-groups might explore in the future.

The past

Suppose we were to turn the problem around and try to conceptualise the last twenty to twenty-five years of the T-group movement. How should we understand the past? A history in terms of the movement itself — an internal, endogenous analysis, gives us one kind of perspective. The origins of group work in education go back to the 1920s in Germany with the pioneering work in group therapy (Moreno, 1947), but the real impetus comes after the Second World War. Both in the US, at the Research Center for Group Dynamics, then at MIT, and in England, at the Tavistock Institute, there were developments in the use of group-orientated techniques of learning and treatment (Back, 1972; Benne, 1964; Bion, 1959). The major thinking at both these centres, compared to the earlier developments in group therapy, emphasised the group process, rather than the individual. Most of group therapy previously had focused on 'therapy on the individual in the group', whereas now the emphasis became the group itself, the way it worked. The orientations of both these centres were nevertheless different. The Tavistock Institute concentrated more on the therapeutic end of the continuum, particularly with the psychoanalytic bias, whereas the Center for Group Dynamics emphasised educational goals and the training of professional people involved in group work (counsellors, social workers, managers, etc.). The Group Dynamics tradition of Kurt Lewin was particularly important. The National Training Laboratory (NTL) emerged out of this latter constellation, and the T-group proper became conceptualised as an educational entity. Also, NTL pioneered work in organisational contexts, attempting to apply T-groups and other group techniques to the specific problems of organisations.

In the 1960s the T-group movement started to expand, and changed in the process. The major impetus for this was in the spread of T-groups in universities in the US, where they were associated with psychology, social work, sociology, and management courses. A whole generation of university students became 'turned on' to T-group ideas, and this was paralleled by a greater social consciousness in general. At the same time, T-groups started to expand in Britain and Europe, and developed into an international phenomenon. The establishment of the Group Relations Training Association in Britain in 1966, and the European Institute of Transnational Studies in 1963 were key factors in this internationalisation.

Out of this increased interest, the T-group as a method of group education started to diversify and develop in different directions. Smith (1971) has identified three major orientations. First, there is the 'straight' T-group, which emphasises interpersonal relations among the members. Second, there are *organisational development* groups, which apply T-group-type methods to specific organisational problems, especially those of management. Third, there are *personal expression* groups, in which the main emphasis is on individual learning, with the individual exploring various aspects of his own behaviour: his feelings, his body, the use of his own senses, and so forth. This latter development became known under a wide number of different names: Encounter groups, *Gestalt* therapy, Syanon groups, Esalen groups, sex therapy, etc. At the present moment, the T-group movement is an extremely diverse phenomenon with little overlap in goals, orientation, and methods between one group and another. The concept of 'T-group' is a very broad and all-encompassing one, and really does not convey very much in terms of what any particular group will emphasise.

Common values

Nevertheless, there are a number of common values across most groups, which distinguish them from other types of group. These have been elaborated in detail elsewhere (Levine, 1971, 1972). The most basic value is a strong emphasis on *involvement* — encouraging the group members to be intimate, warm, and fully integrated with each other. A second value is on *interdependency* — encouraging mutual co-operation, effective decision-making, and the creation of a group structure that is adapted to the individuals' needs. A third general value is on the *development of awareness* — the individual becoming aware of his impact on others and others' impact on him. Other values also emerge in some groups, though not all. For example, some groups place an emphasis on the members' *relation to the outside environment,* whether this is a specific institution or a more general context. In this case, what happens inside of the group is partly related to its effects in the outside environment. This type of value is likely to emerge in groups where the members come from a specific environment (e.g., students, managers, social workers). Another value which is mostly associated with personal expression groups, and which is often unstated, is a *testing of social taboos,* often with the individual being encouraged to develop a greater tolerance toward unconscious feelings and behaviour.

Taken together, these five values can be seen as a broad characterisation of the T-group as a type of social group which differs substantially from other types of group. Many groups encourage intense involvement by their members, though not all. A number of groups encourage interdependency and the sharing of decision-making responsibility, though certainly not all. Most formal groups and institutions, where there are limited resources, in fact, tend to encourage the opposite — elite leadership and hierarchical structure. Further, very few groups encourage participants to explore their impact on others and others' impact on themselves openly; most of the time, people's ideas about each other are conveyed through gossip and 'behind-the-back' comments. A number of groups encourage relationships between a small group and a larger social context, though this rarely involves personal and emotional issues. Finally, very few groups encourage the testing of social taboos, and where this is done it usually involves ritualised expressions of semi-repressed feelings (e.g., New Year's Eve or special holidays). Thus, in spite of the wide diversity of group orientations and techniques within the T-group movement, it is meaningful to talk about these groups as a particular type of social group. We will, therefore, use the term 'T-Group' in this manner to refer to a general acceptance of these five values.

Common social elements

However, a characterisation of T-groups in terms of themselves, either through an elaboration of the history of the movement or in terms of the acceptance of specific social values, leaves much to be desired. We cannot easily explain why the movement developed as it did, nor why it occurred when it did or where it did. All we really have is a description of the chain of events of the group movement, and a statement of the underlying assumptions. What is missing here is a structural interpretation whereby the movement is interpreted in terms of general social variables, rather than by itself. The fact that the parts of the whole society are related to each other and affect each other surely should point us toward the need to understand the effect of external, exogenous variables on the development of the movement.

We are, therefore, going to conceptualise T-groups in a manner in which they normally are not viewed. We are going to look at them as economic phenomena, or, more correctly, socio-economic phenomena (Back, 1974). By doing this, we hope to be able to explain certain characteristics of T-groups which cannot be explained by an internal view of the movement. T-groups can be seen as an educational service provided by social psychological specialists. Like all economic phenomena the spread of this service is a function of the demand for such a service and the supply of trained personnel. We are hypothesising that four major socio-economic variables are critical in explaining the creation and development of the T-group movement — in providing the necessary supply and demand conditions. Further, when it comes to prophesying the future, the direction that these variables take will substantially alter the future development of T-groups.

Anglo-American orientation

The first of the socio-economic variables which affected T-groups was the fact that they were heavily Anglo-American in their inception and early development. As we saw, the origins of the T-group movement lay elsewhere, in Germany with the Group Therapy movement, yet the T-groups as an educational form blossomed in the US and Britain. Why? There are probably two basic reasons. After the Second World War, the vast majority of social science theory and research was conducted in the US and, to some extent, in Britain. Europe was devastated and would take years to rebuild her universities and social sciences. The rest of the world was too underdeveloped to have yet built up effective social sciences. America and Britain, on the other hand, not only had their universities intact, but they also had absorbed many social scientists from Europe who had migrated during the 1930s and 1940s. Thus, the social science heritage from Europe became concentrated in the US and Britain. In addition, the United States was economically prosperous after the war, and was able to expand universities and educational institutions to an unprecedented extent. For fifteen years after the war, therefore, most social science development was in the US and Britain.

Also, the Anglo-American intellectual social science culture had an empiricist and pragmatist tradition, reflecting a positivistic approach to data and an experimental approach to phenomena. The European tradition, on the other hand, was far more theoretical and philosophical. Thus, the practical, semi-experimental, adaptive approach of T-groups was far more consistent with the Anglo-American tradition than with the European. According to Benne (1964), the T-group emerged slowly out of a set of educational experiments, where the emphasis was on experimentation, feedback and reassessment. It was not the kind of technique to be developed theoretically, nor to follow logically from an understanding of the social structure. On the contrary, it was just the opposite. The fact that there are today few general theories of T-groups point clearly to an empiricist intellectual orientation, and a somewhat *laissez-faire* one at that.

A product of an advanced, capitalist economy

A second socio-economic variable that was important in affecting the inception of T-groups was the fact that they emerged in developed countries in an advanced stage of capitalism. It is inconceivable that T-groups could have developed 100 years earlier, during the early stages of industrialisation. Out of the Second World War, only the US emerged with all its industrial capacities fully utilised; European industry had been partly destroyed and Britain was in a state of extreme austerity, with a definite capital shortage. Further, not only was the US business community fully intact, but it was typified by the twentieth century form of industry — the huge corporation (Baran and Sweezy, 1966; Galbraith, 1952). In the nineteenth century industrialisation was carried out by relatively small firms under the direction of entrepreneurs (Hobsbawn, 1968). Though in the twentieth century, all industrialised countries had big corporations to some extent, it was in the US that this was most evident. There are many characteristics which distinguish corporate industrial capitalism from entrepreneurial industrial capitalism, but two important ones for us concern the financing of investment and research orientation. The big corporations had sufficient profits to allow sustained investment and the freedom to use these profits as they chose, whereas previously the dependency on banks, limited partnerships, and other such arrangements by entrepreneurial organisations had meant that there were continual capital shortages, less autonomy and short-run thinking (Galbraith, 1952; Glyn & Sutcliffe, 1972). The corporations could finance projects and could guarantee the continuation of a project, in spite of small recessions. Further, the big corporations started to develop their own research and development programmes, involving not only applied research but theoretical research as well. The effect of both of these was to place an increasing importance on technical skills and technical competence. The complexity of these big organisations required new management skills, and new approaches toward organisation. At the same time, the universities in America started to expand enormously after the war, emphasising new relationships between science and industry, and particularly between social science and industry. It was a new era of science-based industry, and there was an increased demand for skilled, technically-rooted personnel (Galbraith, 1967).

This context was very critical in the emergence of T-groups after the war, as Bradford *et al.,* point out (1964, esp. pp.4—8). If there is a new approach to industry, then there also has to be a new approach toward management. Further, the expansion of government during the 1930s had meant that social services were now on a far larger scale that previously, again necessitating the need for new organisational techniques. It was in this context that the T-group was born. Even the name, 'T' (for training), indicates this applied, technical orientation, and the early groups concerned themselves with training people in bureaucratic contexts in the techniques of good leadership. Even today, the 'straight' T-groups, and especially the organisational development groups, maintain this applied educational orientation.

The effect of the age structure

A third social variable which became critical in the 1960s for T-groups was the age structure. After the Second World War, the age structure of the US and Britain was relatively old (Bogue, 1969). This was due both to a declining fertility rate since the beginning of the century and to a very low fertility rate during the 1930s and the war years. But the post-war 'baby boom' altered the age structure; it became younger. In the 1960s, the post-war cohort arrived in the universities and there was a subsequent shift in the orientation of T-groups. They became more education- and personal-orientated, focusing more on individual problems than on organisational applications. Further, this change in T-groups was paralleled by a general 'youth culture' which characterised the 1960s, both in Britain and the US and elsewhere. While it would be very mechanistic to argue that this youth culture and change in T-group focus were solely the result of a bulge in the eighteen to twenty-five age group, the two are not unrelated, a point that has been made elsewhere (Hauser, 1971). The 1950s were associated with unlimited job opportunities for university graduates, whereas in the late 1960s graduate unemployment suddenly became a problem. The 1950s were characterised by an unquestioned belief in the supremacy of American-type industrial society, whereas the 1960s saw the beginnings of major criticism of this way of life. The civil rights movement and the Vietnam war had a lot to do with starting this criticism, but the sheer weight of the young generation, in numbers, made it more meaningful. Thus it was not an accident that there was a shift in the focus of T-groups away from the applied, organisational orientation toward an individual, personal problem focus. The exciting employment prospects offered to this generation early in the 1960s, the vulnerability experienced by the men to the possibility of being conscripted to fight in an unpopular war, and the numerical dominance of this generation (which encouraged a belief that their social values were the correct ones for American society), had much to do with shifting the technocratic ideology of American society in the 1950s toward a more critical, individual, and, perhaps, more idealistic ideology in the 1960s.

The expression of middle-class needs

A fourth socio-economic variable which affected the development of T-groups was the fact that the vast majority of trainers and participants were middle class. This partly relates to a technical factor whereby only those institutions which could pay for their members to attend T-groups did so (corporations, universities, some social service organisations), but this also reflects the individual orientation of the middle classes. Only the middle class in America, after the Second World War, were wealthy enough to shift their attention away from the acquisition of material goods toward more psychological needs. Prior to the Second World War, even the majority of the middle classes felt marginal, economically, a state of insecurity which is not conducive to asking meaningful psychological questions about individual choice. Previously, only the very rich were secure about material things. Thus, after the Second World War, particularly after the mid-1950s, the American middle class improved their standard of living. Parallel to this growth of affluence was an increase in interest in psychological issues; there was a growth in numbers of people going for therapy, there was an increase in books about personal 'being' and 'effectiveness', there was an increase in films about emotional problems, there was an increase in the understanding of sexual behaviour, and there was an increase in T-groups. All of this must be seen as part of a general affluence being extended to a large part of the population of America and, to a lesser extent, Europe, to the degree that their needs began to change. By the 1960s, the young generation going to the universities consisted of those born *after* the Depression and *after* the war — they were brought up in an era of affluence, and those most affected were keenest on exploring new ways of behaviour and thinking. That T-groups reflect this should be clear. The early T-groups were aimed at improving group effectiveness, on making group leaders more sensitive to the emotional issues underlying group decision-making (e.g., the hidden agenda). These assume that participants are in positions of leadership. The later T-groups were more concerned with individual issues: achieving individual social flexibility, becoming more aware of one's feelings, experimenting with new ways of behaving, and achieving a greater sense of 'liberation' — breaking the restrictive, emotional bonds of social relationships. These values, however, assume that one is economically 'liberated'. Both sets point to a middle-class orientation.

The picture that emerges, therefore, is that the typical participant in a T-group is someone who comes from a highly developed society, most likely British or American, who is in his/her twenties or thirties, and who is either a university student, a middle-class manager, or a middle-class professional. This person is a very specific social type, when all the world's social types are considered, who reflects a particular situation in a particular historical era. That T-groups manifest the needs of these people should be evident, for the trainers of T-groups are of the same population. This is not to deride the value of T-groups, nor to indicate that they should not exist. On the contrary, they have great value, as sufficient research has indicated (Cooper & Mangham, 1971). Nonetheless, we should try to understand T-groups in their structural context, and not try to pretend that they apply to all people, in all societies, in all historical eras. The emergence and development of T-groups has been a result of an external, socio-economic logic as well as the product of its own internal consciousness.

Predicting the future of T-groups

Let us return to the original question 'what kind of changes will occur in T-group-type learning situations over the next twenty years?' For predicting the future, it is much easier for us to extrapolate the external dimensions affecting T-groups than the internal ones. We cannot know what T-group trainers will do in twenty years' time, but if we assume that what they do will be consistent with the state of society at that time, as we have argued, then we can say something about the limits of their actions and the social framework they will use. In the last few years, a literature arose which is concerned with predicting the general changes that will occur in the world over the next few decades. While this literature on 'futurism' is certainly not without disagreements, and is partly ideologically usurped, future trends for some dimensions are known within reasonable limits and on a number of other dimensions, which means we can make some fairly good guesses about the trends that will occur.

In doing these projections, we must consider the effects

separately for developed and underdeveloped countries. This distinction is not an absolute one, of course, as it hides all kinds of quantitative and qualitative differences. Nonetheless, the terminology is fairly widespread and does reflect certain realities about the distribution of the world's resources, including many latent aspects of societies (Levine, 1974; Seers, 1971; Streeten, 1971). As our purpose is to view the T-group in the broadest possible context, this distinction will be maintained. Up to now there have been only few T-groups in underdeveloped countries, though the numbers seem to be growing.

Changes in the international context of social science

Taking the first variable, the Anglo-American tradition, it should be clear even now that the Anglo-American dominance of social science is lessening and will continue to decline. The empiricist tradition is, after all, not an Anglo-American monopoly, and the ideas gained from this tradition have been and will be transmitted elsewhere. De Solla Price (1963) provides some evidence of a trend in the direction, among the developed countries, of a more equal balance of natural and social science research publications.

There are two major reasons for this development. First, the diffusion of information is increasing through the media. As the media becomes more and more international, the ideas expressed in the social sciences are also diffused. Second, since science (both natural and social) is a function of the total wealth of a country (De Solla Price, 1963), then as wealth is created elsewhere, more centres for social science research and teaching will be established. The UN World Economic Survey (1969—70) shows a trend in the redistribution of wealth among the developed countries which bodes well for a wider proliferation of the social sciences. However, since the Second World War, increases in per capita GNP have been much higher in the developed countries than the underdeveloped countries (Meadows, Meadows, Randers, & Behrens, 1972; Kuznets, 1971; UN

1969—70). This poses a question, then, about the extent to which social science will develop in the underdeveloped countries. Unless there is an alteration in the present distribution of living standards, the underdeveloped countries will be unable to support very much social science. Nonetheless, we should expect a certain diffusion toward the underdeveloped countries, as well as some degree of independent discovery.

A particular aspect of this internationalisation of social science will be that the stylised American way of running T-groups should lessen because American dominance in the world economy is also lessening. It is not an accident that the adoption of T-groups elsewhere, especially in Europe, was a response to the need to emulate American techniques in social science. We find that the expressions that are meaningful in American slang, and which have been applied to T-groups, show up in countries where they are inconsistent with the use of language that existed previously. Expressions such as 'feedback', 'felt needs', 'inter group', 'fishbowl', 'one-shot T-group', 'community', the use of letters for words such as T for training, OD for organisational development, are expressions that are highly consistent with American slang. We can expect, therefore, that with the growth of T-group methods elsewhere, there will be a diversification in approach, with possibly national styles emerging.

Changes in the world economy

The second factor, a product of an advanced capitalist economy in a stage of expansion, is likely to be less effective over the next twenty years. As everyone certainly knows now, there is a serious question concerning the extent to which an industrial economy can continue to expand (Meadows *et al.,* 1972). There have been a number of studies which have documented the limited resources available in the world, and the increased competition between countries for these resources (Boerma, 1970; Boulding, 1966; Hudson, 1972; Mishan, 1967). How long it takes to reach these limits is, of course, a vast unknown, but one thing which is sure is that continual, unlimited expansion is no longer possible. Again, the effects on developed countries are liable to be different than those on underdeveloped countries.

For the developed countries, let us assume that the rate of economic growth will tend toward an equilibrium rate of near to or just zero. Of course, 'equilibrium' is an ideal notion whose realisation requires major political, organisational, and structural changes (Boulding, 1973). But if it is not achieved, then quite catastrophic developments will occur at some point in the future. Therefore, if this state is reached, what changes can we expect? For one thing, the economy will shift more toward services and away from material production. This has been happening anyway in virtually all developed countries (Clark, 1940), but we might expect that the shift will be accentuated. In addition, the tendency in developed countries for the labour force to shift toward higher skill levels will also increase (Dahrendorf, 1957). Aside from the enormous consequences this will have on the structure of present-day production, which is mostly capitalist, profit-orientated production, in time the vast majority of the working population will be employed in services, at a fairly high skill level, and productivity will increasingly have to be assessed in terms of this human effort, rather than in terms of the quantitiy of material goods produced. In twenty years' time, these tendencies will be more evident than they are today, though they certainly will not have reached this ideal equilibrium state. In the developed socialist countries, we should expect the same tendencies toward high skill, service development, where, because of the absence of profit motive as a basic economic rationale, it should be, in theory, easier to accomplish.

In all the developed countries, therefore, these tendencies will probably have three effects on the employment situation. First, there will still be a need for highly skilled employees (though not to the same extent as before). Competition between corporations (in the capitalist countries) is liable to be less intense, with stable cartel-like arrangements being reached more easily than before. In addition, corporations will have to learn to adjust in an economic era of greater uncertainty about markets, raw material sources, and rates of return, and with fewer opportunities to export into new areas and make windfall profits. Demand for many goods may stabilise, and the effect of this will certainly be that the rate of growth of the managerial groups will slow down and might even level off (Marris, 1963). This will also mean that the need for organisational T-groups might saturate, if not decrease. On top of this, if a rigidity sets into big corporations due to stricter economic controls, then there will be less scope for managerial experimentation with the consequent drop in demand for T-groups and related educational services. As the private sector moves toward stability in production and employment, we might argue that more and more employment will be in the public sector. None of these things bodes well for the use of T-groups in industrial situations. On the positive side, as industrial production in the developed countries slows down, there will be a shift toward more social services, with the consequent increase in demand for skilled social scientists. Thus, we can predict that the external demand elements affecting T-groups are likely to shift away from production and sales orientation towards a social service orientation.

In the underdeveloped countries, the tendencies will be slightly different, although these countries are part of the same world system. Right now, the rate of expansion of GNP in underdeveloped countries is reasonably high, but the growth of per capita income is very slow and lags well behind that of developed countries (Nortman, 1974; Seers, 1971; UN, 1969—70). There are three reasons for this. First, the underdeveloped countries show higher population growth, which absorbs much of the new production, especially with respect to social services and other infrastructural investments (Berelson, 1974). Second, dual economies persist which are rigidly specialised in agricultural production, lacking links to other sectors, in which the impulse to a sustained domestically based industrial growth is not evident

(Myint, 1964). The rate of growth of GNP could be much higher if this interconnected industrial structure existed, as the base line is low. This further limits the ability of the state to put money into educational experiments or even to improve the quality of education. Further, unlike the industrialised countries' pattern of growth, much of the growth of employment in the 'modern' sector is in services, rather than industry (Sutcliffe, 1971). 'Services' in this case is a slightly misleading label, as most of these services show extremely low increases in productivity: excessive employment in government bureaucracies, streetsellers, petty services for the rich, etc. (Bhalla, 1973; Kiray, 1970). This makes it again difficult for both the state and the private sector to invest in educational experiences like T-groups; for the private sector, organisational development is a very low priority for a number of reasons, among which are the generally small sizes of organisations that exist, while for the state sector the pressure exerted from the population for jobs makes it extremely difficult for investment to be put into organisational analyses which might put people out of work, and such action politically risky (Alavi, 1972). In addition, the distribution of income in underdeveloped countries has tended to become increasingly unequal in the last twenty years, so that the vast majority of the population receives little out of the process (Fishlow, 1972; Paukert, 1973). Again, this limits the extent of educational experimentation to only the wealthier parts of the population.

A third reason has to do with structural imbalances which shift resources disproportionately away from the underdeveloped countries to the developed countries — continuing trade deficits, repatriation of profits by foreign firms, aid repayments, continuing disequilibrium in exchange rates (Amin, 1974; Baran, 1957; Jalee, 1965). Thus, a critical factor is the extent to which the underdeveloped countries can alter this present structure of growth. One possibility is by altering the terms of trade of raw materials, as the OPEC countries did recently. But if the neo-Malthusian economists are correct, even here there are limits. Therefore, assuming the most optimistic growth potential for the underdeveloped countries, they still will be short of capital for a long time. Thus, it should be clear that T-groups will continue to be a luxury for underdeveloped countries unless they can be directly related to development efforts.

Changes in the age structure

Changes in the age structure over the next twenty years are more predictable. In a 'closed' population, the age structure is a function of the given fertility and mortality rates (Lotka, 1939). Even allowing for small changes in the population through international migration, the age structure will not be altered very much unless the migration takes on enormous proportions. As Coale (1963, 1966) has shown, the shape of the age structure (i.e., the proportion of the population in each age group) is more a function of fertility than mortality; high fertility is associated with a young population, and conversely.

So far, the tendencies in population change appear to be following the same pattern. Mortality has decreased in virtually all countries, with the gap between developed and underdeveloped countries closing rapidly (Berelson, 1974). In the developed countries, this has been followed by a drop in fertility, a phenomenon which has been sanctified with a title 'demographic transition' (Notestein 1945; Thompson, 1944). At present, only a few underdeveloped countries have shown a drop in fertility (Berelson, 1974). But if we assume that these tendencies will continue, since those factors inducing low fertility are spreading — income, education, health services, urbanisation (Bogue, 1969; Friedlander & Silver, 1967), then the age structure in all countries will relatively age. However, there will still be differences between the developed and underdeveloped countries.

In the developed countries, fertility has dropped rapidly over the last fifteen years and has almost reached replacement level (Davis 1973; Hauser, 1971). Therefore, asuming that this low fertility will remain for the near future, then the age structure will continue to (relatively) age until demographic equilibrium is reached (Coale, 1966). The dominance of youth, thus, is slowly receding with a consequent shift toward the middle and elderly age groups. If we further assume that service expenditures will be orientated toward those groups which are most in need *and* which can exert more political pressure on governments, then the middle to elderly age groups will receive relatively more attention than they do now. Whether T-groups will reflect this is hard to say, but if a higher proportion of the population is older than now, this is very likely.

In the underdeveloped countries, though fertility will be falling (as we assume will happen), the population will still be relatively younger than the developed countries for a long time to come. There are two reasons for this. First, age-specific fertility rates can be expected to decline over a fairly long period, and, second, the crude birth rate will drop slowly because of 'momentum' in the population (Berelson, 1974). That is, since the majority of the population in underdeveloped countries is young now (40 — 45 per cent under fifteen years of age, compared to 25 — 30 per cent in the developed countries), because of their parents' high fertility, then when these young cohorts reach the fertile ages they will produce a larger number of children due to their sheer bulk, even if their age-specific fertility rates are reduced. The population of underdeveloped countries will continue to remain 'youngish' for a long time, at least a hundred years (Frejka, 1973). Thus, there will continue to be an enormous pressure on the educational, job and housing markets, a fact that will hinder individual development. A youth culture is liable to remain for many years to come, though a youth culture raised on the experience of underdevelopment, so that if T-groups ever grow in underdeveloped countries, they are liable to aim at a younger population.

Changes in the class structure and class orientation

The fourth socio-economic variable, the dominance of middle-class values in the T-group movement, is liable to be the most critical for the future of T-groups, as well as the most difficult variable to predict. In the developed countries, there has been a widening of the middle classes (proportionately) since the turn of the century (Dahrendorf, 1957; Mills, 1951). Subjectively, in terms of an identity with a middle-class life style, the argument has been made that a large proportion of the working classes also share this identity, though it is questionable how much of it is an identity with being middle class and how much an identity with a 'good life'. (Goldthorpe & Lockwood, 1963; Rainwater, Coleman, & Handel, 1959). Nonetheless we can safely say that there has been an expansion in life-style opportunities over the last thirty years.

Whether this expansion will continue in the future is, however, another matter. If the kinds of economic difficulty that we suggested materialise, then opportunities for mobility and large increases in standards of living look more dismal. If the developed countries are forced to slow down their rate of growth, in order to rationalise raw material consumption and limit the polluting of the atmosphere, then this is liable severely to restrict the growth of individual incomes and the creation of consumer goods in seemingly unlimited quantities. This will probably lead to a perception of the social structure as being restrictive in terms of social mobility, compared to the high-mobility expansion period of the 1950s and 1960s. A substantial proportion of the population will start to feel economically marginal again, feelings which are not conducive to the individualistic orientation of T-groups. In the last few years, graduate unemployment has increased in the developed countries, already producing this marginal feeling among the most literate group in the population. Though this should balance out in the long run as the population ages and pressure on the job market for the twenty to forty-year-olds decreases, still there is liable to be a close fit between job creation and job absorption by the educated. This will most certainly lead to increased class conflict as political pressure from the working classes builds up for the limited educational opportunities and for the standard of living that they have been led to believe was available. Again, this situation will not be particularly suitable for T-groups as they have existed up to now.

In the underdeveloped countries, the situation is more acute. Certainly, in most underdeveloped countries, aspirations have risen very fast, especially among the urban population, so that it is meaningful to talk about ideals for a high standard of living (see, for example, Blaug, 1973; Levine, 1973b; Myrdal, 1968). But the job situation has been problematic. For those countries which have experienced a fast urbanisation, this has been associated initially with an increase in job opportunities in the cities (ILO, 1970). But as the rates of immigration have tended to exceed the rate of job creation, a large increase in unemployment and disguised employment has developed (Bairoch, 1973; Jolly, De Kadt, Singer, & Wilson, 1973). Also, the increased aspirations in the population have led to a fast expansion in education (Blaug, 1973), which in turn has led to an increase in graduate unemployment (Myrdal, 1968; Coombs, 1968); again, the rate of change of job creation lags behind the rate of change of higher education. There are many side effects of this high unemployment rate, but one clear effect is the maintenance of dependency by individuals on their families (Bruner, 1970; Bryce-Laporte, 1970; Gutkind, 1973). Young individuals, who might normally in a developed country leave home and make their own way in the world, are forced to maintain interdependencies with their immediate families; if the person lives in the same city as the parents, then he/she lives with the parents until marriage. If the person becomes a migrant, then obligations are created concerning the sending of money back home, the maintaining of support for family members who follow, and a whole host of other obligations (Abu-Lughed, 1961; Levine, 1973a). This is particularly true for the poorer sections of a society, but it is also true for the middle classes. High graduate unemployment, the lagging behind of demand for housing, as well as the need to create marriages which reinforce class positions, all tend to tie young middle-class people to their families. In short, the economic environment presented to the population of an underdeveloped country is very restrictive indeed. This means that T-groups run in such countries can only have limited effectiveness, especially if they are run as carbon copies of the present-day developed countries' T-groups, and can only survive if they adapt to the different conditions.

Future effect on the T-group movement

We are suggesting, then, that, rather than T-groups expanding continuously over the next twenty years and becoming part of the general educational process, they are instead liable to suffer a rapid deterioration as the social forces limit their use. The question really is, 'Can T-groups survive if they do not represent the needs of their society?' T-groups have been successful in the US (Back, 1974), Britain (Cooper, 1972), and northern Europe (Lennung, 1974) because they raise meaningful questions about personal orientation. If there is choice in social relationships, then one can meaningfully pose alternatives, and a T-group is as good a place as any to raise these questions, given its permissive climate. The background of high job absorption for university graduates in developed economics has allowed for the consideration of personal goals. If these elements change, however, or are missing, is it still meaningful to talk about personal choice? With an economically restrictive environment, a personal orientation becomes dysfunctional and social norms become restrictive on the individual in order to protect the economic unit, in this case, the household family.

Thus, there are liable to be three general consequences of all these factors for T-group development. First, there will be a general contraction in the demand for T-groups by those private-sector organisations which presently finance them.

Second, the demand for groups in the public sector is liable to increase, but the demand is apt to come from the older age groups, the social services, and, probably, the more underprivileged economic groups. In other words, there will be a qualitative shift in demand away from production toward services. While this might seem socially desirable, it may nevertheless bring a real crisis for T-group people. Since T-groups are an educational service, they nonetheless have to be paid for like any other service. At the moment, the two major sources of income for T-group trainers are the corporative business sector, which employs trainers either as outside consultants or as in-company training personnel, and universities, which finance T-groups through employing staff. The government to some extent also finances T-groups. But if there is a shift in demand toward the more elderly, the social services, and the more underprivileged groups of the society, then these are the groups which will least likely be able to afford the 'luxury' of T-groups. T-group people normally do not like to discuss these things, for the whole value system of T-groups is ostensibly anti-materialistic. Yet, if there is a drop in the demand for T-groups by those who are most likely to pay, how many T-group trainers are going to continue to work for the kind of income that these groups which do have a demand can provide? For that matter, the same issue applies today. There are undoubtedly many groups in society today who could gain something from a T-group experience, but cannot afford it. How many groups do we see run with these populations? Very few indeed (for exceptions, see Klein, Thomas, & Bellis, 1971; Olmosk & Graverson, 1972; Walton, 1970). This does not mean that the future is totally dismal, but it will mean the T-group trainers will have to face up to these issues and learn to explore a number of different possibilities. There are, of course, always the universities, which could be used as a base for T-groups for populations which want them, as part of a general research orientation. Naturally, this could also be done today. There is also the government. If the social services expand, then there is liable to be an increase in spending by the government for

T-group education. But the T-group trainers will have to persuade the government that such training is in their interest. Naturally, this could also be done today. T-group trainers could also do something which is very anti-materialist indeed. They could give their time to various groups for token payments. In this sense, they would be substituting moral criteria for economic ones. In effect, the shift in demand for T-groups in the future will do nothing more than reveal the present. There are today many groups which have no access to the advantages of T-groups and these same groups will exist in twenty years time, too.

A third consequence will be that the individual orientation of T-groups must change if these forms of education are to survive. It will become increasingly difficult to talk about individual freedom and choice in the absence of social considerations. The strong necessity of adjusting to society, which first and foremost means economic adjustment, will restrict the individual from changing jobs continuously. There is still liable to be more choice available in personal issues, but even here this cannot be examined independent of the economic choices available. If jobs are hard to find, marriage takes on a greater economic value, especially if men and women are competing equally on the market. Couples will be very careful to maximise their joint income, and there could be an absolute drop in divorce. Social sexual freedom is limited by the choices available, and if strong norms for marital stability develop, then strong norms for non-marital relations will also stabilise. We might even see a slight reversal of the present social-sexual permissiveness. Further, as fertility becomes increasingly under the influence of economic 'abstinence' with parents limiting the number of their children, then socialisation may increasingly emphasise social stability and adaptability, rather than individual choice and decision.

Directions for T-group growth

Given these restrictions, what kind of directions can T-group people work towards? First, T-group people must come to grips with economic realities, their own and others. Social psychologists, educationalists, and to some extent sociologists have too long ignored economic structure. But T-group trainers cannot continue to push the *laissez-faire* 'it's not important to me' philosophy and make a meaningful impact on the society twenty years from now. Thus, there is a need by T-group trainers to explore the problems of collective responsibility, and to examine dimensions of learning that are group-orientated, rather than individual-orientated; learning to work with others, learning to protect others, learning to participate in unions, learning to negotiate, etc. This is not a throwback to the Machiavellianism and ideology of aggressive competition which T-groups tried to get away from initially. Instead, new social values can be defined and new techniques developed. Instead of 'openness in general' being advocated, perhaps the emphasis should be 'openness to one's friends or one's workmates.' Instead of 'individual feelings', there should be 'group feelings'. Individualism is not necessarily the only alternative to alienation.

Second, there is the need to explore the problems of the older age groups. In the US and Britain, this will mean going up against social taboos where youth is everything. In many other countries, however, being old is not a crime and the old are respected and accepted. But there needs to be a movement toward this by T-group people. Whether T-groups will take the specific form of age groups (e.g., thirties groups, forties groups, geriatric groups), or whether they will focus in on specific problems (e.g., young couples with children, grandparents, the elderly) is impossible to say, but there are a lot of possibilities here.

Third, T-group practitioners and others interested in educational experimentation must also come to grips with social realities, especially in underdeveloped countries. Those who attempt this kind of approach cannot ignore the fate of the large numbers of people who cannot share much of the developed wealth. This is also true for those in developed countries who also share little in the wealth. Thus, trainers must learn to work with social consciousness, whether this means political T-groups or something else. Being practical, it is always difficult for middle-class intellectuals to work with the working classes. There is distrust on both sides, and there is usually little chance for mutual contact. But social consciousness can be encouraged, in whatever capacity T-group people work. T-groups in primary and secondary schools would be obvious places to contact all people. T-groups with unions and other workers' organisations would increase contact. In working with the middle class in universities, T-group trainers could emphasise social consciousness they now push aside. This will mean advocating social values that are now considered unfashionable: social flexibility, learning to work inside systems, learning to try to change things slowly. While this lacks the dramatic and radicalising effect of 'instant personal change', which T-groups in the Sixties were so good at, in the long run this is liable to be a much more effective strategy for being useful to people and to society.

Unless T-group trainers face up to these issues, T-groups will become an archaic remnant of a forgotten era — the 'flashy Sixties'. The practitioners will slowly age and will come to represent only themselves and a few privileged people. And when that happens, T-groups will have died a natural death.

References

Abu-Lughod, J., Migrant adjustment to city life: The Egyptian case, *American Journal of Sociology,* 1961, *67,* 22-32.
Alavi, H., The state in post-colonial societies: Pakistan and Bangladesh, *New Left Review,* 1972, *74 (July-Aug.),* 59-81.
Amin, S., *Accumulation on a world scale* (2 Vol), New York: Monthly Review Press, 1974.
Argyris, C., Explorations in interpersonal competence—1, *Journal of Applied Behavioral Science,* 1965, *1,* 58-84.

Back, G.R., Marathon group dynamics: I. Some Functions of the Professional Group Facilitiator, *Psychological Reports,* 1967, *20,* 995-999.
Back, K.W., *Beyond words,* New York: Russell Sage Foundation, 1972.
Back, K.W., Intervention techniques: Small groups, *Annual Review of Psychology,* 1974, *25,* 367-387.
Bairoch, P., *Urban unemployment in developing countries,* Geneva: International Labor Office, 1973.
Baran, P.A., *The Political Economy of Growth,* New York: Monthly Review Press, 1957.
Baran, P.A., & Sweezy, P.M., *Monopoly Capital,* New York: Monthly Review Press, 1966.
Bass, B., Reactions to Twelve Angry Men as a measure of sensitivity training, *Journal of Applied Psychology,* 1962, *46,* 120-124.
Benne, K.D., History of the T-group in the laboratory setting. In L.P. Bradford, J.R. Gibb, & K.D. Benne, (Eds.), *T-group theory and laboratory method,* New York: J. Wiley, 1964.
Berelson, B., World population: Status report 1974, *Report on population and Family Planning,* 1974, *No. 15. (Jan.).*
Bhalla, A.S., The role of services in employment expansion. In R. Jolly, E. De Kadt, H. Singer, & F. Wilson (Eds.), *Third world employment,* Harmondsworth, Middlesex: Penguin, 1973.
Bion, W.R., *Experiences in groups,* New York: Basic Books, 1959.
Blaug, M., *Education and the employment problem in developing countries.* Geneva: International Labor Office, 1973.
Boerma, A.H., A world agricultural plan, *Scientific American,* 1970, *223, No. 2. (Aug.),* 54-69.
Bogue, D.J., *Principles of demography,* New York: J. Wiley, 1969.
Boulding, K.E., *The economics of the coming spaceship Earth.* In H. Jarrett, (Ed.), *Environmental quality in a growing economy,* Baltimore: Johns Hopkins Press, 1966.

Boulding, K.E., The shadow of the stationary state, *Daedalus,* 1973, *102, No. 4 (Fall).*

Bradford, L.P., Gibb, J.R., & Benne, K.D., Two educational innovations. In L.P. Bradford, J.R. Gibb, & K.D. Benne (Eds.), *T-group theory and laboratory method,* New York; J. Wiley, 1964.

Bruner, E.M. Medan: The role of kinship in an Indonesian city. In W. Mangin, (Ed.), *Peasants in cities.* Boston: Houghton-Mifflin, 1970.

Bryce Laporte, R.S., Urban relocation and family adaptation in Puerto Rico: A case study in urban ethnography. In W. Mangin, (Ed.), *Peasants in cities,* Boston: Houghton-Mifflin, 1970.

Burke, R.L., & Bennis, W.B., Changes in perception of self and others during human relations training, *Human Relations,* 1961, *14,* 165-182.

Clark, C., *The conditions of economic progress,* London: Macmillan, 1940.

Coale, A.J., Population and economic development. In P.M. Hauser, (Ed.), *The population dilemma,* Englewood Cliffs: Prentice-Hall, 1963.

Coale, A.J., *Regional model life tables and stable populations,* Princeton, New Jersey: Princeton University Press, 1966.

Coombs, P.H., *The world educational crisis: A systems analysis,* London: Oxford University Press, 1968.

Cooper, C.L., T-group training and self-actualization, *Psychological Reports,* 1971, *28,* 391-394.

Cooper, C.L., *Group training for individual and organizational development,* Basel: S. Karger, 1972.

Cooper, C.L., & Mangham, I.L., *T-groups: A survey of research,* London: J. Wiley, 1971.

Dahrendorf, R., *Class and class conflict in an industrial society* (English ed., 1959), London: Routledge & Kegan Paul, 1957.

Davis, K., Zero population growth: The goal and the means, *Daedalus,* 1973, *102, No. 4. (Fall),* 15-30.

De Solla Price, D.J., *Little science big science,* New York:

Columbia University Press, 1963.

Fishlow, A., Brazilian size distribution of income. *American Economic Review,* 1972, *62,* 391-403.

French, J.R.P., Sherwood, J.J., & Bradford, D., Changes in self-identity in a management training conference, *Journal of Applied Behavioral Science,* 1966, *2,* 210-218.

Frejka, T., *The future of population growth,* New York: J. Wiley, 1973.

Friedlander, S., & Silver, M., A quantitative study of the determinants of fertility behavior, *Demography,* 1967, *4,* 30-70.

Galbraith, J.K., *American capitalism,* Boston: Houghton-Mifflin, 1952.

Galbraith, J.K., *The new industrial state,* Boston: Houghton-Mifflin, 1967.

Glyn, A., & Sutcliffe, B., *British capitalism, workers and the profits squeeze,* Harmondsworth, Middlesex: Penguin, 1972.

Goldthorpe, J.H., & Lockwood, D., Affluence and the British class structure, *Sociological Review,* 1963, *11,* 133-163.

Gutkind, P.C.W., The unemployed and poor in urban Africa. In R. Jolly, E. De Kadt, H. Singer, & F. Wilson (Eds.), *Third World employment,* Harmondsworth, Middlesex: Penguin, 1973.

Hauser, P.M., The census of 1970, *Scientific American,* 1971, *225 (July),* 17-25.

Hobsbawn, E.J., *Industry and empire,* Harmondsworth, Middlesex: Penguin, 1968.

Hudson, H.V., *The diseconomies of growth,* London: Pan/Ballantine, 1972.

International Labor Office *Towards full employment. A programme for Colombia,* Geneva: International Labor Office, 1970.

Jalee, P., *The pillage of the Third World,* (English ed., 1968) New York: Monthly Review Press, 1965.

Jolly, R., De Kadt, E., Singer, H., & Wilson, F., *Third World employment,* Harmondsworth, Middlesex: Penguin, 1973.

Kiray, M.B., Squatter housing: Fast depeasantization and slow workerization in underdeveloped countries, Paper presented at the 7th World congress of Sociology, Varna, Bulgaria, 1970.

Klein, E.B., Thomas, C.S., & Bellis, E., When warring groups meet: The use of a group approach in police/black community relations, *Social Psychology,* 1971, *6,* 93-99.

Kuznets, S., *Economic growth of nations,* Cambridge, Massachusetts: Harvard University Press, 1971.

Lakin, M., Some ethical issues in sensitivity training, *American Psychologist,* 1969, *24,* 923-929.

Lennung, S., *Meta-learning, laboratory training, and change,* Stockholm: Swedish Council, 1974.

Levine, N., Emotional factors in group development, *Human Relations,* 1971, *24,* 65-89.

Levine, N., Group training with students in higher education. In C.L. Cooper (Ed.), *Group training for individual and organizational development,* Basel: S. Karger, 1972, 40-67.

Levine, N., Old culture—New culture: A study of migrants in Ankara, Turkey. *Social Forces,* 1973a, *51,* 355-368.

Levine, N., Value orientation among migrants in Ankara, Turkey: A case study, *Journal of Asian and African Studies,* 1973b, *8,* 50-68.

Levine, N., Why do countries win Olympic medals? Some structural correlates of Olympic Games success: 1972, *Sociological Social Research.* 1974, *58,* 353-360.

Lotka, A.J., *Theorie analytique des associations biologiques,* Paris: Hermann, 1939.

Marris, R., A model of the 'managerial enterprise', *Quarterly Journal of Economics,* 1963, *77,* 185-209.

Meadows, D.H., Meadows, D.L., Randers, J., & Behrens, W.W., *The limits to growth,* New York: Potomac Associates, 1972.

Mills, C.W., *White collar: The American middle classes,* New York: Oxford University Press, 1951.

Mishan, E.J., *The costs of economic growth,* New York: F.A. Praeger, 1967.

Moreno, J.L., *The theatre of spontaneity,* Boston: Beacon

House, 1947.

Myint, H., *The economics of developing countries,* London: Hutchinson, 1964.

Myrdal, G., Labor utilization outside traditional agriculture. In G. Myrdal, *Asian drama,* Vol. II, 1968.

Nortman, D., Population and family planning programs: A factbook (6th ed.), *Report on Population and Family Planning,* No. 2. (Dec.), 1974.

Notestein, F.W., Population—The long view. In T.W. Schultz (Ed.), *Food for the world,* Chicago: University of Chicago Press, 1945.

Olmesk, K., and Graverson, G., Group training for community relations: The community workshop. In C.L. Cooper *Group training for individual organizational development,* Basel: S. Karger, 1972.

Paukert, F., Income distribution at different levels of development: A survey of evidence, *International Labor Review,* 1973, *108,* 97-125.

Rainwater, L., Coleman, P., & Handel, G., *Workingman's wife,* New York: Oceana Publications, 1959.

Runin, I., The reduction of prejudice through laboratory training, *Journal of Applied Behavioral Science,* 1967, *3,* 29-50.

Seers, D., Rich countries and poor. In D. Seers, & L. Joy (Eds.), *Development in a divided world,* Harmondsworth, Middlesex: Penguin, 1971.

Siroka, R.W., Siroka, E.K., & Schloss, G.A., *Sensitivity training and group encounter: An introduction,* New York: Grosset and Dunlap, 1971.

Smith, P.B., The varieties of group experience, *New Society,* March 25, 1971, 483-485.

Streeten, P., How poor are the poor countries? In D. Seers, & L. Joy (Eds.), *Development in a divided world,* Harmondsworth, Middlesex: Penguin, 1971.

Sutcliffe, R.B., *Industry and underdevelopment,* London-Reading: Addison-Wesley, 1971.

Thompson, W.S., *Plenty of people,* Lancaster, Pennsylvania: Jacques Cattell Press, 1944.

United Nations, *World Economic Survey,* New York: United Nations, 1969-1970.

Walton, R.R., A problem-solving workshop on border conflicts in Eastern Africa, *Journal of Applied Behavioral Science,* 1970, *6,* 453-489.

Endnotes

The following chapters were published by the author in the following scholarly journals:

1. *Psychology Teaching,* 1974, 2 (1), 105-112.

2. *Advances in Experiential Social Processes,* 1978, Volume 1, 1-29 (London: John Wiley & Sons).
   (With N. Levine)

3. *Annual Handbook for Group Facilitators,* 1976, Volume 3, 157-169 (La Jolla, Calif: University Associates).
   (With K. Harrison)

4. *Human Relations,* 1977, 30 (12), 1103-1129.

5. *Human Relations,* 1969, 22 (6), 515-530.

6. *Group and Organization Studies,* 1976, 1 (1), 43-56.
   (With N. Levine and K. Kobayashi)

7. *Interpersonal Development,* 1971, 1 (2), 110-127.
   (With I. Mangham and J. Hayes)

8. *Interpersonal Development,* 1975, 5, 71-77.

9. *British Journal of Social Work,* 1974, 4 (1), 39-49.

10. *Interpersonal Development,* 1972, 2, 50-60.

11. *Interpersonal Development,* 1977, 6 (4), 188-191.

12. *Psychological Reports,* 1973, 33, 451-454.

13. *Interpersonal Development,* 1975, 5, 203-212.

14. *Human Relations,* 1976, 29 (1), 1-23.
    (With N. Levine)

The author would like to thank the above mentioned journals and their publishers for permission to reprint the above papers in this volume.

Index

Experiential learning is abbreviated to EL within index entries.

Minnesota Multi-phasic
  Personality Inventory
  (MMPI) 105
Mishan, E.J. 271
Mitchell, R.R. 186
MMPI 105
Modelling *see* Simulation
Models of values 25-6
Moreno, J.L. 260
Moscow, D. 81, 220
Motorway catering study 208-22
Myint, H. 274
Myrdal, G. 278

National Training Laboratory
  77, 212, 260
Nature of man-constructive
  138f, 141, 143, 145
NDS scale 199
Neuroticism 196-7, 199-202, 245
Nie, N.H., *and others* 89
Non-verbal communication 41f,
  69
Normality, psychological 20-1
Nortman, D. 273
Notestein, F.W. 275
Nurses, EL study of 195-205

Odiorne, G.S. 203
Olch, D. and Snow, D.L. 102f
Old people 282
Olmosk, K. and Graverson, G.
  19, 280
Openness 22-3, 44, 194, 200,
  202, 282
Organic approach 57-8
Organisational development 16,
  25, 29-30f, 39, 136, 185, 210-
  11, 261, 266, 274
Organisations, values of 16, 21-
  5, 35f

Osgood, C.E., *and others* 220

Participants *see* Members
Particularism 23-5
Paukert, F. 274
Pearson product-moment
  correlation 200f
Pederson, D. and Breglio, U.
  234
Peer/self ratings of disturbance
  80-1, 91-4, 100, 102, 245, 247,
  250
Perceived status 18-20
Perception measures for social
  skills training 220
Perceptual Inventory 116-17,
  120
Perceptual isolation
  experiments 195, 242
Personal aims 51
Personal Description
  Questionnaire (PDQ) 84-5
Personal expression groups 25,
  136, 261
  see also T-groups
Personal growth groups 9, 30,
  58, 241
  see also Personal expression
    groups
  T-groups
Personal Orientation Inventory
  (POI) 135, 138-46
Personality inventories *see*
  names of specific inventories,
  e.g. Sixteen Personality
  Factor (16PF)
  Questionnaire
Personality profiles of members
  and trainers 228-31
Peters, D.R. 111
Pfeiffer, W. and Jones, J.